THE
HERO
WITHIN

Also by Deborah L. Grassman

Peace at Last: Stories of Hope and Healing for Veterans and Their Families

THE
HERO
WITHIN

Redeeming the Destiny
We Were Born to Fulfill

Deborah L. Grassman

VANDAMERE
PRESS

Published by
Vandamere Press
P.O. Box 149
St. Petersburg, FL 33731
USA

Second Printing February 2016

ISBN 978-0-918339-76-8

Disclaimer Statement
   Unless otherwise noted, the names and identifying features
of all people have been changed to protect their privacy.

Dedication

There are many heroes in my life. They are people who have loved me in spite of myself and have encouraged me to be myself. This book is dedicated to them. Not all of them are cited on these pages, but I want to identify those who are. You will read their stories and understand why they have inspired me. In order of appearance in the book, they are: Marie Bainbridge, Dan Hummer, Marlene Lewis, Sheila Lozier, Pat McGuire, Ferol Martin, Lorraine Acompora, Shaku Desai, Sarah Grassman (my daughter), and Edwin Jones (my father).

My heroes also include those who had the courage to heal their lives through therapeutic letter-writing. Some of these letters are in this book. You will read them, and they will inspire you too. Not only will you understand their pain and its redemption, the letters will help you understand your own. The authors of the letters are: Victoria Curtis, Drew Delmore, Rob D., Suzanne Foster, Abi Katz, Linda O'Keefe-Wood, Clarice Steiner, and Vicki Tangney.

I've also been fortunate to have many people enrich my life, some of whom are on these pages. In order of appearance, they are: Suzanne Greacen, Diane Johnstone, Buzz H., Suzanne Bauer, Macy Grassman, John Hull, Joy Easterly, Ed Chaffin, Sherie Graham, Amy McDonald, Audrey Chiarenza, and Patty Surprenant.

Acknowledgements

Although I am the sole author of this book, it has not been written alone. I've had the support of many people who have encouraged the development of my ideas and have participated in groups and courses that I have facilitated. The honesty, courage, and humility they have demonstrated in healing their lives have inspired me so that I can heal my own. They are the reason this book exists.

I'm also grateful for a group of colleagues, friends, and family who have willingly been readers, editors, and collective memory-keepers with me. They've joined me on my journey, providing valued feedback and support in the process. My gratitude is beyond words. They include: Lorraine Acompora, Colleen Almas, Marie Bainbridge, Jan Bucholz, Linda Burke, Enid Clarke, Shaku Desai, David Grassman, Sarah Grassman, Evelyn Harley, Gail Horsley, Kevin Householder, Nikki Kirk, Karen Lindsey, Ruth Maddox, Mary McCoy, Pat McGuire, Charles Mirasola, Gail Moore, Linda O'Keefe-Wood, Mary Ellen Smith, Patty Surprenant, Tracy Thatcher, and Dan Tobin. I can only feel gratitude, warmth, and humility in accepting the help of so many generous friends, colleagues, and fellow travelers as we make the heroic journey home unto ourselves.

Table of Contents

Prologue

Helping veterans face the end of their lives has been my role as a Hospice and Palliative Care Nurse Practitioner with the Veterans Administration (VA) Healthcare System. From this vantage point, I have been given the opportunity to observe the responses of the human spirit as it struggles to bring congruity and integrity to lives that have been lived wholly or partially with the brokenness that is part of our human experience. I have endeavored to make the journey of these veterans my own. In the process, I have been changed.

When people learn that I work with dying veterans, they will often say, "I can't imagine working in hospice." To help you imagine my everyday world, let me tell you the stories of the nine patients on the Hospice and Palliative Care unit at the time of this writing. Then, you can understand the context from which my lessons are derived. You will also understand the privilege that it is to care for veterans. Military experiences changed them in fundamental ways that shape, mold, destroy, and redeem the rest of their lives. Many are able to confront their sufferings successfully. In one aspect of their lives or another, they have been able to redeem portions of their suffering so that it can be used for healing as they face the end of their lives.

Mark is dying of liver failure from alcohol abuse, his skin yellow as a low-glowing lamp. He came to the Hospice and Palliative Care unit semi-comatose; we won't get to know him except through his brother's eyes. I comment on his brother's devotion. The brother responds, "I look at Mark and know why I'm in Alcoholics Anonymous." I behold one brother willingly serving the suffering of the other.

Donnie is 50 years old and has lung cancer. He's been a quadriplegic since he was 27 when an automobile accident derailed his career as a professional football player. "I spent three years in despair. Then I found God and salvation," he tells me. He says he is thankful for his suffering: "I never would have found Jesus if the accident hadn't happened." Twenty-three years of redeemed suffering is a story worth beholding.

In the next room, an embittered, lonely man sits sullenly. Alcohol has estranged Zachary from his family. At 82, he's angry at his body for failing him. He's been afraid of death since he was 10 years old when a neighbor died falling through a skylight. Bitterly, he tells me, "My only solace is in knowing that someday all the rest of you are going to be in this bed too." A gathering of team members provided a turning point as Zachary experiences the concern of the four staff members who were willing to love him. "Why aren't we talking about my breathing, and the 16 pills I'm taking?" he asks us. "Because you are more than just your breathing, and we are more than just pill-givers," I reply, leaning in and daring to touch him tenderly. A tear forms; his features soften for the first time. "I can't argue with that," he says quietly. I can't tell you the ending of his story, but once the crack starts hope emerges.

In the room next to Zachary is Marvin.[1] He was a photographer to a general in World War II. He has been a physician, sailboat racer, and builder of piers, driveways, and roofs "made with my own hands." Marvin's wife and four children sit at his bedside supporting his journey into the next world and supporting one other. Near death, he says little except the Lord's Prayer. There's no need for us to intervene. We just get out of the way and behold a life well lived.

In the adjoining bed is Jim, a Vietnam War veteran who has lived a colorful life. He's intermittently confused; sometimes he's argumentative. He has no family; a few close friends are his source of comfort. His first days on the unit were filled with agitation. He was convinced the Vietcong had put a bomb in the stereo. Nurse Suzanne responded creatively. She called the security officer and said, "I want you to inspect the stereo and declare it bomb-proof. Tell the patient you're pulling guard so you've got his back and the perimeter is safe. Let him know that another guard will be on patrol when you leave duty." The police officer responded convincingly, and Jim's agitation subsided.

Then there's Bruce, a 67-year-old man who came for pain control. He hadn't wanted to come to our Hospice unit because, he said, "I'm afraid I'll never get out." His early days of anxiety and impatience were manifested with frequent summons on the call light. Probably because he realizes he's in a safe, loving environment his spirit is now emerging bright and full. He simply needed a little time and a little love to know that he need not fear. He has grown closer to his family as he approaches death and tells us, "I wouldn't trade these last few weeks in my life for anything."

Bruce's roommate, Richard, suffers respiratory distress from a tumor encroaching on his breathing tube. He awaits his daughter's arrival from Indiana. He says his suffering will be redeemed when he can rejoin his wife who died two years ago. "That will be a happy day," Richard says with tears. We share his anticipated joy.

Ben has a history of drug use and actively continues with alcohol abuse. He identifies himself as a loner who has witnessed much violence. "My family doesn't care about me," he told me. We've had some difficult sessions confronting his suffering. He's going to be discharged next week. I don't know what's going to happen with him. What I *can* tell you is that his brow unfurls after prayer, he plans to go to Alcoholics Anonymous meetings, and he wants to reach out to a faith community. Seeds planted and good intentions, however, are still not enough to withstand the ravages of alcohol. Ben's redemption awaits a courageous decision that only he can make every day for the rest of his life.

The last patient, Edwin, has severe chronic respiratory disease and is ready to die but he worries about his wife of 54 years. His needs are increasing rapidly, but he doesn't acknowledge them because he doesn't want to worry her. "I can't hold on much longer though," Edwin says while making plans to hold on for his wife's sake. We talk about the advantage of letting go so he can prepare himself and his wife for his death; we talk about the damage his denial is causing them both. Edwin cries as his grieving begins. Stories of sacrifice in the name of love are always worth beholding.

As these stories depict, paradoxically, there's probably more intense living on the Hospice and Palliative Care unit than in most of our own lives. In my first book, *Peace at Last: Stories of Hope and Healing for Veterans and Their Families*,[2] I wrote about veterans like the ones cited above. I told how they experienced healing as they near the end of their lives.

I've used the proceeds from the sale of that book to give more than

2,000 books to veterans. However, my own gift is frequently reciprocated with generosity. For example, I noted a World War II volunteer helping staff members at a Jacksonville hospice event. Slight of frame and doddering in gait, he set up food trays, opened doors, and performed clerical duties. After I had completed signing books for participants, the volunteer handed me a 20-dollar bill.

"Oh, no. You don't need to pay for your book. It was my gift to you," I protested.

He smiled kindly, saying, "You gave me a book last year when you were here. This year, I want to pay for my book so that you can buy more books for your veterans."

I could only smile and accept this 88-year-old man's graciousness. These acts, small as they may seem, are not small acts. They perpetuate a grace and energy that propel the work that I do.

At another hospice event, a funeral home director told me that he had worked with two different families who had lost sons in the Iraq war. "I bought each family one of your books. Both of them called me later to say how much it helped."

I handed him two more books. "Find two more families for these two books."

"You mean it?" he said incredulously.

"I would feel honored for you to do so."

He cried. I could only sit and marvel at the love and sense of responsibility that he felt toward the veterans he served. His was a gift much greater than the two books I had just given him.

I was getting on an airplane and noted a Vietnam vet by the insignia on his hat. Unfortunately, my books were in a checked suitcase. After we deplaned, I kept the veteran in view as we approached baggage claim. His suitcase came before mine so I tried to detain him.

"Wait, sir. Don't leave yet. I have something I want to give you."

He looked at me with suspicion, probably worried I was going to sell him something. Luckily, I spied my suitcase inching toward me on the carousel.

"Really. Hold on for just a minute," I pleaded as I ripped open my suitcase and produced the mysterious gift I referenced.

He accepted the book readily enough, but warily looked over its cover until he saw the words, *Stories of Hope and Healing for Veterans and Their Families.*

"I wrote this book for you. I want you to have it," I explained

"You wrote this book for me? I'm a Vietnam vet. No one's ever done *anything* for me," he said with sad guardedness.

"I know. I love Vietnam vets. You are the exact reason I wrote this book," I said sincerely.

"You're really the author of *this* book?" he pressed.

"I really am, sir."

He dropped his head and then fumbled in his pocket, producing a pen. "Then would you please autograph it for me? I never knew anyone who really cared about us."

I took his pen and inscribed my hope for his peace.

Six months later, my website received a message from this man's son. It read: "You gave my father a copy of your book at the luggage terminal at the Louisville airport last year. He had the Vietnam Vet hat and lots of tattoos. My father could not sleep that night at our lake house, which is nothing new, so he started reading your book. He told me he cried, which is something he rarely does. He said he finally realized he has PTSD. I would like to thank you personally for sharing your insight and helping those who are suffering."

Though I've had these kinds of responses countless times, I'm still enthralled and humbled every time they occur.

I had given a book to another Vietnam vet who sought me out when I was presenting in a nearby city. "I had to find you to tell you what a difference your book made," he told me as he introduced himself.

I said nothing, waiting for him to proceed.

"I've always been ashamed of my service in Vietnam. I took my uniform off in the airport as soon as I came Stateside. Only my family knows I served there. Now, I'm letting the secret out. I am no longer ashamed, and I'm proud. Thanks to you, I don't have to hide anymore."

He could only cry and hug me. I could only cry and accept his grateful homecoming.

These moments are profound. They are profound because they signify shifts in perspective that precipitate healing. I have had hundreds of veterans tell me how their hearts have been opened because the words on the pages bring peace to their hearts. Their peace has brought me great joy. However, it can sometimes feel overwhelming as portrayed in the next two stories.

Buzz was a World War II veteran who came to see me after he had read *Peace at Last.*[3] He lived locally and sought me out on the Hospice unit. He carried a German war helmet in his hands; it had a bullet hole with cracks radiating outward. Haltingly, he handed me the helmet. I was reluctant to accept it until he told me the story of how he had acquired it.

"I was a company commander on maneuvers in Germany near the Dachau concentration camp," he said, carefully choosing his words. He had joined his men digging a trench when he uncovered a foxhole with the remains of a German soldier, helmet, rifle, and pieces of a parachute. "His rifle was dismantled, so he must have been cleaning his weapon and was surprised by an American soldier."

I looked at Buzz unknowingly. I wasn't grasping the significance of the details he was offering.

"He shouldn't have been shot. He should have been ordered to surrender."

Still, I was perplexed. "But, you weren't there Buzz. How do you know what happened?"

His voice became low, and it was hard for me to understand him at first. "I don't know what happened, but I can imagine because I know what I saw. I took the helmet home with me as a reminder."

"A reminder of what, Buzz? I don't understanding what you're saying."

"Guilt. I took on the guilt for what was done to him. I felt I had to. We shouldn't have shot him. He should've been taken prisoner. Then, he'd still be alive today." Slowly, I was starting to understand. "I've kept this helmet in my closet for sixty years. I haven't told this to another soul, but after I read your book, I had to let you know that I've decided to let the guilt go. I had to find you to let you know the heaviness in my chest is gone, and I feel free now."

Buzz H. holding the German helmet of guilt along with a parachute fragment.

I could only feel wonder and relief as I felt the weight of the load he'd carried for so long. Although his guilt seemed irrational, there was a rational motive behind it. As he hugged me, I whispered, "Thank you for caring about the death of that German soldier, Buzz. Thank you for holding the space of forgiveness in the American heart for him. You've carried it long enough. I'm glad you've decided you can let it go now."

Like Buzz, guilt weighed heavily on Barry, another World War II veteran. Barry lived at a State Veterans Home. Stein Hospice provides end-of-life care at the facility. They give a copy of my book to every veteran upon admission to the facility. The staff also asked me to train them in how to better care for dying veterans. They wanted me to meet with Barry because he had aggressive and combative behaviors that had caused his removal from one section of the Veterans Home. I met with the 92-year-old veteran, along with 10 Hospice staff who were observing the interaction. Barry had read my book, and he was eager to meet me.

Initially, Barry and I talked about his relationship with his three estranged sons and his anger at being confined to a nursing home. Then,

I asked him about his military service.

"Wanna hear about my three Purple Hearts and two Bronze Stars?" he asked me proudly.

"No. We can talk about your medals later," I said gently. "Right now I'd be interested in hearing about things from World War II that might still be troubling you."

Barry's pride quickly turned to hostility. "All of it!" he said fiercely, wheeling quickly around to bring his face close to mine. I said nothing, but my eyes opened in surprise, and I motioned for him to proceed.

"Do you know what it's like to put a gun in the middle of a forehead and pull the trigger?" he asked intently, putting his forefinger in the middle of my forehead, pushing my head back.

Even though I had heard these kinds of stories from other veterans, I was unprepared for the intensity and directness with which he had responded. I summoned inner strength so that I could remain steadfast. My eyes never diverted from his. I shook my head "no," acknowledging that I didn't know what that was like.

"Ya wanna hear more?" he asked in a taunting manner.

I didn't indicate yes or no. I simply remained open to the anger and bitterness he was directing toward me.

He paused before he proceeded. "Do you know what it's like to tie a noose around a man's neck and watch him hang?" He leaned forward peering even more intently at me.

Again, I met his steely blue eyes that were piercing my soul with a steady gaze that belied the inner quaking I was experiencing as I imagined the horror that he had seen and done.

"Wanna hear more of what I did?" he challenged me.

Again, I said nothing, but my unwavering gaze let him know I could take it.

Barry then retracted his stance slightly and told me that he and a buddy had been ordered to patrol an occupied city. The names of the occupants were posted on the doors of the houses. They had gone into one house, however, and found three teenage boys whose names were not on the list.

"They weren't supposed to be there. They were just lying on their beds jeering at us with their arms behind their heads." Barry put his arms behind his head to show me how the boys looked. "The other soldier I was with asked me what we should do with 'em. I told him that we gotta peel 'em."

I narrowed my eyes quizzically, indicating that I didn't know what he meant.

Barry came close to my face, pushing back the bill of his Army hat so he could get even closer. "You split their heads open with the bullet. Their brains come out."

Tears came to my eyes as I imagined the shockingly intimate carnage.

"Yeah. Ya see? Want to hear more *NOW?*"

I shook my head no. "I can't hear any more," I told him without averting my gaze from his. "I've heard all I can hear."

Seconds ticked by as we sat locked together in silent wartime memories. The room was reeling, and I wasn't sure what to do next. Instinctively, I placed my hand firmly on his heart while my eyes peered closely into his soul, a place beyond the anger and venom he was spewing forth.[4] "Barry, I am so sorry that you were put in a position to see and do the things that you had to see and do at that young, tender age. I am so sorry that you had to experience that."

I felt Barry relax under my hand. Then tears came to his eyes, and we cried together. "I'm shaking," he said.

"That's okay, Barry. Let yourself shake, just breathe deeply as you shake. Breathe and shake."

Barry had great trust in the chaplain, so I motioned for Chaplain Vern to stand behind Barry and encircle him in a hug that could contain the trembling. I motioned for the other staff to draw in closely as well.

"Barry. We're here to encircle you with love while Chaplain Vern prays for you. Is that okay with you?"

Barry indicated consent, and Chaplain Vern prayed for peace in Barry's soul. Barry continued to cry and shake, even making low guttural noises. Afterward, he looked up with amazement at the team surrounding him, a team who had the courage to bear witness to his story. A look of relief came over Barry's face. Softness crept in to replace his furled and fierce brow.

Marie, a Vietnam War veteran who is one of my colleagues and had traveled with me, came forward. "Barry, I have a pin I want to honor you with." Marie showed him an American flag pin inscribed with "honored veteran." Barry remained silent, but held his gaze into Marie's eyes. "You deserve this. You have carried the guilt long enough. It took a lot of courage to do what you did here today. I want you to have this." Marie pinned his shirt collar and then enveloped him in a hug. Once again, Barry cried. In fact, all of us did. We were witnessing a soldier brought home from war at last.

Barry maintained his softness for the many months he lived. He was smiling, and even seemed light-hearted. He reconciled with two of his sons. Staff members were astounded with the change in him; I was not surprised by the change. Combat is like that. It can create mean and ugly places in peoples' souls, and those places can be covered up during much of a person's life. At the end of life, however, redemption awaits if people have the courage to avail themselves of the opportunity the way Barry did.

I didn't always know about the redemption of suffering at the end of life or at any other time in life for that matter. When I first became a nurse 30 years ago, I was naive and thought I could eradicate my patients' suffering. By rescuing them, I thought I would become a hero. Now I realize that suffering is inevitable and that heroism arises when I dare to encounter its distress. More importantly, I learned that I couldn't help my patients' suffering until I learned how to encounter my own. Ironically, it was my patients who taught me how to cultivate courage so that I could face affliction. They have been my heroes, showing me how to navigate through the labyrinth they courageously face at the end of their lives.

I'm certainly not the hero I had originally envisioned when I started my nursing career, and my path has been everything except what I anticipated. This unimagined experience is fortunate because the unexpected experience has yielded treasures I would otherwise have never known. This second book is about those treasures. Although the context for many of the stories is provided by my experience with veterans, this book is not about veterans. The principles are applicable to anyone, veterans and nonveterans alike; suffering and its redemption are universal. Accessing the interior hero is an assignment we are all tasked to fulfill.

Chapter One

Accessing the Hero Within: A Paradoxical Process

We are all here for a single purpose:
to grow in wisdom and to learn to love better.
We can do this through losing as well as through winning,
by having and by not having,
by succeeding or by failing.
All we need to do is to show up openhearted for class.[1]
-Rachel Naomi Remen, M.D.

No one taught me how to fail. No one showed me how to lose, and because I never learned these things, I felt alone when they occurred. Sometimes, I felt more than alone. I felt incompetent if I didn't win; I felt rejected if I wasn't the chosen favorite. I felt worthless or guilty if I couldn't please someone. Certainly, I never considered opening my heart for a class on how to experience losing and failing.

Winning and success have also been mine. Some achievements came from blind determination and relentless work. Other successes came my way because of sheer luck or the fortune of those around me. However, my real successes, the ones that give me the most personal fulfillment, have come from opening up to my "losings," "not havings," and "failings." I spent the first half of my life running from them. I've spent the last half learning how to show up for the hidden lessons they contain. I discovered that, paradoxically, the things I had been so fearfully fleeing were the very things that would free me to grow into my larger self.[2]

I learned these secrets from people I admired. I realized they knew something that I did not. When I looked very carefully at what set them apart, it was that they knew how to lose and fail. They had

1

not learned these traits from educational systems or advertisements. Schools tell us how to succeed; they show us how to hold on and control. Likewise, ads don't show us how to let go of people, places, or things. In fact, they teach just the opposite: We can have it all, more is better, and we can do whatever we want. Ads create a no-need-to-fail illusion that we are seduced into believing is true. It's no wonder that we feel like losers when we discover that we can't have it all, that more doesn't make us happier, and that we can't do whatever we want. This book seeks to counter that illusion. The people you are going to read about on these pages have allowed themselves to encounter failure; they even use it to reach depths within themselves. This deeper aspect of self that they access sometimes seems mysterious to me. Some people might call this deeper self the soul; others might call it the Self, the divine spark, or the kingdom of God within. I call it the "hero within" because it is the place inside ourselves that touches God. This inner giant is like the giant oak tree mapped within the proverbial acorn: an imprinted destiny or purpose that we are born to fulfill if we have the honesty, courage, and humility to do so. I've come to realize that each of us possesses this goal-directed vitality that tries to grow the seed of ourselves into fruition.

What I notice about the heroes in my life is that they allow the destiny imprinted in their personhood to mold and shape their lives. As they learn to trust this vision and rely on the inward vitality to attain it, they become less dependent on other peoples' approval, appreciation, love, and acceptance. Whether or not they are afraid also becomes less and less relevant. What becomes most relevant is living from a place of deep integrity.

Rather than becoming broken down by their hardships, my heroes are broken open. They show me how to successfully encounter failure and loss so I can develop resiliency. You will meet my heroes on these pages. You will encounter people who show us how to stop running from painful experiences. They invite us to open up to hardship so we can redeem our suffering with lessons that help us manifest the unique destinies we were born to fulfill. Then, we can inhabit ourselves more completely.

Carefully scrutinizing these heroes, I realized that trials and tribulations offer us opportunities to develop qualities that can help us become more like our true selves. To solve complex personal problems, we learn to let go of the illusion that the problem doesn't exist or that we aren't contributing to it so that we can live honestly. To have life-giving relationships with others, we develop the courage to speak authentically without fear of disapproval. Illness and aging help us let go of pride and vanity so we can develop the quality of humility.

Whether they were my patients or people in my personal life, I have noted common patterns and processes described above. Through stories, explanations, and the proper tools, I hope to articulate these processes so that readers will be able to use them because, within our depths, a hero is waiting to be born. Accessing the hero is a rather straightforward process, but it requires honesty, courage, and humility to do so. Although the process is simple, it is not easy. When we complete the process, however, we redeem our destiny; we materialize our God-given potential by expanding into our full capacity.

John's Destiny and Its Redemption

One of my former patients, John, highlights the process.[3] By most anyone's definition John was a failure. He had been an alcoholic since age 13. Rather than *feel* painful experiences, John numbed distressing emotions with alcohol. Because of his drinking habits, he had not achieved much success in his career or his relationships. In fact, he had a 6-year-old son he had not even met. When John was 37 years old, he lost his health. He was diagnosed with stomach cancer. His father and grandfather had also died of the disease at young ages. John plunged into despair. However, his poor health served as the wake-up call he needed to get his life on track.

The first thing John did was stop drinking. Sober and confronting a life-threatening illness, he saw things anew, and he opened up to his bleak and tumultuous feelings. His priorities shifted. He contacted his son's mother, Donna, and made arrangements to meet his son, Baily. John and Donna had been in love, and they found their feelings were still the same when they reunited. A few months later, they decided to marry. John moved his new family to Florida, so he could be near the VA hospital where he received his chemotherapy treatments.

I met John on one of his numerous readmissions to the hospital for complications from his illness. "Cancer saved my life," he told me. He had a new-found innocence. He was no longer afraid to encounter distressing feelings, so he had no need to numb them with alcohol. His new world looked very different. Not only did he now have a wife and son to share his life, but also he formed stronger bonds with his widowed mother and his four sisters. He became an active member of our cancer support group, helping other patients "save their lives."

John also had moments of despair and loneliness. He told me about a recurring nightmare he'd been having. "This grotesque-looking travel agent keeps asking me what I want. I keep dodging her, but she always manages to find me. I wake up trembling."

I often use imagery from dreams to help people understand experiences they may be avoiding. "Next time you should ask the travel agent what she wants," I told him. I proposed that he try to meet her while he was awake, and I was with him. "Close your eyes," I said quietly. "Bring her image to your mind." When he'd done that, I suggested that he tell her that the next time she came, he was going to ask her what she wanted.

John sat quietly for a few moments before opening his eyes and nodding. "If you don't ask her in the dream," I said, "ask her as soon as you wake up. Stay in that twilight sleep of a relaxed frame of mind and ask her what she wants. See what impressions come to your mind."

A few weeks later, John came to tell me the travel agent had visited him in the night.

"What'd she tell you?" I asked, fascinated. I should have been prepared for his answer, but I wasn't.

"She said she wanted to help me get ready for my trip. She wanted me to be comfortable. She asked what I needed."

My heart sank as I realized that his "trip" was his own death. "How do you feel about what she told you?" I asked him warily.

"Good. I'd never thought of her coming to help me. I only thought she was coming to take something away. Now I know I don't need to be afraid of her."

My disappointment with my own realization that John would soon be facing death turned into hope as we talked about what he needed to get ready for his "trip," focusing on end-of-life strategies that could successfully prepare him. Understandably, most of John's concerns focused on preparing his now 8-year-old son for his death. He didn't want Baily to repeat his own mistakes. He was especially hopeful that he could provide some guidance for Baily's sexual maturity. "That's when a boy really needs his father," John said. He wanted to compress a lifetime of fatherhood into their remaining months together.

John made a videotape teaching Baily how to shave and tie a tie, along with other fatherly advices he would not be able to provide in person. I also helped him write six letters that Donna was to give their son at milestones in Baily's life. These are some excerpts from each letter:

Dear Baily,
Surprise! – a voice from your past (and present and future). You have to remember not to go anywhere until your homework is done. Also, do the extra credit because it's like that magic card in the pocket you can redeem if the dog eats your homework. I hope you'll always learn that others can take a lot of things away from you, but they can't take away your education. I want you to remember not to compare yourself to others, but to do your best. Remember to pick good classes that will keep you interested. Consider science club. You always said you liked space. Go to the planetarium. Ask for a tutor if you need one. Find people who will help you. Lots of people want you to excel. Want that for yourself. Schools are wild now. You will have many temptations.

Be strong enough to resist the temptation so you don't betray yourself or undermine your goals. I want you to read this letter at the start of each school year from now on.

Dear Baily,
You're probably getting taller now and getting some hair on your body. Your penis may be growing, although it may not be as big as you want. Don't let anyone tease you about it. I remember taking a shower with a bunch of boys and trying to pull on mine to make it look longer. Now, I realize I need not compare myself with anyone else. I know you're not kissing girls yet, but you prepare by learning how to shave without razor stubble. Girls don't like razor stubble. You have to respect girls. Baily, love is not a game. Sex is not a game. God gave sex and love as a gift of pleasure. If you're going to start seeing a girl seriously, ask to meet her parents. That's a courtesy you should provide. Your virginity is a gift, and it's not going to go away unless you give it away. My advice to you is to wait for sex and don't give your love to just anyone. That would be irresponsible. At least wait until you are in college, even better until you marry. Sex can change everything. There are lots of other ways to sexually express yourself than intercourse. You are the one who will suffer the consequences of poor sexual choices. So be prepared for the consequences if you make poor choices.

Dear Baily,
I'm going to be watching over you. If you try to smoke, I'll be saying "No! No! No!" in your ear. Smoking is one thing that will keep you from blowing out your candles. If you get a car, I hope you will always remember it's a privilege. A policeman or court can take that privilege away. So follow the rules, including the golden rule. You see, when you have a car, you have a lot of mature decisions to make.

Dear Baily,
I hope this marriage is not a spur of the moment decision and you've put a lot of thought into it. A bad marriage is hard to deal

with. Don't do it if you're not prepared to do it for the rest of your life. Good communication skills are important. Talk about the little things like, "Would you ever consider living in Alaska?" Make sure you can compromise on issues. Be like the reed that can bend with the winds. I wish you a long and happy marriage with lots of children. Give my love and hello to your bride-to-be. Anytime you need me, if God will let me interfere, I'll be there. I wish you both all the happiness life has to offer.

Dear Baily,

Congratulations! I hope and pray your baby is healthy and well and that you understand the miracle you've been handed and the responsibility you are about to undertake. If there are potholes in the road, or if the child needs special care, I send even more prayers for healing your way. I hope you are happy parents because then you'll raise happy children. I hope your children bring you as much joy as you have brought me during these few years we had together. You can't see me, but I'm not far away. If there are any trials with your kids, I'll pray to God that you find the help you need. Don't be afraid to ask for help.

Dear Baily,

This is the last letter you will receive from me. I haven't had the wit of Johnny Carson or the love of Mother Teresa, but I do pray. I pray that in the place where there is extra love, that you will use it to shine a light on someone in the dark today who has forgotten that God is in their heart. I pray for people who want help. Since I first met you, Baily, you told me "When I grow up, I want to help people who are in trouble." I hope you have continued to keep that mission, and if you haven't, that you might reconsider it now. It will bring much peace, meaning, and fulfillment to your life.

After John's Death

John died a few weeks after these letters were written. I attended his memorial service. Chaplain Dan invited people to speak. As others shared their thoughts, I thought carefully about the many lessons John had taught me. Then, I shared my musings with his family: "If John had died three years ago, he would have just sort of fallen off the face of this earth. Many probably would have written him off as an alcoholic who got lost in his unused life. However, John's life changed these last three years. He used his loss of health as a means to wake up to the joys and despairs in his life. As a result, John learned how to love, and once he experienced love, his world changed and our world changed. He redeemed the mess he had created in his life. John always said, 'Cancer saved my life,' but I think what really saved his life was courage. John used cancer to summon courage so he could heal his brokenness. John didn't heal his life *in spite of his cancer,* he healed his life *because* of his cancer. Everyone here today bears witness to the hero that John became. He achieved the destiny you all knew that he was born to fulfill. May we each leave here letting John's example influence our own lives. May we each summon the courage to confront our own wounds so they can be used as sources of healing for ourselves and others. May we each change in the ways that we need so that we can fulfill our own destiny."

I still think about John. Had it not been for cancer, there is little doubt that John would still be living the life of a desperate man. Had he not accessed his interior hero, there is little doubt that he would have also *died* a desperate man.

I also think about Baily. I think about the hole in his heart that is healed each time he reads another letter from his father. I also think about the hole in Baily's heart that would still be there today if his father *hadn't* written those letters.

Redeeming Our Destiny by Accessing the Hero Within

I have had an advantage that most people have not had. I have worked for 30 years with people who are dying. Just like John's story demonstrates, possibilities for growth and expansion accelerate as death approaches; dying people become fertile ground for healing.

One reason this change occurs is because perceptions of time change. We all know the phenomenon of the person who says after surviving a potentially fatal accident, "My whole life flashed before me." Past, present, and future are no longer experienced as sequential at the moment of the accident; rather, time collapses into the ever-present now. Experiencing the eternity of the ever-present now is one of the gifts death offers. It's an inward space where past, present, and future coexist. This experience is very different from trying to block the past or defer plans for the future in order to live in the "present moment."

People who are aging often experience the eternity of the ever-present now not in a flash, but in a process of reflection. Elders don't "live in the past;" the past lives in the now, offering opportunities for insight and healing. They review their lives to see what lessons they have learned or what meaning their life contains. It is a natural search for insight before they let go of their earthly existence.

Not all people use life-threatening illnesses to discover meaning the way John did. There are various reactions to serious illness, and these reactions have always intrigued me. I notice that some patients *crumble* under a grim diagnosis, becoming passive and fatalistic. Other patients *fight* the illness; the disease becomes an adversary they are determined to defeat, using positive-thinking, denial, and sheer grit to bolster their morale so they can "rise above" it and go about their lives as if nothing has changed. However, there is a third group of patients who are like John; they neither cave into the disease nor fight it. Rather, they use their disease as a way to encounter life in a larger way. They heal broken relationships and express love and gratitude to others. Though they might be pensive, they are also humorous and even light-hearted. Their outward circumstance does not dictate their inward landscape; in fact, it only deepens it. Rather than fearing their disease, they open up to it. Although sadness and sometimes loneliness may be part of their illness experience, so are wisdom and serenity.

Some of the patients in the latter group come by these qualities naturally; they have learned how to successfully suffer hardships from previous life experiences, and fear no longer controls them. For others the trajectory is not smooth, but takes an up-and-down course. They struggle with moments of despair and loneliness. Rather than running from these moments, they use them as a passageway into the reality of their humanity, encountering their interior hero in the process. These are the patients I watched and let touch my soul so I could learn how to successfully suffer hardships in my own life.

A Three-Step Process

I have come to conceptualize a three-step process that facilitates access to the hero within each of us. I will describe the process in detail in subsequent chapters; however, I will outline them here using John as an example. The three steps are:
- Abiding: Showing up "openheartedly" to all of the emotional dimensions of life: the good, the bad, and the ugly, and more importantly, *embracing the part of self that is experiencing that feeling.*
- Reckoning: Changing our relationship to problematic situations, relationships, or aspects of self by cultivating the honesty, courage, and humility to face the source of distress.
- Beholding: Experiencing a newfound peace with the circumstance because the relationship to the problem has shifted.

Abiding

Abiding is more than just feeling an emotion; it includes *embracing the part of ourselves* that is generating the feeling. Most of us know how to abide with experiences that make us feel happy, hopeful, or loving. We open up to the part of self experiencing these feelings and let ourselves wholeheartedly laugh, relax, and smile. It's more difficult to abide with "negative" feelings such as fear, grief, anger, helplessness, or loneliness. Rather than open up to these experiences, we often numb them with denial, illusion, alcohol, workaholism, and other kinds of addictions or compulsions. Addictions, compulsions, and illusions make us smaller than who we are destined to be because the part of self covered up by the illusions and compulsions becomes isolated in fear and can't contribute to the integrity of the conscious self.

Abiding has two directional foci. Focused inward, abiding allows us to encounter ourselves; focused outward, abiding allows us to experience vicariously the emotional dimensions of others. When turned inward, abiding requires that we open ourselves to our inner experience, no matter what. In fact, one definition of the word *abide* is "to stand fast."[4] Thus, abiding means I "stand fast" with all parts of myself, even those parts that feel "bad" feelings, such as grief, helplessness, fear, and loneliness. I don't abandon or numb the aspects of self with these emotions, nor do I banish them into an imaginary nonexistence. When we shut ourselves off from feelings (including "bad" ones), we lose the part of self that is experiencing them. This is a serious loss.

Focused outward, abiding brings a different dimension to our relationships. The process transforms an empathetic relationship into an *abiding* presence. This distinction is important. The dictionary defines empathy as the "intellectual identification of oneself with another."[5] Abiding includes this meaning and more; it includes heart identification as well. Abiding means, I stand with you in your suffering even if I can't identify with it personally; I'm willing to feel your distress with you; I won't emotionally flee. Abiding your distress also means I'm willing to encounter any personal distress that your situation triggers.

With John, abiding began when he stopped numbing his despair and other "negative" emotions with alcohol. Instead, he opened up to his distress. Once he let himself abide the despair that this aspect of self was experiencing, he used the despair to encounter the meaninglessness in his life. Opening up to despair transported him into a place within his soul that birthed meaning, allowing the despairing, forsaken aspect of self to come home.

I also used the abiding process with John so I could encounter his personhood. This process required more than actively listening to him; it required that I vicariously experience him emotionally. I had to let myself abide the part of myself that was grieving John's antici-pated death; abiding requires me to engage my own "beingness." My willingness to engage my own beingness helped provide John with emotional safety so he could explore his own feelings.

Reckoning

Whereas abiding is a journey of the heart, reckoning is a journey of the head. Reckoning requires that we change; it's a willingness to change our relationship to problematic situations, relationships, or aspects of self by cultivating the honesty, courage, and humility to face the source of distress. Change requires us to do two things: We must let go of our current relationship to the problem and open up to the uncertainty of something new and different. This opening up is not always easy to do, which is why the development of honesty, courage, and humility is essential for the reckoning process.

Reckoning should not be confused with coping; they are dis-tinctly different processes. The dictionary defines the word cope as "to deal with problems."[6] It defines reckoning as an accounting, a getting to the bottom line, a line that often lies below surface con-sciousness. For example, John had spent 25 years *coping* with his problems by drinking alcohol. Once he was diagnosed with cancer, however, he decided to *reckon with what was causing him to drink* in the first place. Instead of being the victim of circumstances that caused him to escape into alcoholism, he decided to change his rela-tionship to his past. He asked forgiveness from Donna and Baily for abandoning them. He sorted out what was important from what was not. He took steps to regain his integrity so that his destiny could be redeemed. He summoned the honesty, courage, and humility to redeem his suffering.

Tools are often needed to help us reckon with the difficulties in our lives. As John demonstrates, forgiveness is often an essential ingredient of the reckoning process. Letter-writing can also be used to discover deeper dimensions the way John did. Forgiveness and letter-writing help us achieve integrity. These tools will be described in detail in Chapters Six and Seven. Dream analysis (like the travel agent chasing John) and mythological stories can also be helpful. (See Chapter Four.) They are surprisingly easy tools to use once we value their effectiveness and then practice using them personally.

Beholding

The result of abiding and reckoning with hardships is what I call beholding, that is, experiencing a newfound peace with the circumstance because the *relationship* to the problem has shifted. Once the shift has occurred, we receive energy from a deeper aspect of self and our integrity is restored. The situation may not be any different, but the relationship to the situation shifts with insight and new meaning. People often verbalize their experience of this shift by saying something like, "A load was lifted off my shoulders."

John's statement, "Cancer saved my life," reflects this shift in meaning. When this shift occurred, John received energy from a deeper place within himself. Recognizing and acknowledging this new meaning helped him act from a dimension of integrity. It also helped him gain confidence in tackling other problems because he learned how to trust resources beyond himself.

The definition of the word *behold* is "to see or look at."[7] Beholding, as I'm using it, means more than this definition. It means developing *inner vision;* it requires using one's soul to see. Thus, when we develop the honesty, courage, and humility to abide the effects of our past and reckon with the cause of our current distress, then we are able to behold a future filled with hope; peace replaces chaos and pain. In other words, we experience healing.

SELF-AWARENESS EXERCISE
Depicting Our Life Story: Identifying the Puzzle Pieces

Create a long scroll using a roll of paper or taping pieces of paper together. Reflect over your life. What have been the significant events that have helped shape and mold your responses to the world? Think of each event or person as a piece of a puzzle containing information that helps you know and understand who and how you are. Think of your conscious self as the central pieces of conjoined puzzle with a homing device calling outlying puzzle pieces that have been lost or forsaken. The more pieces consciously conjoined, the stronger the homing signal. If there are not many conjoined central pieces, the signal will be weak, and you will have to listen closely to hear the self calling broken pieces back into wholeness. (Alternatively, you could create your Life Story in the computer.)

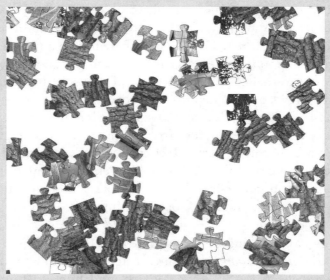

First, write the significant events and people on a timeline that starts with your birth and ends with today. You may want to draw pictures or use stickers, colored markers, or computerized graphics to highlight different events.

Second, using a 1-10 scale (1=minor, 5=significant, 10=major), rate how much your life was impacted by each significant event or person depicted on the scroll. These ratings should include both positive and negative people and experiences.

Third, review your Life Story again. What else needs to go on it? Do any of your ratings seem inappropriate? (For example, if your mother died when you were young, a rating of 3 might be minimizing the impact unless there was another person who heroically filled the gap.) Remember to include seemingly "little" events that took you either away from yourself or toward yourself. (For example: you were called "selfish" when you pursued any personal interests rather than working the family business. This experience caused you to become less you by becoming overly responsible for taking care of others, and not taking care of yourself with "self-ful" hobbies like reading, taking long walks, or going out with friends. On the other hand, a neighbor always told you how creative you were, prompting you to dress uniquely. As a result, you value your individuality, becoming more you.)

You can hide your Life Story so no one else sees it; it's only important that you don't hide it from yourself. It will take honesty, courage, and humility to forthrightly uncover some of the aspects of how you responded to difficult events. You will probably deny the significance of some events; write them down anyway. You will have lots of ways to fool yourself into thinking you felt one way when actually a façade hides the opposite feeling. Have the courage to persevere. Tell yourself you *want* to experience all of yourself, even those parts that you don't want to see because you are afraid or even ashamed. These parts are especially in need of your energy and attention; they need a voice so they no longer need to hide. Welcome this part of self home so you can hear what he/she has to say to you.

It can also be helpful to give your Life Story to someone who really knows you. If they are trustworthy, have them review your Life Story. Ask them to point out events and people you may have overlooked. Seek stories about yourself from them.

Universal Application

I believe that we are born whole with an imprinted destiny we are designed to fulfill. Each time we close down to a feeling we don't like, the part of self experiencing the feeling is disconnected from the whole; we lose our integrity by closing ourselves off from the message this silenced self is trying to tell us so it can be rejoined to the conscious self. We turn away from the very piece of self that we need to be facing. More importantly, we lose the energy of this exiled self.

Failing to gather these lost pieces of self means we do not inhabit ourselves completely. To the extent that we don't completely inhabit ourselves, we live an unused life. The abiding, reckoning, and beholding processes facilitate gathering these lost aspects of self so they can be welcomed back home, and we can regain our integrity.

After you read this book, my hope is that each reader will understand and value the abiding, reckoning, and beholding processes so they can be used to redeem the suffering we have experienced. In redeeming our suffering, we will need to access the hero within. This book will provide you with the tools to find your hero. It will be up to you to cultivate a willingness to develop the honesty, courage, and humility to make the inward journey. This willingness often comes as you participate in the process. You will then be able to use what you learn to completely encounter all parts of yourself. This process will allow you to grow into aspects of yourself that you were previously reluctant to inhabit. You can then use the process to heal abuse, bring peace to broken relationships, lose weight, face death, or any challenging situation. From small, everyday problems to overwhelming dilemmas, you will become empowered.

Unlike many self-help tactics, this book will *not* teach you how to overcome, endure, "rise above," or transcend problems. Rather, you will learn how to use the problem or limitation to transport you into deeper places within yourself to cultivate qualities that will open you to energy beyond yourself. Instead of running from darkness, you will discover that shadows create color and richness in your life. Once you learn how to abide and reckon with difficulties, you will succeed not *in spite* of your limitations but *because* of them.

The first four chapters of this book require some study to grasp the concepts, but the required effort will pay off. You will soar through the last four chapters as you apply the lessons in a life-changing way. Once you become familiar with the process and are willing to use it with personal challenges, you will then be able to use it with others. People will seek your presence because they experience your peacefulness and lack of fear. You will become a healer. Our world desperately needs your healing presence.

Lessons on Accessing the Hero Within

- If you haven't read the Prologue of this book, read it now. It provides the lessons that are the foundation for accessing the hero within.
- We are all here for a single purpose: to grow in wisdom and learn to love better. We can do this through losing as well as through winning, by having and not having, by succeeding, or by failing. All we need to do is to show up openheartedly for class. When we do, we redeem the destiny we were born to fulfill.
- We are born with an imprinted destiny, like the giant oak tree mapped within the proverbial acorn. Each of us possesses this goal-directed vitality that tries to grow the seed of ourselves into fruition.
- As we learn to trust the vision we were born to fulfill, we start relying on inward vitality and passion to attain it. In the process, we become less dependent on other peoples' approval, appreciation, love, and acceptance. Fear also becomes less and less relevant. What becomes most relevant is living from a place of deep integrity.
- Paradoxically, the things we so fearfully flee are the very things that free us, growing us into our larger selves.
- Heroes show us how to encounter failure. They don't "rise above" or endure their hardships; they use their hardships to reach deeper depths within themselves. Then, they are able to inhabit themselves more completely.
- Experiencing the eternity of the ever-present now is one of the gifts death offers. It's an inward space where past, present, and future coexist.
- Within our depths, a hero is waiting to be born. Accessing the hero is a rather straightforward process, but it requires courage, honesty, and humility to do so. The process is simple, although it is not easy.

Chapter Two

Abiding: The First Step in the Healing Process

Neurosis is always a substitute
for legitimate suffering.[1]
- Carl Jung

Abiding starts when we encounter the entire emotional dimension of our personhood. Abiding the "negative" end of that spectrum was difficult for me to learn initially. As I did so, however, I slowly began to realize that feelings, such as anger, fear, loneliness, and emotional pain, were only "negative" because I was afraid of them. By refusing to acknowledge them, I not only cut myself off from these feelings, I also cut myself off from the aspect of myself that was experiencing them. At that time, I did not think this loss was significant; now, I understand its magnitude.

I began looking at how I handled feelings. I realized that I often erected a stoic wall to "fight or flight" emotional pain that I didn't want to suffer; I pretended all was well, foolishly hiding these feelings from myself and others. I used denial to deal with my problems because it perpetuated my illusions about the world being the way I wanted it to be. Rather than letting myself feel anger or emotional pain, I either pretended I didn't have a problem, or I minimized problems by saying, "It's no big deal." Like a callus formed to prevent sensitive blisters, I created a calm, cool veneer.

I was raised in a culture that emphasized putting on a smiling face, and I was not immune to its influence. Whenever a lump came to my throat, I shoved it down along with the embarrassing tears that brought it forth. Anger was just as distressful; I denied its very existence and disowned the aspect of myself feeling it.

Developing the courage to acknowledge my emotional pain and anger, as well as accept the part of me that was experiencing these feelings took time. Experiencing emotional pain was easier to learn because there was no way around it. Working in hospice, I was surrounded with sadness as patients died and their families were left bereft. I slowly learned that stoic walls were of no help to dying people or their families. My stoic wall was no good to myself either. Denying my pain segregated me from the vitality of myself that was generating the pain. As I softened my stance toward emotional pain, my fear of it also softened. I was able to let myself grieve. The adage, "Those who grieve well, heal well," became less of an enigma to me.

Confronting anger was a bit more difficult, yet I knew it was important. I began to realize that it was not about getting rid of anger, but rather hearing what it had to say so that I could come to know that part of myself. I started by telling myself, "It's okay to feel angry, Deborah." This was a big step because I thought anger was a negative feeling that well-adjusted people didn't have. I was afraid of hurting other people's feelings if I spoke my anger. I was worried it would expose something about me others wouldn't like; then, my comfort and security would be disrupted. Instead, I used energy to suppress anger, disguising it by saying I was upset, or lying and saying there was no problem. I wanted to be the peacemaker, and I thought personal anger would only interfere. Not surprisingly, I often relinquished myself in relationships.

I associated anger with violence, which only reinforced my fear of it. I am not a violent person, and I didn't want to become one. Slowly I began to realize that violence toward others or even one's self is, ironically, caused by a lack of connection with anger. Although they have no difficulty feeling their anger, hostile people are unable to make the acquaintance of the aspect of self that is generating the anger. Rather than letting anger transport them into a deeper interior space where they could uncover a more vulnerable feeling, such as emotional pain, violent people keep the anger *away* from their inner selves by fighting that pain. Rather than using their anger to change themselves, they repel it onto a target. The more disconnected they are from the aspect of themselves that generates their internal anger, the more violent they become. As their inward self dwindles, they become more insistent that others change in the mistaken belief that the other person changing will avert having to make personal changes themselves.

Once I realized that acknowledging my anger would take me more deeply into myself, I stopped resisting it and tentatively started expressing my anger to others who cared about me. They didn't stop loving me the way I feared. Although expressing my anger was a risk, it was a risk I was now willing to take because it became more important to be myself than to create facades to please others.

I changed my language too. "I'm angry" was no longer foreign. Then I discovered an important secret about anger that totally changed my relationship with it. Each time I let myself feel angry, I could release it because it had served its threefold purpose of (1) notifying me that I need to define myself in a problematic situation in which I had not been respected, (2) deciding to let the problem go if I determined my anger was unfounded, or (3) using it to examine vulnerable feelings (pain, guilt, fear, jealousy, etc.) that the anger might be covering up. I marveled at the vitality and genuineness I gradually gained as I let myself heal what I hadn't been letting myself feel. I was beginning to appreciate the meaning of the Chinese proverb that says suppression leads to momentary relief and permanent pain, whereas feeling the experience leads to momentary pain and permanent relief. It was yet another reminder that feelings have energy; it's better to feel them consciously than to let them gain power in the unconscious where they can cause neurotic behaviors.

Abiding: Opening Up to Ourselves and to Others

You will remember that abiding means opening our heart to all of the emotional dimensions of life: the good, the bad, *and* the ugly, and more importantly, *embracing the part of self* that is experiencing that feeling. Although feeling emotions is an important aspect of abiding, embracing the aspect of self that is generating the feeling distinguishes abiding as a different process. This distinction is important because simply feeling emotions is a surface process, whereas opening up to the aspect of self *causing* the feeling requires deeper insight. Every time I deny an emotion by covering it up, I'm lying. The part of self that is experiencing the feeling is left stranded, saying, "Can't you hear me? Don't you want to hear what I think? Don't I count for anything?" This aspect of self then gets lost in unconsciousness, taking its energy with it. Recovering this part of self is important because we not only learn the truth it's trying to speak, but we regain its vitality.

Abiding not only includes encountering ourselves, it also includes focusing outward so we can vicariously experience the emotional dimensions of others with whom we want to connect. Abiding ourselves and others is a dynamic process that often occurs simultaneously. The first person who raised my awareness about the dynamic nature of the process was a difficult patient who generated staff complaints.

"He's driving us nuts," Dana, one of the nurses, told me. "He wants us to take him outside to smoke, but he gets mad because we don't have time to take him very often."

Since I eat my lunch outside, I offered to take the patient with me that afternoon. "It will at least get him off your backs during the middle of the day," I told Dana.

So that day, in addition to my brown-bagged lunch, I picked up a disheveled patient with severe emphysema. "Would you like to come out and enjoy the sunshine and a cigarette while I eat my lunch?" I asked.

"Yes ma'am. Yes ma'am," he said, scrambling to assure he had enough smokes.

I pushed him outdoors, parked his wheelchair at the edge of the picnic table, and turned off his oxygen so it wouldn't ignite. I tried to hide my annoyance about people with respiratory disease who don't stop smoking.

While I ate my lunch, he remained silently aside, taking long drags on his cigarettes and looking off into the distance.

Occasionally I'd ask how he was doing, and he'd nod in contentment.

When lunchtime was over and I was about to wheel him back into the hospital, he spoke for the first time. "I just want to know one thing," he said. "What's a woman like you doing eating lunch with a grumpy old man like me?"

I laughed at his question before I responded. "Oh, I don't know. I guess I sort of like 'grumpy old men' like you." I was grateful that I had started learning how to abide my own grumpiness rather than banishing it into denial; otherwise, I would have been tempted to tell him that he wasn't grumpy.

As I pushed his wheelchair into the hospital, I put one hand on the back of his neck and shoulder, massaging his thin muscles as we made our way indoors.

"Oh thank you, thank you, thank you," he said with a loud exhaling sigh of relief.

I wasn't sure if he was grateful for the massage or for taking him outside to smoke so I asked him what he was thanking me for.

"I'm thanking you for..." his voice trailed off without completing the sentence. I said nothing, waiting for him to collect his thoughts. I was unprepared for how he would resume. "I'm thanking you for loving a grumpy old man like me."

I was speechless. I could hardly say, "But I wasn't loving you. I was just doing my nurses a favor by getting you off their backs." Instead, I remained silent and let myself absorb the meaning of his words.

That man, whose name I do not now remember, showed me what he needed and what I did not know. He was showing me how to *abide* with people: how to show up openheartedly to them even though they are different from me. My patients were veterans, and they had a military background I didn't share. Their hard-fisted and sometimes hard-drinking ways didn't always mesh with my softer, teetotaling manner. Sometimes it's easier to feel angry toward them or remain detached. Abiding, however, requires that I open up to the part of myself that is feeling angry or disconnected from others. It's difficult for me to open myself to people who are different from me; it's hard to connect with people I don't always understand. Yet, the process of abiding requires opening up, and the connection that occurs is often exactly what is needed. Some might call this connecting process "empathy," but I call it abiding to distinguish qualities that extend *beyond* empathy. Empathy could be likened to patting a beloved pet, whereas abiding is holding and cuddling it. Both empathy and abiding are good, but the latter is far more satisfying because it connects on a deeper level.

Abiding with other people is more than just passively hearing what they say. It requires experiencing what they say, which requires me to open myself and let myself feel their words. Abiding requires self-awareness coupled with wholehearted listening. Listening with our whole being allows us to experience the other person's beingness. To listen this way, I must also be able to abide with my own self. Eckhart Tolle describes this two-way abiding quality: "When listening to another person, don't just listen with your mind, listen with your whole body. Feel the energy field of your inner body as you listen. That takes attention away from thinking and creates a still space that enables you to truly listen without the mind interfering. You are giving the other person space – space to be. It is the most precious gift you can give…You cannot feel someone else's Being except through your own."[2] This quality of beingness transcends my professional role with patients so that personhood is shared.

I've often thought about the reason we prefer to empathize with others rather than abide with them. The conclusion I've drawn is that empathy feels safer; it doesn't require us to open up to an emotional connection with another person's suffering; therefore, we don't have to learn how to let go of it. Our American culture focuses primarily on how to achieve, gain, control, and hold onto, so learning how to let go of another person's suffering does not come naturally. Therefore, we may not know how to open up to abide with others. Abiding suffering means I'm willing to join you in your suffering. It also means I've got to learn how to let go of it so I don't become overwhelmed or take on things that are not mine to take on. Our fear and ignorance about how to let go causes us to miss opportunities to create openings so that abiding can occur.

Rather than staying detached, I believe we can learn how to open our hearts to people *without* losing ourselves. Maintaining ourselves without letting other peoples' problems drain our energy is a letting-go process that requires understanding three things. First, we have to become comfortable with our own losings, failings, and sufferings. Second, we have to recognize that other people have a hero inside too. We can't access it for them. They must find their own way. Third, we do not need to be afraid of uncertainty; in fact, we should learn how to befriend it when it accompanies change. When we are reaching out to people who are undergoing change, our job is to *en-courage* them to abide the insecurity of uncertainty while the change is occurring so that they can resist the temptation to return to the comfort of "the way it used to be."

While we are abiding with someone we wear their moccasins with them. We store their footprints in our soul, but when it's time to leave, we give their moccasins back so they have protection for their soles as they walk without us. Otherwise, we become enablers.

When I find myself wanting to protect someone from the pain or hardship they are experiencing, I have to tell myself, "Let go, Deborah. *En-courage* them. Cheer them on. Help them open up to their loss. Hold the space of hope for them, but don't do it for them." Enablers have a hard time seeing how much damage they do when they prevent people from discovering their hero within.

Rather than trying to change someone, abiding means being willing to let the person change *me*, to touch me. It means developing a willingness to hear the good, the bad, and the ugly, including stories I'd rather not hear about, such as childhood trauma, wartime experiences, or how difficult it is to be sick or face death. As I learned how to abide my own feelings of loss and failure, I became better able to abide with other people such as Christine. She chronically suffered from lupus, a disease of the skin, muscles, and joints. At age 43, she had suffered a stroke. Although she lived with her husband and two teenage sons, she had spent most of her recent months in the hospital. Each time she was admitted to the medical unit, I was consulted to help manage her pain and suffering.

Our first meeting was difficult. I heard her before I saw her; her screams were echoing down the hallway. "Jesus help me!" she kept shouting over and over again.

The staff felt utterly inadequate. They were also afraid that Christine's screams would impact other patients on the unit. "We're giving her high doses of pain medications, but it doesn't help," one of the nurses told me. "Do something for her," she begged.

They were right. Pain medication relieves pain; it doesn't always relieve other forms of suffering. No amount of morphine could alleviate what Christine was going through.

While the nurses were trying to contact the physician for more medication, I tried to assess Christine's pain. Conversation only heightened her agitation; my assessment would have to wait. She kept her eyes squeezed shut as if blocking out the world would block out the pain it held.

I sat quietly at Christine's side for several minutes, letting myself absorb her suffering, waiting for an inner cue to prompt me into response. I felt my helplessness, and I was trying to learn to accept that feeling without getting frustrated, so I remained calm and didn't rush to do anything. In doing so, I surprised myself by starting to hum *Amazing Grace*. Slowly I sat on the edge of her bed humming softly; it seemed to help. Though she kept yelling, her tone grew less frenzied. Gradually, I got in bed with her, slipping my arms around her, cradling her head on my chest where her ear could absorb the soothing vibration of my hum. It was an odd thing to do, but I could feel her relax.

I started taking slow, deep breaths, hoping the rhythm would soothe her. Meanwhile, I stayed open to her pain. I placed my palm on her sternum, a technique that is usually very calming.[3] Soon her shouts turned into whimpers, then her whimpers turned into sighs.

When the nurse came in ten minutes later with more pain medication, Christine was asleep in my arms. I gently slid out from underneath her. We brought the comfort cart (a rolling stand that

holds both a CD player for peaceful music and an aroma therapy dif-
fuser that produces calming scents) to her bedside. This portable station can transform a hectic environment into a peaceful oasis.

When I returned the next day, Christine seemed less overwhelmed. Neither of us mentioned our time together the previous
day; I wasn't even sure she recognized me. She was able to talk, and
I was able to assess her pain and suffering. She said her physical pain
extended over her chest and arm, and she had muscle pain throughout her legs and hips so severe that even the pressure of the sheet
hurt. Harder than her physical pain, though, was her loneliness.
Although her children and other family members visited when they
could, she still had long hours alone.

She realized that she might die and feared that she might not be
able to help her children through their teenage years. I told her I could
bring a tape recorder so she could give messages of encouragement and
motherly advice that would survive her death. That idea brought her
comfort. We talked about her spiritual concerns, and I said that I
would make arrangements for the chaplain to visit. I also promised to
bring her a CD recording of the Bible as she had requested.

As I was about to leave, I asked her about our time together the
day before.

"Christine, do you remember my visit yesterday? You were in
a lot of pain. I got in bed with you and held you. I hope that was all
right with you. If it wasn't, please tell me."

"Was that you?" she said. "Oh, heavens yes! I thought you were
my Mama holding me and singing. I thought she'd come from heav-
en to make my pain go away."

This kind of physical abidement that I did with Christine sym-
bolizes the emotional and spiritual abidement I try to cultivate in all the
relationships that are important to me. I've come to realize that abiding
can respond to suffering in ways that empathy and medications cannot.

Practical Skills That Can Be Learned

When I first encountered Christine's suffering, I was afraid. I wanted to hear what she was experiencing, yet I felt helpless. I knew that giving false hope or useless platitudes such as, "Things will get better" would not ease her pain. What Christine needed was for me to listen *with an open heart,* which meant I had to encounter my *own* pain. That's when I recognized the relationship I had with my own suffering. I had banished all the Deborahs who were frightened, angry, lonely, sad, and ashamed. I didn't know what they were seeing, thinking, or feeling because I was too scared to ask. I didn't like those aspects of myself, and I didn't know how to confront them or listen to what they had to say to me. Ironically, I had perpetuated the very thing that others had done with me: ignored and neglected the displeasing Deborahs. This self-awareness empowered me. I could beckon these parts of myself back home by simply opening up to them and nurturing them. I began to understand that looking outside myself for a source of strength, love, and courage sabotaged my ability to meet my interior hero who generated these vitalizing qualities.

I also realized that feelings, such as anger, fear, shame, loneliness, and helplessness, were not the source of my suffering. My suffering came from forsaking those aspects of myself that were experiencing the feelings. I was cutting myself off from the vitality and truth about who I was. I began to realize that I needed to seek an open relationship with the part of self experiencing unwanted feelings. I realized that I could take one of three stances with a threatening feeling:

- Deny the feeling, unconsciously lying to my conscious self
- Pretend a different feeling exists, consciously lying to my self
- Acknowledge the feeling, listen to the self that is generating it, and decide to restore my integrity by opening up to it.

With these new awakenings, I also realized how I had misapplied "positive thinking." I used it to deny the authenticity of my feelings, thinking it would make me feel better and create a more upbeat environment for everyone else. In reality, using positive thinking in this manner invalidated my feelings, and I became less authentic, losing an important aspect of my integrity. I gradually learned how to open up to my feelings by simply affirming them with a different kind of positive thinking every time I felt "negative" feelings: "Stop resisting Deborah. Your job is to feel your _____ (grief, anger, fear, etc.)" Paradoxically, this often helped me feel less helpless in the situation because real "positive thinking" means having the confidence to open up to "negative" aspects of self rather than being afraid of them. When I can accept my limitations, I no longer have to fear what will come or feel guilty for what I cannot do. Instead, I grow into myself with confidence of who I am and who I am not.

SELF-AWARENESS EXERCISE
Understanding Our Relationships
with the World, Others, and Ourselves

This awareness assignment has two parts. Both parts have relevance to how you orient yourself in relationships, roles, and problematic situations today. This assignment will help reveal puzzle pieces that may be missing from your whole *self*.

The first part of this exercise will help you discover the emotional response you had to events that shaped you, as well as the part of

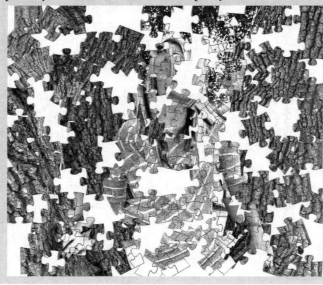

self that might still be trapped in the experience. Review your Life Story from Chapter One. Carefully look at how you emotionally responded to significant events and people. (Remember, we have all of these feelings; it's part of our humanity. It's not about erasing the feelings; it's about hearing what they have to say so that you can make the acquaintance with the part of yourself generating the feeling. Your job is to show up for the human experience.) By each event or person on the scroll, draw or write out how you emotionally responded. (Emotional responses include feelings such as anger, fear, pain, happiness, uncertainty, security. Thoughts are *not* feelings.) You can use words or pictures to express your response. (For example, Edvard Munch's painting, *The Scream*, might best depict a trauma you've experienced.)

The second part of the exercise will help reveal the relationship you have chosen to have with the event because of the emotional response it generated. Review your emotional responses. For each response, ask yourself these questions:

- What feelings were banished into the shadows because you were afraid of them when the event occurred? How did you numb "negative" feelings? (For example, overeating, staying busy, erecting a stoic wall, or putting on a happy face are common coping mechanisms.) What did you hide from everyone else, even yourself? (You have lots of ways to fool yourself into thinking you felt one way when actually a façade hides the opposite feeling. For example, you may have used anger to cover up emotional pain; conversely, you may have used sadness or depression to cover up anger. You might hide happiness, thinking you aren't worthy of it. Make a list of feelings in others that scare you. What do you do with these feelings in yourself?)
- Carl Jung says that neurosis is always a substitute for legitimate suffering. Ask yourself: "What do I use as a substitute for legitimate suffering?" (e.g., denial, blame others, cover up unwanted feelings with more acceptable feelings, build stoic walls, overeat, etc.)

Remember that to the extent that you blame others or deny your own experience, you lose yourself, and the vitality of your authentic self dwindles. Have the courage to persevere. Tell yourself you *are willing* to see all of yourself, even those parts that you have been denying are even there. When you are done, go back and review your responses. Ask yourself, "What else?" Dig deeper.

- A part of yourself might still be trapped in the experience, consuming energy unconsciously. On a 0-10 scale, rate how much aspect of self is still trapped in each experience. To help you determine this number, consider two things:

  ❑ Have you really talked about the experience and let yourself experience the feelings that occurred? (If not, there's a part of you that is still stuck feeling the feelings *unconsciously* because you refuse to open up to the emotions that are there. The energy of those feelings is blocked and segregated from self, so you would score yourself a high number because much of that aspect of self is still consumed with the experience.)

  ❑ On the other hand, you may have allowed yourself the honesty of the associated feelings without encountering the part of yourself that is generating the emotion. If so, you might be mired in your anger, grief, guilt, etc. *without encountering the part of self generating that feeling.* (In other words, the feelings are on the surface but the aspect of self feeling them is still left alone and untended, so you would, likewise, score yourself a high number.)

Wholeheartedly Listening for Peoples' Truth

Anyone who wants to abide with others can develop the skill to do so. The desire to learn coupled with the willingness to change allows the process to occur. The first step is to learn how to abide with ourselves. Once I became more aware of my own pain, I was able to listen to others more carefully; I wanted to hear what they were saying and, as importantly, to what they were not saying. I refrained from speaking so intensely or giving advice so matter-of-factly. I let go of the need to control my own fear of helplessness and inadequacy and instead let myself experience these feelings. I stopped trying to rescue people from their feelings of anger, fear, pain, guilt, loneliness, helplessness, and uncertainty they were trying to express, and instead help them feel whatever they were feeling.

Helping people feel whatever they are feeling is like an archaeologist on an excavation project trying to discover whatever might be hiding beneath the surface. When I'm abiding with someone, I join the person in a search for their authentic experience. I'm not only helping them feel their feelings, I'm helping them open up to the part of themselves that is generating the feeling.

Sometimes, I'm unwilling to be with another person's experience. I want them to smile, be compliant with my agenda, or make me feel good. When I do this, I lose my power because I'm creating an illusion of what I want rather than accepting reality. Abiding is a nonjudgmental process that requires honesty to see what we don't want to see and humility to open our heart to what we previously blocked. Abiding often requires courage to face fears and experience feelings; bravery is the courage to face whatever is. My role is often to act as an *en-courager,* with others and with myself.

The reason abiding can be so effective is because it provides safety for people to explore their fears and the parts of themselves that they've discarded. An abiding presence fosters connection and engenders trust. Connection and trust are essential elements in a therapeutic relationship; they often have to be gained quickly on a hospice unit because patients don't have long to live. Connection and trust are also hard to gain with people who have experienced trauma. They have been emotionally wounded, and it can be difficult for them to reach out to others or let others in. Thus, learning how to *abide* with people sometimes facilitates connections that would not otherwise be possible.

Learning how to listen with our whole being is difficult. I can be like the fickle friends of a man named Job in the Old Testament of the Bible. Job suffered what we now call Posttraumatic Stress Disorder (PTSD) when his 10 children were killed, he lost all his possessions, and his health painfully failed. He became angry with

God for his sufferings. When three friends heard of Job's adversities, they traveled to his side "to come and mourn with him and to comfort him. And when they raised their eyes from afar and did not recognize him, they lifted their voices and wept; so they sat down with him on the ground seven days and seven nights, and no one spoke a word to him, for they saw that his grief was very great."[4]

For that first week, his three friends *abided* with Job. It's not clear what happened to change their minds, but after a week, they modified their tactics. They started telling Job that he brought on his troubles by sinning and he needed to repent. In other words, they stopped abiding and started advising. As a result, Job felt abandoned, angry, and forlorn.

Sometimes I'm a good listener the way Job's friends were initially; other times I'm not a good listener. "I'm too busy;" "I've got better things to do;" I've got a hundred excuses why I can't, don't, or won't listen. I can also be lazy. It takes work to listen so I can hear what's said and, equally, what's not said. It takes work to turn off the distractions of a hospital environment and my inward environment. I get absorbed in my own world with my own agendas. Because of the tension that accompanies coming to grips with a problem, abiding can become even more difficult; I'm a fixer and advice-giver, and I want that tension relieved so I don't have to suffer it.

Listening with an open heart means paying attention. The better listener I become, the more I realize what a good listener I'm not. A quadriplegic patient who had been institutionalized for 40 years helped me understand. He said that he could tell which staff members didn't want to hear him by looking in their eyes.

"What do you see there?" I asked.

"I see deafness," he said.

As he said it, a chill had gone up my spine. I knew there were times when he saw deafness in *my* eyes, especially when he was telling me things I didn't like to hear. After that, I discarded the part of my training that had taught me to maintain an expressionless face. Instead I let my feelings show through my facial expressions. If patients were happy, I let my face lighten and eyes brighten as I felt their lightheartedness. If they were confused and trying to sort things out, my face became tense as I joined in their search. If they were sad and lonely, my eyes sometimes filled with tears. They could see I was changed by what they were saying.

One day, I was with a group of staff around a patient's bedside. I had been silently absorbing and vicariously experiencing everything the patient was saying. A nurse came in late, apologizing to the patient and asking what she had missed. He pointed to me and said, "Ask her. She hasn't said a word, but she hasn't missed anything I've said. It's written all over her face." His words validated the value of abiding.

I used to think that as long as I stayed empathetically focused on another person, then he'd feel supported, but empathy keeps me on the periphery because my heart doesn't have to be engaged with the person. I don't have to experience him. Abiding, on the other hand, has a slow, quiet, absorbing energy that soaks up the person's experience. When I abide with a person, it's like a switch that's flipped from "task" to "abide" mode, from the "me" or the "you" mode to the "us" mode. It's easiest to notice this process in my personal relationships. My closest friends not only hear my pain, they *feel* it too, and I no longer feel so alone and inadequate.

Helping People Feel

Abiding includes listening with my posture. It means sitting down rather than standing over people. In fact, our Hospice and Palliative Care team put casters on our chairs so we could roll to patients' bedsides to be with them at eye level; it helps equalize the power. Abiding includes leaning forward to engage in the listening process. It means meeting patients where they are, even if it's on the floor. A nurse colleague gave me that insight. A man was sobbing in the fetal position on the floor of the room where his father had just died. Marlene said nothing; she simply lay down on the floor with him. I categorize her action as abiding of the highest order. Later, the son wrote a note telling us how meaningful Marlene's action had been.

Unlike empathy, abiding means helping people feel whatever it is they are feeling or are afraid to feel. I was explaining the importance of feelings to a patient, when he poignantly asked, "Will I ever be able to feel again?"

"You will," I had responded. "And it starts by telling yourself that it's okay to feel."

Abiding feelings can be especially effective with people who have complex issues. Our Hospice and Palliative Care team met with a patient who was so difficult that staff didn't want to care for him. Nothing they did seemed to satisfy him. He filed numerous complaints with supervisors. Initially, Mark didn't want to talk to us, but finally he relented. He identified some legitimate complaints about his care that we could resolve. After he saw we were willing to respond to his needs with things we could control, he revealed more: a messy divorce, a move to a new state and new VA hospital, numerous new health issues. He summed up his spiritual needs with these words: "I worked hard all my life and now to have it all stolen from me doesn't fit my benevolent God theory. I don't have trust in God anymore."

Chaplain Dan validated his suffering. "You've been through a lot of changes this past year. That's not easy," he said. Then Dan asked him about the psychological baggage Mark might be toting; he pointed out that Mark's anger at the staff might be related to his fears and emotional pain. At first, Mark was startled. However, as he looked around his bed at four nonjudgmental faces who were willing to abide his fear and pain, he acknowledged his feelings. His anger dissolved before our eyes as he was able to give voice to the fearful aspect of himself that his anger was hiding. Later, he reckoned with the damage his anger had caused by writing notes to each of the nurses and their supervisor, apologizing for his actions.

This experience with Mark reminds me of a story about a six-year-old boy who was late coming home from playing at a friend's house. His mother asked him what had caused his tardiness. He said he was helping his friend fix his tricycle.

"You don't know how to fix tricycles," his mother said skeptically.

"I couldn't fix it, but I could help him cry," the little boy said.

This makes me wonder: At what age do we start losing our ability to abide with others and even with ourselves?

Abiding Lessons

- Neurosis is always a substitute for legitimate suffering, or as a Chinese proverb says, "Suppression leads to momentary relief and permanent pain, whereas feeling the experience leads to momentary pain and permanent relief."
- Abiding is showing up openheartedly to all of the emotional dimensions of life: the good, the bad, and the ugly, and more importantly, embracing the part of self that is experiencing that feeling. Focused inward, abiding allows us to encounter ourselves; focused outward, abiding allows us to vicariously experience the part of the other person that generates the emotion. Our abiding presence provides safety for the person to also experience their feeling self.
- Feelings are only "negative" when we close down to them by cutting ourselves off from the aspect of ourselves generating the feeling, a significant loss. This reaction often perpetuates what others have done to us to create these feelings in the first place. We become the abuser, the shamer, the neglector of our own self.
- Every time I deny an emotion by covering it up, I'm lying. The part of self that is experiencing the feeling is left stranded. Recovering this part of self is important because we not only learn the truth it's trying to speak, we also regain its vitality.
- We can nurture the parts of ourselves we have exiled with our shame and neglect. This process begins when we open up to these scattered pieces of broken self so they will no longer be feared and, therefore, forsaken. Having the courage to give voice to these hidden parts of self releases their silent, unconscious power over us.
- Not letting other peoples' problems drain our energy requires understanding three things. First, we have to become com-

fortable with our own losings, failings, and sufferings. Second, we have to recognize that other people have a hero inside too. We can't access that hero for them. Third, we do not need to be afraid of uncertainty; in fact, we should learn how to befriend it when it accompanies change.

- While we are abiding with someone we wear their moccasins with them. We store their footprints in our soul, but when it's time to leave, we give their moccasins back so they have protection for their soles as they walk without us. Otherwise, we become enablers. Enablers have a hard time seeing how much damage they do when they prevent people from discovering their heroes within.

Chapter Three

Reckoning: The Second Step in the Healing Process

Grant me the Serenity to accept the things I cannot change,
the Courage to change the things I can,
and the Wisdom to know the difference.
Living one day at a time,
enjoying one moment at a time,
accepting hardships as the pathway to peace.[1]
– Reinhold Niebuhr

It's surprising how the simple act of abiding often helps us come to peace with hardships that we face. Many people need nothing more than giving themselves permission to have a safe emotional environment in which to express themselves. That, in and of itself, creates peace and opens vistas for hope and new perspectives. On the other hand, abiding is not always enough; ventilating feelings might feel good, yet accomplish little, especially if the aspect of self generating the feeling is ignored. Facing the difficulty and strategizing ways to effectively reckon with it are also important so we can change our relationship with the problem by *integrating the part of self* dealing with the situation. This is a different process than simply trying to "move on" or "get beyond it."

Confronting difficulties helps us let go of perspectives that may be contributing to a problem and opens us to new possibilities so we can be changed for the better. Confronting problems requires a deeper process that I call reckoning. Reckoning is changing our relationship to problematic situations, relationships, or aspects of self by cul-

tivating the honesty, courage, and humility to face the source of distress. Cultivating these qualities often occurs by discovering a needed
lesson; however, the purpose of the lesson is not to teach, but rather
to help us be. The lesson is only the vehicle to achieve qualities of
"beingness:" honesty, courage, and humility.

Abiding is a journey of the heart; we open our heart to our feelings and to the aspect of ourselves generating the emotion. Reckoning,
on the other hand, is a journey of the head. Reckoning helps us let go
of our need to forget, minimize, rationalize, justify, or deny; we
become more able and willing to let go of coping mechanisms and
open up to the truth of who we are and who we are not. Reckoning
requires that we look at more than behaviors; we have to examine the
cause of behaviors. For example, alcoholics have to quit drinking in
order to restore their lives. After they remain sober, they have to
address what caused them to drink in the first place. If they are unable
to reckon with the source of their distress, they become "dry drunks;"
they may not be getting into the trouble that intoxication previously
caused, but they still numb their feelings and fail to develop honesty,
courage, and humility to live their lives effectively.

It might be tempting to jump right to reckoning without first
abiding with the accompanying feelings. We want to fix problems and
find solutions. Reckoning without abiding, however, might mean
incomplete healing because the emotional dimension is not engaged.
Although will power might accomplish the goal, it's not heartfelt nor
is it long-lasting. Jumping too quickly to reckoning means we minimize our suffering and gloss over the strength and courage it takes to
face and carry our burdens. Reckoning without first abiding might
mean that the aspect of self generating the unpleasant emotion is left
stranded and silenced.

On the other hand, abiding without reckoning might mean that
I stay stuck in a victim mode. A victim perspective keeps us bitter and
powerless (if the feelings relate to guilt, anger, fear, sadness) or irresponsible and cowardly (if the feelings relate solely to maintaining
happiness and comfort). Appendix A provides a chart that contrasts
the abiding and reckoning processes.

It is easy to confuse reckoning with coping; yet, they are distinctly different processes. Coping is like cutting the tops off our weeds whereas reckoning pulls our weeds out by the roots. Coping is a passive process, whereas reckoning is an active process. Coping often includes denial, an unconscious process that keeps us from seeing reality. Some people even say that denial is an acronym for "**D**on't **E**ven k**N**ow **I A**m **L**ying." Reckoning inserts consciousness into a problem, whereas coping diminishes consciousness. Diminishing consciousness is often done by pretending that everything is "fine." (Fine is an acronym for "**F**reaked out, **I**nsecure, **N**eurotic, and **E**mpty.") Coping closes down to the problem whereas reckoning opens up to it. A patient told me, "We need to have a come-to-Jesus meeting." He explained that what he meant was that his family needed to stop sugar-coating the prognosis and, instead, get honest so they could face his death together. In other words, he needed them to stop coping and start reckoning.

In describing coping in this light, I don't mean to imply that coping is bad. We can't be on the reckoning path all the time. All of us need times to chill out, numb out, and go into neutral. Too often, however, we *misuse* coping as an avoidance mechanism that shields us from uncomfortable feelings and realities. Appendix B helps clarify the distinction between coping and reckoning.

Reckoning means being willing to endure the discomfort that accompanies making internal change. Rather than coping with the situation by fighting or "flighting" the discomfort, reckoning means struggling with the discomfort as part of the "coming-to-grips" process. Although I've mentioned the discomfort that accompanies change, it bears repeating. The transition period that occurs after we let something go and before we have incorporated something new is fraught with tension, fraught with urges to return to old habits. Morton's description of navigating this "awful abyss that occurs after the shattering, and before the new reality appears" is a key element in successful reckoning.[2] The struggle is necessary, however, because it allows larger lessons to surface.

Coping with a problem rather than reckoning with it means that my suffering is in vain because I didn't figure out the lesson I need. Wasting suffering means that I miss an opportunity to grow in honesty, courage, and humility. It's not easy to change from coping to reckoning; coping feels comfortable, like an old pair of favorite shoes we're used to wearing. It's no wonder that it takes effort and resolve to "break in" new reckoning processes.

Most stories you read in my books depict people who shifted from coping to reckoning. Some stopped coping with their problems by "flighting" into alcohol before they started reckoning with the feelings that made them want to drink in the first place. Others coped with their impending death by pretending their illness was not terminal, but at some point they started reckoning with their mortality by courageously preparing for death. Some people in my stories stopped coping with their trauma by isolating themselves, and they began to reckon with their trauma by reaching out for help or helping other people. As a result, they often become "wounded healers," repairing harm they caused, preventing similar harm from recurring, and sharing their wisdom with others who have been similarly afflicted.

I frequently use the words honesty, courage, and humility throughout this book; I do so consciously because they capture the qualities I believe we each need to cultivate if we are going to be heroes in our own lives. It requires honesty to let go of illusions, denials, and pretenses so that we can open up to our authentic self, including the aspects of ourselves we'd prefer to hide. It takes courage to let go of our fears and instead show up for things in our life we'd prefer to fight, flight, or freeze. Paradoxically, humility empowers us; we gain real power when we let go of pride and will power and open up to acknowledge our needs and ask for help; a humble heart is a teachable heart.

Joe is a patient who demonstrates a teachable heart. He shifted from coping to reckoning. Rather than continuing to cope with his problems by numbing their impact with alcohol, he decided to use his problems as a passport into his deeper self where he discovered honesty, courage, and humility. Joe was 58 years old. He had both bladder and colon cancers. He didn't know what to do or where to turn;

often he came to the VA hospital. Each time he came, I was consulted. No matter the ward to which he was admitted, the story was the same: his pain was out of control and so was he. Angry at what was happening to him, Joe lashed out at staff members. Staff felt helpless, and Joe would go back home without effective treatment for his distress.

It was Joe's utter loneliness that struck me. He spoke of his physical pain, but pain of non-physical dimensions echoed in his voice. He was filled with bitterness. Each time I met with him, a different aspect of his suffering self emerged. His mother had abused him as a child and eventually abandoned him. Her efforts to reach out to him in his adult life only angered him further. When she phoned him, Joe wouldn't talk to her. Although his children lived close by, he seldom saw them. He still loved his ex-wife, but his drinking had driven her away. His sister visited occasionally, but he thought she was bossy and discouraged her visits. As he talked about his life, he cried. I listened, validating his suffering. I let myself feel his pain, abiding his anguish, fear, anger, and despair.

Joe became weaker and was no longer able to stay in his mobile home alone. He was behind in his bills. His pain remained out of control. I knew if he was ever to move from coping with his suffering to reckoning with it that he would need love and patience beyond what I, alone, could provide. Admitting him to our unit, I asked for help from our Hospice and Palliative Care staff.

Joe remained aloof and suspicious, continuing to lash out. Nothing satisfied him. He tested our patience with his demands. He remained a loner. Much of the day and night, he rode the unit's electric scooter outside to smoke.

I asked Joe about his faith. Yes, he believed in God. No, he didn't feel God's love. Yes, he was angry at God. No, he couldn't feel God's presence in his life. Yes, he wanted to explore non-religious spiritual dimensions of himself. Yes, he wanted prayer. I hesitated about praying for him right then, but I offered it anyway, and he accepted. I took a deep breath to let myself abide his sufferings before I started.

"Dear God. This man comes before you feeling broken and used. He has suffered the brokenness of the world and feels lost and forsaken. He needs your love and your light to show him how to walk in darkness. Help him feel your mercy and your grace, so he can feel whole again. Help him feel worthy. Help him know he is valued and important. Give him the courage to open up to your love and the love of others he can trust. Help him let go of the wall he's built to keep others away. Help him start depending on you. Help all of us caring for Joe to be trustworthy. Help us listen carefully to his needs. Help us respond with patience and kindness even when we don't want to do so. When we fail him, help us acknowledge that failure, so we can change. I pray all these things this day. Amen."

Joe cried throughout the prayer.

Little by little, with staff who were willing to abide his pain and suffering, Joe began reckoning with his unfinished business. First, he focused on his relationship with his ex-wife. He wrote to her acknowledging how he had let her down. She began visiting on weekends. They talked about getting married again. Soon his sister and his daughter began visiting. He was able to ask for forgiveness for the pain that his anger and bitterness had caused. He confronted his mother about the abuse he had suffered. Although she wouldn't apologize as he had hoped, he forgave her. At first, he forgave her because he thought it was the right thing to do for her sake. Later, he came to realize he had to forgive her for his own.

Joe wrote a letter to the staff. It read:

> I have had a bout with cancer for a long time. I wasn't going any place with the curing or the pain. I was very depressed and at the end of my rope until I met you all in hospice. Before this, I was always promised this and that, but here I was treated with compassion and love I never had. You knew when I was in pain and I was taken care of right away. I was screaming and you would come and touch me and before long, my pain was relieved. I wish I was a rich man so I could help hospice out with their needs, but all I can do is look toward hospice and have a heart because you have a heart, and I love you all dearly. This is hard for me to say because of the past. Thank you for listening.

His unfinished business completed, Joe said he was ready to die. A few days later, he asked one of the nurses, Sheila, to read the 23rd Psalm. As she read the passage, *"Yea, though I walk through the valley of the shadow of death, I will fear no evil for You are with me,"* she noticed that Joe was staring toward the ceiling. She asked what he was seeing.

"God," he replied.

"What does God look like?" Sheila asked.

"Beautiful, swirling colors like a rainbow," he said, and closed his eyes. Sheila continued her reading. When she was done, she looked up and saw that Joe had died.

The meaning of Joe's life did not stop with his death. A patient who had often smoked with Joe came to the unit. He spoke about the transformation he had witnessed. "Did you all know that Joe initiated prayer circles with other patients outside in the smoking area?" he asked. We were surprised and not surprised.

We also received a request from Joe's daughter: "Dad changed so much in the last few months. He wasn't the same man that people in our hometown knew. Could you contribute to his eulogy to help people understand Dad's transformation?" So Pat, one of the nurses, wrote an account of Joe's final journey to redeem his suffering. (The complete eulogy can be found in Appendix C.) It was through Pat's account that people became privileged witnesses to a man's journey into holiness.

Two days after the funeral, we received another letter from Joe's daughter:

To Everyone at Hospice:
You were firm when you had to be firm and you were soft, but not too mushy, when Dad would allow you to be soft. I am so thankful he had you. I am thankful you gave him the unconditional love he needed and the tools, when he was ready, to let go of his anger and his hurt, which allowed him to forgive and ask for forgiveness. He grew so much in your care. I am also thankful you were there for him right up to his last breath. It was such a comfort to know he saw God as beautiful, swirling colors. The

letter you sent for Dad's eulogy was wonderful. Otherwise, no
one would have known how Dad changed. That letter was an
incredible testimonial that amazed and comforted everyone.

The work Joe did to abide his feelings and reckon with his suffering birthed the hero hidden within him. He was able to redeem the destiny he was born to fulfill. However, his work could not begin until he
felt safe enough to do it. Surrounding him with staff who were willing to
abide his distress provided the safety he needed. Once he realized that he
no longer needed to cope by running from himself and others, he let
himself become vulnerable, owning his feelings so that segregated pieces
of self generating the emotion could be coaxed out of hiding. As a result,
new-found hope inspired him to change his relationship to his bitterness.
He decided to let the bitterness go and open up to developing a teachable heart. He asked and received help from others who were willing to
abide with him. This courage forged his journey into heroism. He
became a hero not only for himself, but for all of us who were privileged
to witness his transformation. We even named two hallways on our
Hospice and Palliative Care unit in honor of his bravery. "Forgiveness
Street" and "Peace Boulevard" remind us that we, too, are called to do
the work Joe did in our own lives. We, too, are called to become heroes
for ourselves. We, too, have the opportunity to redeem the destiny we
were born to fulfill. In fact, Viktor Frankl writes that we have a *responsibility* to discover and fulfill our unique destiny.[3] When we fail to discover our unique destiny, our passion dries up and our efforts toward personal fulfillment are thwarted because we've lost the power of the destiny
seed implanted in our very being. However, when we sensitize ourselves
to the calling to be whole, we recognize hardships as guideposts for coming home unto ourselves. Our suffering encourages us to let go of a non-
productive path so that we can merge onto a deeper, interior path that
leads to a bona fide destiny.

The Reckoning Qualities

Joe used the despair of his illness to encounter his interior hero. It wasn't will power, control, or pride that transported him there; it was honesty, courage, and humility. He didn't "rise above" or transcend his illness; he moved into its depths. He was willing to see who he was and who he was not; he was willing to acknowledge his limitations and ask for help. He didn't "put his past behind him," he integrated his past so it could be used for healing. Joe was willing to change. Once he changed, a new world opened up to him because he now had access to the energy of his deeper self.

I commented on the quality of humility that I saw Joe develop as he used his emotional pain as a passport into his interior hero. He expressed regret that he hadn't learned the lesson sooner. "It was pride," he said. "Until now, I've been arrogant. I was unteachable because I wasn't willing to change, so my suffering increased. But when I'm humble, I become teachable and my suffering eases." Change is like that; it always requires that we let go of something (usually something that is safe and familiar) and open up to something different (which doesn't yet feel safe and familiar). This is why change often requires courage. It took courage for Joe to let go of the arrogant self who protected his inadequate self. Until Joe let his arrogant self go, he couldn't *open up* to his humble self. Once his humble self was set free, Joe grew. Change also requires honesty. All of us have an arrogant self (although most of us are too arrogant to acknowledge that). Joe was not only able to acknowledge his arrogance, he was able to use it as a passport into his humble self so he could experience healing.

Healing is not the same as management of symptoms. Although managing symptoms minimizes distress, it does not require inward lessons and changes. Healing is not the same as "cure" either; healing doesn't require the distress to be removed. This distinction is important because there are many problems that can't be erased. Healing means we are able to open ourselves to the distress so we can change our relationship with the problem. This is an important concept because when a problem recurs, it can be tempting to think that no healing occurred. For example, Joe still had times when he felt insecure. His impoverished childhood could not be erased, and he was not magically "cured" of the distress of feeling inadequate. Because he still experienced inadequacy, however, does not mean that he did not experience healing. By letting himself encounter his inadequacy and reach out for help with it, he was able to develop an open relationship with his inadequate self; his inadequate self was then no longer alone. He was also able to infuse his inadequate self with new messages of self-worth, thereby gradually changing his experience.

Honesty allows us to perceive the illusions that we generate so we can experience the world the way it is rather than the way we want it to be. Illusions effectively shield us from our deeper selves. For example, because Joe lived in the illusion that he was unlovable because of his mother's abuse, he treated himself as if he were worthless. His drinking numbed his feelings of rejection. Ironically, even though he was angry at his mother for treating him so disrespectfully, Joe treated himself with the same disrespect and abuse. However, when he was willing to reckon with the illusions he had maintained, Joe then accessed his interior hero. That hero supplied him with the truth that he was worthy of respect. When we open up to our illusions, we can use them to encounter truth. Reckoning is the means by which we find truth. Reckoning requires that I become more honest, courageous, and humble. Paradoxically, I have to open up to the ways that I am dishonest, cowardly, and proud to achieve this. Otherwise, I'll create illusions that keep me from owning these very human qualities that are part of my truth.

Reckoning requires mindfulness about the many ways we have of fooling ourselves into thinking that we've participated in the reckoning process when we haven't. Excuses such as, "I rose above it" or "I'm not going to let that get to me," can effectively delude us into *excusing* ourselves from doing inner work. Reckoning requires honestly discerning the distinction between a "reason" and an "excuse." Joe kept excusing his self-abusive usage of alcohol and his angry abuse of others with the statement, "No one cares about me anyway." When he got honest with himself, his excuse changed into an honest reason: "I drink because it's easier than figuring out the ways that I'm worthwhile and important. Drinking is easier than learning how to develop an internal mother who knows how to nurture me."

It requires courage to discern reasons from excuses, but healing doesn't happen until we dig deeper to discover the reasons. Not only that, "rising above" a hardship means that I become less "me;" I use will power and control to keep the vitality of "me" stifled. However, when I *open up* to the hardship or my limitation, I become more myself and the resources of that self become available.

It's easy to deceive ourselves into thinking that we've learned a valuable lesson by reckoning with a problem when we have actually coped by sweeping the problem under the carpet of fear. One patient, Evelyn, swept a bitter divorce under the carpet by adopting an "all-men-are-jerks" stance. As a result, she never remarried; instead, she had numerous transient relationships with untrustworthy men who reinforced her "all-men-are-jerks" lesson which she thought she had learned. Evelyn only knew how to cope with her rejection and disappointment rather than abide and reckon with her feelings of hurt, inadequacy, and rejection. She didn't yet know how to use her anger to transport her into herself so she could meet her rejected self – an interior aspect who needed her love and attention rather than her fear and neglect. Therefore, she let fear control her subsequent decisions relating to male relationships.

Evelyn started developing courage. She started working through issues relating to her birth mother who had placed her for adoption. By the time Evelyn became an adult and searched for her mother, her mother had died. Nevertheless, Evelyn learned how to abide and reckon with her feelings of loss and abandonment. She was able to reckon with lingering resentments and achieve a level of forgiveness. Her previous lesson of "I'm not worthwhile or lovable because I was given away" yielded to a more mature lesson of "I was innocent. My mother giving me away had nothing to do with who I am. I am worth knowing and loving. Some people may reject me, but that won't keep me from seeking trustworthy people who can accept me." Needless to say, this new insight affected her subsequent relationships with men; she was able to see both their good and not-so-good qualities, which empowered her. She was then able to let go of her supposed lesson that all men were jerks and, instead, seek reliable men who treated her respectfully. Although initially Evelyn thought she could change the men she dated, she subsequently learned how to let that illusion go so she could open up to the truth of the need to change herself.

Evelyn's new perspective meant that her suffering was not wasted, but rather used to help her personal growth. Unfortunately, it's easier to blame others for causing us to feel ugly feelings than it is to use those feelings to take care of the aspect of self experiencing them. Paradoxically, we become empowered when we abide those feelings and seek opportunities to learn from them by reckoning with the lessons they are trying to provide.

Discerning coping from reckoning is necessary to learn these lessons. Discernment isn't always easy, however, because outcomes don't make the distinction. For example, Evelyn divorced her husband because she coped with difficulties by running away, rather than reckoning with internal changes that were needed to develop a successful relationship. Many people, however, might do just the opposite. They cope with a bad relationship by staying in it rather than reckon with the discomfort of making needed internal changes so they can let go of the relationship. Sorting out coping from reckoning is important and the distinction depends on whether someone is opening up or closing down to interior aspects of self. Coping keeps unwanted aspects walled off; reckoning brings them home. Reckoning leads to healing.

Although reckoning requires that we journey into the wilderness of our soul, a cautious pace should be maintained. The trick is to be able to maintain enough of ourselves in the wilderness so that we don't flee to the security of marked paths. Proceeding too quickly or haphazardly allows the briars and brambles of unmarked paths to rip apart our emotional skin.

SELF-AWARENESS EXERCISE
Changing our Relationship with Lost Aspects of Self

This awareness assignment has five parts to help gather outlying puzzle pieces of self:

Review your Life Story from Chapter One. With each significant event, think about the lessons you learned and the qualities you cultivated. Write down or draw the lessons and qualities beside the picture or words on your Life Story.

Review your Life Story more closely. It will take scrutiny to realize which lessons were not really lessons but merely shields to keep you from feeling inadequate, hurt, rejected, angry, or other difficult feelings. (See Evelyn's story above.) The result is not a lesson, but rather a fear that is probably controlling you and keeping you from a more expanded self. When you discover a fear, ask yourself how this fear is now controlling you and keeping you from a more expanded self. Which areas are you using a coping process rather than a reckoning process? (Review Appendix B.) How does this relate to the "lessons" you have learned?

In what ways are you perpetuating what others did to you to cause you to lose yourself. (For example, if your father abused or neglected you, in what ways are you now abusing or neglecting yourself?) In what ways do you need to develop healthy interior aspects of your own? (For example, growing an internal father who loves and protects you.)

Review each event and relationship on your Life Story. In what ways have you used illusion, cowardice, and pride to keep you from achieving healing? (We all do this. It's a survival mechanism. There's no need to be ashamed. If anyone thinks that they do not do this, it just means that they are too dishonest, cowardly, and proud to see it.)

Select one event or relationship that you feel ready, willing, and able to change. What are you going to have to let go of so the change can occur? What will you need to open up to?

Acknowledge and Validate Limitations and Suffering

When I can accept my limitations, I grow into myself with confidence of who I am and who I am not. Validating our limitations is a willingness to acknowledge and bear witness to our difficult experiences. It means resisting the urge to tell ourselves, "Don't be so negative" or any of the other things that indirectly communicate, "I don't want to hear about your problems. Don't let yourself feel human. Put up that stoic wall and hide behind it." Validating suffering means that we acknowledge when we have a problem, which is not always easy for people who are proud. Recognizing our human frailties, however, can be done with a light-heartedness so that we don't get into a prideful, "I'm such a terrible person" syndrome whenever we're not perfect.

At a young age, Viktor Frankl learned a wisdom about suffering that takes a lifetime for most of us to appreciate. While in a German concentration camp, Frankl said that there was "no need to be ashamed of tears, for tears bear witness that a man has the greatest of courage, the courage to suffer."[4]

Once we're able to validate our own suffering, we are more able to validate others. A 41-year-old, newly admitted hospice patient once told me about a conversation he had with a nurse who had transported him from another unit. "I said it was hard to come here to hospice," he said. "And her answer was, 'It's not so bad here. Look at the pretty pictures they have on the walls.' I'm about to die and she's telling me about pretty pictures!"

People often bear heavy sufferings, especially at the end of life. Platitudes about smiling or keeping their chins up are just another way of telling them to look at the pretty pictures on the walls. Saying these kinds of things can also erode their self-confidence. One patient told me, "I'm scared and miserable, but everyone keeps telling me that things are going to get better. I must be weak or I wouldn't feel so miserable." We sell people short when we don't respect their capacity to suffer. We miss the opportunity to affirm their courage in carrying their load.

Simple statements that affirm their suffering can have the opposite effect. Statements such as, "You've had a hard go of it" or "It takes a lot to go through all of this" tell people that someone understands how hard their situation is. These kinds of statements also indirectly validate their resiliency and the sheer courage it has taken to carry their load. People have told me how grateful they are when I validate their suffering and how it lessens their sense of isolation. Validating suffering helps people develop genuine appreciation and respect for what they've been through and the enormity of what they have accomplished just to get through it.

Validating personal suffering was important in prisoner-of-war (POW) camps. Some former POWs have told me that optimistic prisoners had the most difficult time during confinement. Frankl writes about similar experiences in the concentration camp that he was in: "It was the incorrigible optimists who were the most irritating companions," he writes.[5] They were also the most vulnerable, living in the naïve hope that they would be home in a few weeks. When weeks passed and nothing had changed, they despaired. "Disappointment overcame them, which had a deleterious effect on their powers of resistance; many died."[6] Those who did best were not cynical, just fiercely realistic. "We refused to minimize or alleviate the camp's tortures by ignoring them or harboring false illusions and entertaining artificial optimism. Suffering had become a task on which we did not want to turn our backs. We had realized its hidden opportunities for achievement."[7]

Opportunities for achievement can even be measured. The

American Psychological Association uses a Posttraumatic Growth Inventory to assess negative and positive changes sustained after life-altering events like Frankl experienced in the concentration camp. However, the scale is useful in assessing a person's relationship to any event, even if it's not traumatic. Five categories of change that occur after significant events are identified as: relating to others, new possibilities, personal strength, spiritual change, and appreciation of life. The inventory (Appendix D) helps determine the relationship we keep to the hardships we've borne. It can also provide clues to changes we might want to make so we can develop a more enlightened perspective.

Enlightened perspectives are not gained by blotting out experiences or numbing emotional responses with "positive thinking." An experience become positive when we are not afraid to embrace it and struggle with the internal changes that the experience requires. The deleterious effects of "artificial optimism" that Frankl describes with prisoners cause just as much damage when used to solve everyday problems. Rather, positive thinking should focus on giving ourselves *en-courage-ment* to have confidence that we can navigate the difficulties of life. Then, we don't have to take "quick-fix" paths that temporarily relieve discomfort. It's not about making my pain go away, but about making me competent enough to access the hero within me to learn from my distress. I may not be responsible for the pain, but I am responsible for reckoning with it.

I used to fear that validating suffering would encourage patients to sit on the "pity pot." Then I realized that self-pity was not a bad thing as long as it wasn't used to avoid facing problems. I realized the goal was to be able to get on and off the "pity pot" as needed. People who are stoic, in fact, often needed help acknowledging their own suffering. I also feared that validating suffering with whiny people would foster more whining. I was surprised to discover that many people complain in an attempt to get someone to validate their suffering. Once heard, they often don't need to whine as much.

I've also learned that just because people can talk about their trauma doesn't mean they are reckoning with it. People sometimes cope by shielding themselves with an emotional detachment from the trauma. One woman told me she was in the grocery store when she overheard a soldier talking on his cell phone. "He had just gotten back from Iraq, and he was talking about gruesome things as if he were describing beans on the store shelf!"

When I heard this, I wasn't surprised. Staying detached, almost as if it happened to a different person, provides emotional survival and prevents feeling overwhelmed with horror. However, talking detachedly about trauma does not mean that the trauma is integrated into the person's experience; in fact, it may mean just the opposite.

Reaching out for Help

Healing requires that we open up to the ways we are victims and the ways we are heroes. To open up to all aspects of our humanity, we have to let go of who we are so we can open up to who we are capable of becoming. However, letting go of our current self causes ambiguity and uncertainty. Developing tolerance for uncertainty during times of transition is a struggle. It's why transitional times, such as teenage years, midlife, or the time before death, can be so difficult. We want progress to be continuous. Instead it's marked with indolent periods while new thoughts and behaviors are incubating. Conditioned for instant gratification, we are vulnerable to return to old habits. As one woman told me, "I'm determined to change today – at least until it becomes unpleasant. When it becomes unpleasant, I'm going to go back to eating cookies." I often counsel people to develop a strategy for times of transition because that is when we are most vulnerable for going back "to eat the cookies."

"This quest you are on is hard, but it's important," I sometimes say to patients to *en-courage* them not to take an easy way out. I also encourage them to take deep breaths. I've found that deep breathing increases our tolerance for struggle; breathing gives space to our demons so they loosen their choke-hold that cuts off our air and our power. Breathing allows us the opportunity to relax and open up to possibilities beyond our fear. The trick is remembering to do it when we feel overwhelmed with uncertainty.

The other trick is to ask for help when we are vulnerable to betraying ourselves. Pride, independence, and need to control make asking for help difficult. The difficulty usually involves feelings of inadequacy, which we tend to bear silently. Much of my work with people includes helping them understand the importance of identifying needs and asking for help from trustworthy people. This strategy might mean something as simple as reaching out to family members and talking about the difficulties they are having. For many, participating in a Healing Community is therapeutic; I will describe this process in detail in Chapter Eight. For others, it might mean reaching out to professional staff. It might mean joining a church or social community. Sometimes, it requires more formal venues for help, such as joining a 12-step recovery program or obtaining a good counselor. Pride, need for control, and stubborn independence interfere with reaching out.

When we reach out for help with our limitations and suffering, we develop the honesty, courage, and humility to change. When our perspective changes, our world changes. It reminds me of a story that Rachel Naomi Remen writes about in *Kitchen Table Wisdom* in which three fourteenth-century stonecutters build a cathedral.[8] Though each performed the same tedious and methodical task, each offered a different perspective on his work. One stonecutter bitterly complained that his job was to cut stones into blocks, and he was going to be stuck doing it the rest of his life. Another worker warmly reported that he was earning a living for his beloved family; stonecutting allowed him to create a home they could fill with love. "But it is the third man whose response gives us pause," Remen writes. "In a joyous voice, he tells us of the privilege of participating in the building of this great cathedral, so strong that it will stand as a holy lighthouse for a thousand years."

I find it ironic that I have spent so many years searching outside myself for just the right bricks so I could build a holy lighthouse, one that everyone would admire, when all along I was holding the bricks in my own hands and my job was to develop the honesty, courage, and humility to discover the unique lighthouse I was destined to create.

Lessons in Reckoning

- The Serenity Prayer used in recovery programs is a good recipe for reckoning with life's difficulties, especially when the second sentence is included: "Grant me the serenity to accept the things I cannot change, the courage to change the things I can, and the wisdom to know the difference. Living one day at a time, enjoying one moment at a time, *accepting hardships as the pathway to peace.*"
- Reckoning is changing our relationship to problematic situations, relationships, or aspects of self by cultivating the honesty, courage, and humility to face the source of distress. By doing so, we live from a more authentic self and our decisions are less controlled by fear.
- Coping is like cutting the tops off of our weeds; reckoning is pulling our weeds out by the roots.
- All change requires that we let go of something (usually something that is safe and familiar) and open up to something different (which doesn't yet feel safe and familiar). This is why change requires courage.
- The secret for learning how to create inward change is to develop a tolerance for ambiguity and uncertainty while we are letting go of old habits and perspectives so that we can open up to new insights and experiences. Deep breathing helps during transitions because it gives space to our demons so they loosen their choke-hold on us, cutting off our air and our power. We should also reach out for help during these times.
- Living from a dimension of integrity often occurs by discovering a needed lesson. The lesson is simply the vehicle to achieve the honesty, courage, and humility because the purpose of the lesson is not to teach, but rather to help us *be*.
- We have to open up to the ways that we are dishonest, cowardly, and proud. Otherwise, we create illusions that keep us from

owning these very human qualities that are part of our truth. Recognizing our human frailties can be done with a light-heartedness so that we don't get into a prideful, "I'm such a terrible person" syndrome.

- When helping other people, we have to remember that reckoning is the other person's journey. We shouldn't enable avoidance behaviors by trying to solve problems for them. Providing *en-courage-ment* and support are a better way to help. We have to have the courage to ask some hard questions, but it's up to them to provide the answers. Otherwise, we rob people of the opportunity to meet their interior hero.

- Validating suffering means that we acknowledge when we have a problem. It is a willingness to acknowledge and bear witness to our difficult experiences. We sell people short when we don't respect their capacity to suffer. We miss the opportunity to affirm their courage in carrying their load.

- Enlightened perspectives are not gained by trying to blot out experiences with "positive thinking." An experience becomes positive when we are not afraid to embrace it and struggle with the changes the experience requires of us.

- To grow, we have to let go of who we are so that we can open up to who we are capable of becoming.

- Reckoning is the means by which we discover truth.

Chapter Four

Beholding: The Birth of the Hero Within

The heroes of all time have gone before us.
The labyrinth is thoroughly known.
We have only to follow the thread of the hero path,
and where we had thought to find an abomination, we shall find a god.
And where we had thought to slay another, we shall slay ourselves.
Where we had thought to travel outward,
we will come to the center of our own existence.
And where we had thought to be alone, we will be with all the world.[1]
-Joseph Campbell

Our weaknesses and faults are not the abominations that we imagine. Our limitations are not the things that set us apart, but rather the things that unite us in our humanity. When we blame, gossip, or violate another person, it's because we've not allowed ourselves to encounter aspects of our own selves that we don't like or accept. Once we open up to these "negative" aspects of ourselves, we can use them to transport us into the center of our existence where we behold healing.

The beholding step of the healing process occurs once we abide and reckon with our hardships and personal liabilities. Beholding is experiencing a newfound peace with the circumstance because the relationship to the problem has shifted. Once this inward shift has occurred, we receive energy from our deeper selves; our integrity is restored because the aspect of self dealing with the problem is reintegrated into the conscious self. The situation may not be any different, but the r*elationship* to the situation shifts with insight and new meaning. People often verbalize the shift of energy by saying something like, "A load was lifted off my shoulders."

As we continue applying the abiding, reckoning, and beholding processes to confront problems rather than trying to deny or escape troubles, we gain more confidence to use this energy to tackle other challenging areas in our lives. Once we access this energy on a regular basis, we are able to live from a dimension of integrity; fear no longer drives our decisions.

Learning how to let go of my fear and open up to my emotional distress so I can behold healing has not been easy for the recovering coward that I am. Yes, I am a recovering coward; no doubt, I always will be. I like to pretend otherwise, but my fear keeps me tethered to my cowardice. There are still times when I don't confront someone because I don't want to suffer possible dislike or rejection; instead, I talk to other people about what someone has done to me or I pout resentfully. I don't speak up about an issue because I don't want to suffer being wrong or appearing stupid; I then have to work hard to resist the urge to criticize and complain about an outcome that occurs without my input. Sometimes, I want to emotionally bully other people so I don't have to suffer not getting my way; this bullying is just as cowardly as maintaining silence. I don't like confrontation, and I don't like to hurt other peoples' feelings; then I realize that this attitude is just an excuse for not taking responsibility for my own feelings or stances. What I often forget is that each time I fail to take responsibility, I am actually betraying myself; a piece of me becomes hidden and I lose access to that part of my vitality. When I was betraying myself habitually, there came a time when there was hardly any "me" left; I was just a shell, although I didn't recognize it at the time. I was still thinking that if everyone else changed, my problems would be solved.[2] Rather than slaying others, I had, indeed, slain myself.

My patients showed me how to cultivate courage to let go of my fear of experiencing the things in my life I'd prefer not to confront. I began to realize the honesty that is required to let go of my illusions, denials, and pretenses so I could open up to my inner self, including the aspects I'd prefer to hide from myself. Paradoxically, I found that humility empowers me; I gain real power when I let go of pride and will power and allow myself to be broken open to acknowledge my needs and ask for help.

It's difficult to describe the energy that the beholding process accesses. Knowledge doesn't necessarily use this energy, but wisdom does. Knowledge can be instilled, but books and teachers can't instill wisdom; wisdom can only be gained from the energy of the hero within. The brain does not depend on this energy, but the mind does. Will power may not access the energy, but grace and graciousness do. Pride doesn't depend on this energy, but humility does.

Many people use sheer grit and determination to "rise above" limitations; their pride, control, and will power are publicly validated. Other public heroes use a different route; they access the energy of the beholding dimension. Mother Teresa was one who accessed this energy. After she died, her diaries were published; they revealed the doubt she sometimes experienced. Many people were surprised that a woman of such faith could be plagued with doubt. I wasn't surprised. She had used her doubt to propel her into the intimate places of her soul from which her heroic work emanated. Her faith was courageous *because* of her doubt; it reflected her humility. She was not afraid to completely inhabit herself, including her doubting self. As a result, her service to others was authentic because it emanated from a place of integrity.

Ordinary Heroes

Our team was struggling with a difficult staff issue that triggered gossip and backbiting. I sent an e-mail to staff members describing the issue and what was needed for us to deal with it healthfully and effectively. I asked for a change in behavior, a heroic change so we could forthrightly reckon with the problem. One nurse responded: "We are all heroes already. It takes a hero just to get up in the morning. It takes a hero to come do the work that we do." She was essentially saying, "I don't need to change."

I thought about what she said. I think she was right, and she was not right. There is no doubt that to do any job with vitality and integrity requires accessing aspects of our interior hero on a daily basis. Heroes, however, are also able to recognize and own their hostility, not an easy thing to do in a society that thinks that simply showing up for work is a heroic act. Gossiping and backbiting are hostile acts in which we all participate at one time or another (although we often turn a blind eye to it and feel justified doing it). Fortunately, in this situation, there were staff who humbly came forward to acknowledge their hostility; they took responsibility for it with an apology and a change in behavior. *They* were the heroes, and I could only sit back and behold their honesty, courage, and humility in doing so. That's the paradox that occurs with the healing process. The humble become empowered; the prideful become more blind.

I have had people call me a "hero" for the advocacy work I have done for veterans, but I don't think speaking publicly about what veterans have taught me necessarily qualifies me as a "hero." When I scrutinize personal acts that I might classify as "heroic," they are usually small acts that took courage to execute: standing up for a family member or employee unfairly treated even when it meant risking condemnation myself, not maligning someone who deserved it, keeping my heart open to someone who wronged me, or reaching out to nurture an aspect of my own self that I had left exiled in unconsciousness. Sometimes, it's simply acknowledging my greed, vanity, and hostility; it's saying "I was wrong," "I'm sorry," "Forgive me."

Macy, my granddaughter, told me I was her hero because I participate in triathlons; she was wooed by the medal of participation around my neck. I told Macy that being in the race did not qualify me as a hero, but there were other things that did: the decision to start taking care of myself, half-drowning during my initial attempts to swim in the ocean and yet not giving up, being willing to participate in consistent training, and enjoying being in a race even though

I come in last every year. I wanted Macy to know that most acts of heroism go unnoticed, and I wanted her to know that heroes know how to lose. The truth, however, is that most days I'm not a hero. I coast through my day on automatic pilot, not paying attention to the inner giant that silently awaits my attention while I arrogantly proceed in my egotistical illusion that control and will power are all I need to reach my destiny.

Mostly, I think the term "hero" has become misused in our society. The media reports on the single act that scores a 10 on a 0-10 heroism scale. After that act is completed, however, "heroes" might resume a life of cowardice, failing to confront personal fears that keep them from completely inhabiting themselves. The heroes who inspire me, however, are not usually featured in the media because their heroic acts may only measure a 1-2 on the scale. For example, many of my patients are recovering alcoholics who have not only been able to resist the urge to drink each day, but have also reclaimed their lives by working the steps of recovery. Their acts, repeated on a daily basis, culminate in a life filled with courage, honesty, and humility. These are the heroes whom I allow to inform my life. When I'm providing counseling with these people, I confer a Ph.D. upon them, a **P**ersonal **H**ero **D**egree. It's an award that my colleague, Pat McGuire, created to recognize the heroic journey people have taken when they abide and reckon with difficult problems.

Most of my heroes wear the faces of ordinary people who live in my home, school, and community. One of my heroes lived right next door to me. She even knew me the day I was born. Her name is Ferol Martin.[3] I remained close to her and her husband, Jim, even after I grew up and moved to Florida. Jim had developed dementia the last 15 years of his life. As I watched how Ferol tenderly cared for Jim, she became one of my heroes. Just getting Jim up in the morning required tireless effort and infinite patience. "I had to do things in stages," Ferol told me. She'd remove a blanket and tell him it was time to get up. Half an hour later, she'd say, "It's time to get up Jim," and another blanket would come off. Half an hour later, she removed the sheet. More time elapsed before the bath, more time before the dressing ordeal.

Sometimes, Jim was cooperative; other times he was stubborn, or so Ferol thought. "Once I started researching dementia, I realized it was not stubbornness. It was fear," Ferol told me. "I learned that fear of making decisions is the real problem for people with dementia."

Ferol said she also learned that people with dementia fear not remembering. Not knowing which way to turn or how to proceed makes the fear escalate. "Everything in the environment could be overwhelming and frightening for Jim. It was easier for him to just stay in bed and let the world go by."

Ferol told me how thankful she was to be able to care for Jim. "As I grew older, I realized how much Jim had given me over the years. I realized how selfless he had been so that my needs could be met. I realized how selfish I had been sometimes. In these later years, I had an opportunity to love and comfort him in a way I'd never quite done before, and I was so grateful to have the chance." I had listened, beholding Ferol's wisdom.

I didn't plan on flying to my hometown in Indiana for Jim's funeral. Then, I started thinking about his eulogy. I knew that the struggle with dementia and Ferol's loving, ennobling response to its suffering was a moving story, a story that could inspire others as it had inspired me. I also knew it was a story that would probably not be told. Eulogies usually delete these kinds of "negative" elements; they often minimize suffering. I realized that if the story was going to be told, I would be the one to tell it, so off I flew.

Ferol eagerly agreed to my participation in the eulogy. I listened carefully in the days prior to the funeral as she spoke with family members. I jotted down lessons she learned, asking questions that focused on discovered meanings that birthed her wisdom.

At the funeral, the minister cited the many achievements, successes, and virtues of this upstanding man in their community. Nothing was mentioned about the 15 years of suffering Jim and Ferol had not only endured, but redeemed. When the service was opened to the congregation for participating in the tribute, I filled in the gap. I described the tedious details of Jim and Ferol's daily life with dementia, validating their suffering and the ways Ferol had abided and reckoned with it. Then I revealed the noble way in which Ferol responded to Jim so she could exchange that suffering for wisdom:

> Ferol says Jim taught her much over the past several years. "Mainly I grew up," she told me. "I came to the realization that the things I wanted were really insignificant compared to the love in human relationships. I realized what Corinthians 13 means when it says love bears all things and endures all things. Dementia robbed my husband of his ability to think. It robbed him of his capacity to do many things, but it never robbed him of his capacity to love. Jim's illness taught me you don't love someone less because he's ill. You love him more. Illness of the mind is no different from illness of the body. It's just that we fail to respect illnesses of the mind. That's sad. We miss a lot by doing that. My 75-year-old sister had told me, 'By the time you know how to live, you die.' It took me a long time to grow up, but I'm grateful I learned how to live before Jim died. Otherwise I would have missed the gift these last few years have been.

Like a stilling enchantment, the 200 people present at Jim's funeral were able to behold Ferol's healing as she accessed the hero within herself so she could respond to Jim's suffering. Rather than wasting their suffering, Ferol was able to use it as a doorway to personal awakening.

Beholding

Ferol used the disappointment, grief, fear, and loneliness that she experienced while caring for her husband to take her into the energy that was in her very depths, even beyond her depths. This heroic journey unto oneself to encounter, transform, and integrate all the scattered pieces of broken self so we can be restored to wholeness requires this transcendent energy. I've come to believe that these beholding experiences are products of hard work and human sweat combined with God's grace. I say hard work because our outer self must be courageous enough to make the journey. Our outer self has to be humble enough to recognize and acknowledge our weaknesses and liabilities to transport us into our depths; otherwise, we think we have no need for energy beyond ourselves. Our outer self has to be humble enough to relinquish control of all the illusions it has created so we can encounter truth. I say, "God's grace," because there is also an element utterly beyond our control, a natural force of life that propels us toward integration, healing, and beholdenment if we have the courage to stay open to it. This force is the hero that resides in each of us; the hero within is the place inside ourselves that touches God.

Beholding experiences are not a guaranteed outcome of the process of abiding and reckoning. First of all, some people don't have the interest or energy to do the work of abiding or reckoning. Some try to do the work, but for unknown reasons, experience no shift in perspective nor gain any meaning. People who have psychiatric illness may not be able to fully participate in the process unless their illness is controlled with medications. However, many people engage in the process with an outcome worth beholding. I often see extraordinary shifts in consciousness as my hospice patients near death; they can see a bigger picture. This type of wholeness or healing is independent of physical cure. In fact, people who are unable to be cured are especially fertile ground for such healing. They often discover inner dimensions that reveal personal meanings that had previously been obscure. Once they stop pinning their hopes solely on external rescues and open up to internal rescue, peace reigns again. Most stories in this book culminate in a beholding moment when fear, brokenness, or bitterness is transformed with new meanings. It's as though they can see the forest now that they are no longer muddling about in the trees. They can even appreciate the purpose of each tree and understand meanings not previously understood.

Certainly, some of the most beholding moments I witness are times when people become renewed through self-forgiveness or when broken relationships are healed through forgiveness. However, meaningful moments worth beholding can be very simple moments: a tear escapes from behind a stoic wall, an unspoken fear is verbalized, a guilt is released, or an orphaned feeling is re-owned and welcomed home. Almost always, a new relationship with the suffering is created. This new relationship is filled with meaning and wisdom, creating peace and hope.

Hope should not be confused with wishes. Wishes are whims without any expectation of fulfillment. Fulfillment of hopes, on the other hand, requires an inward commitment and exterior resources in order to accomplish. For example, a person might *wish* to win the lottery, but he doesn't really expect it to come true and doesn't depend on it to pay the bills. His *hope* for a good job, however, is put into action by going to school, studying, and working hard to pay the bills. A person might *wish* to live forever; however, he can *hope* for a peaceful death and therefore do things that will increase its likelihood. People often *wish* to escape suffering. Paradoxically, this can actually decrease hope. "Hope does not lie in a way out, but in a way through," writes poet Robert Frost.[4]

Beholding the birthing of peace and hope after people abide and reckon with difficult issues, such as death, is probably best described by Leo Tolstoy in the final chapter of his classic book, *The Death of Ivan Ilyich*.[5] Ivan lived a respectable life, contributing to his family and community. He becomes terminally ill, however, and his fear about dying becomes overwhelming. When he approaches the last few days of his life, Ivan Ilyich "felt that with every minute, despite his efforts to resist, he was coming closer and closer to what terrified him." Ivan's agony about being "shoved into that black hole" of death caused him to scream and flail for three days. Then, an hour before his death, Ivan's son crept into the room. "One hand fell on the boy's head. The boy grasped it, pressed it to his lips, and began to cry. At that very moment Ivan Ilyich fell through and saw a light, and it was revealed to him that his life had not been what it should have but that he could still rectify the situation." With his broadened perspective, Ivan then grieved for his son and wife and tried to express his apologies for the way he had let them down. "And suddenly it became clear to him that what had been oppressing him and would not leave him suddenly was vanishing – all at once." He waited expectantly for his pain and wondered where it had gone. "Ah, there it is. Well, what of it? Let it be." He then discovered that "instead of death there was light." Tolstoy says this discovery left Ivan exclaiming, "So that's it. What bliss!"

Using fear and despair to discover bliss is something I am privileged to see daily, or I should say behold daily. The word "see" just can't capture the experience of these moments. These are moments when I feel connected to the realness of another human being who is simultaneously both like and unlike me. They are moments when I feel connected to truth and deeper dimensions of myself, even dimensions beyond myself. Beholding moments transport me outward, only for me to discover that I'm at the center of my own existence. They are moments of awe when I am both humbled and *en-couraged.*

When beholding moments come, I stop, experience, and marvel. It is a time of sacred silence. I let my energy become still and low. I resist urges to say or do. It is a time to open myself and let myself resonate to the healing in which I am participating. It's a time when I allow myself to experience the situation, stay connected with it, and feel beholden to it. In that moment, I know I'm in my larger self, and I inhabit myself more completely than I normally do. In that expanded moment, I realize that I am not just saying a prayer, I *am* prayer, and what I am experiencing is the love of the universe. These moments can be so captivating that I sometimes forget to even breathe. My soul tingles and my back shivers because I know that in some small way, rather than facing an abomination, I am glimpsing the face of God.

Beholding God-filled moments seems like a passive process, but it's not. To recognize, acknowledge, and appreciate these life-giving moments is an active process that creates space for more of them to occur. Beholding moments are often missed in busy hospital environments that value activity; they can be missed in cultures that value stoicism or in environments that shy away from soulfulness.

Moments are missed in cultures that worship knowledge or value data rather than the meanings they contain.

Myths Awaken Heroic Qualities

Myths are ancient stories that paradoxically depict *truths* beyond mere words or explanations. Just as parables convey truths beyond facts, myths transcend known material reality, extending into deeper meanings and immeasurable dimensions. With my worship of science and technology, I had previously dismissed the value of myths, mistakenly calling them falsehoods or reducing them to superstitions.

Clarissa Pinkola Estes, a Jungian psychologist, changed my perception. She opened my eyes to the value of using mythological stories to precipitate healing. Almost all of the myths in her book, *Women Who Run with the Wolves,*[6] depict the hero's journey into hardship. The heroes use hardship to redeem their destiny.

One tale, *The Crescent Moon Bear,* seemed to have particular relevance to my work with veterans. In this story, a warrior husband returns from combat behaving distant and cruel to his loving wife. The wife turns to the village healer for help. The healer tells her she must find the Crescent Moon Bear who lives at the top of a treacherous mountain pass and bring back a single hair from its throat for a magic potion that will make her husband loving once again.

The trip up the mountain is perilous, and there are numerous boulders, forests, and snowstorms the wife has to face. As she overcomes each obstacle, she expresses gratitude for making her way. She finds the bear, but its antics are fearfully intimidating. The wife shakes in terror, but stands her ground, feeding the bear every day until the bear becomes used to her and trusts her. Finally, she is rewarded by obtaining the hair. Exhausted but excited, she returns to the village and gives the hair to the healer. The healer takes it, nods and smiles, and then throws it into the fire where the hair is instantly consumed.

"No!" cries the young wife in horror. "What have you done!?"

"Be calm. It is good. All is well," says the healer. "Remember each step you took to climb the mountain? Remember each step you took to capture the trust of the Crescent Moon Bear? Remember what you saw, what you heard, and what you felt?"

"Yes," said the woman, "I remember very well."

The old healer smiles, and says, "Now, go home with your new understandings and proceed in the same ways with your husband."

Meeting Our Crescent Moon Bear

Estes emphasizes that the story is not what it seems; it is not about loving someone who has experienced trauma. She says the story is really about the journey of emotional healing made by any person who has experienced trauma or neglect. After the physical self comes home, the emotional self has to come home, and that can be an arduous journey.

Each character in the story actually represents different aspects of our own selves: husband (angry and traumatized self), wife (loving self), healer (wise, calming, healing self), bear ("great compassionate self"). Estes says the story depicts what must be done "in order to restore order in the psyche, thereby healing the angry self:"

- Seek help from a wise, calming, healing, inner force, while recognizing that its help is not magical nor instantaneous (going to the healer within)
- Accept the challenge of going into mental and emotional territory not approached before (being willing to climb the inner mountain into uncomfortable territory that scares us)
- Recognize illusions that makes the self want to fight, flight, or freeze (being willing to face the boulders, forests, and snowstorms that threaten inner growth)
- Solicit the great compassionate self (patiently feeding the inner bear and finally receiving its kindness)
- Understand the roaring side of the compassionate self (recognizing that the inner bear is not tame. Accessing our bear

requires patiently getting to know it and knowing when we are ready to approach more closely.)

Estes says the story demonstrates our desire to have something (a hair from the bear) or someone (healer) magically erase trauma. Instead, healing comes when we come down off the mountain and apply the lessons learned from having reckoned with our hardships.

The myth resonated with my own experience with suffering. For many years, I had avoided, denied, or reacted against the suffering in my life. I now realized that what I had been doing was avoiding making the trek to meet my Crescent Moon Bear. Instead, I had tried to get people who caused me suffering to meet *their* bear so I wouldn't have to meet mine. I read about suffering and how to transcend it, hoping my knowledge would magically make my suffering disappear. I had been willing to do everything except set foot on the path to meet my Crescent Moon Bear. I had lots of excuses why I didn't need to meet that bear. After reading about the Crescent Moon Bear, I realized that the myth provided a map for how I could personally access the hero within me. This insight provided the impetus for me to gather the courage to embark on the arduous journey to meet my bear. Paradoxically, I discovered that vitality began to be slowly birthed into my life.

I often do workshops with people who desire personal healing. The workshop is based on the exercises in this book and helps people abide and reckon with their suffering. After they complete their Life Stories, I recruit them to do roles in the Crescent Moon Bear myth. I then read the myth from Estes' book while they act out what I'm reading. Afterward, they each identify areas in their Life Stories in which they've faced their Crescent Moon Bear, as well as areas in which they haven't. We talk about what they need to do to stand their ground when the Crescent Moon Bear roars and makes them want to run back down the mountain without the lesson they are seeking. "You can always tell those people who've met their Crescent Moon Bear," I tell them. "Those who have met the Bear know how to abide and reckon with walled-off pieces of self and integrate suffering instead of running from it. They have a peace beyond worldly understanding. They learn not to run from the very thing that will free them up."

SELF-AWARENESS EXERCISE
Redeeming Suffering: Integrating the Puzzle

Review the pieces of your Life Story. Your awareness assignment
has five parts:
  1. Reflect on the following three perspectives about suffering:
     • In the opening of this chapter, Joseph Campbell asserts,
       "And where we had thought to slay another, we shall slay
       ourselves. Where we had thought to travel outward, we
       will come to the center of our own existence."
     • I decided to learn how to not waste my suffering in a very
       practical way. I began jogging. Exercise physiologists say
       that aerobic conditioning doesn't begin until one jogs for
       twenty minutes -- I was ready to quit after ten minutes.
       My side hurt. I was hot and sweaty. I couldn't get my
       breath. Now, however, I persisted because I didn't want
       the suffering I'd already endured to be wasted. I was will-
       ing to abide my suffering and reckon with the excuses
       that I created to avoid it. I can now proudly say that I
       behold cardiovascular health; my suffering has not been
       in vain.
     • In the next story you are going to read, Lorraine talks in
       a more profound way about redeeming suffering: "I felt
       privileged to have witnessed the redeeming of a tortured
       soul, and I realized that in a very important way my own
       soul had also been redeemed."
  2. Use Appendix D, the Posttraumatic Inventory, to determine
the relationship you are keeping with the three top-rated events
or relationships on your Life Story.
  3. Mark each event and relationship in which you have not
yet become a hero because you are still coping with the
hardship rather than reckoning with it, thus missing the
opportunity to redeem your suffering by growing into your
larger self.
  4. Consider ways in which you haven't yet made the acquaintance of your Crescent Moon Bear. Are the interior boulders too
difficult to mount? Are you afraid of the roar of the bear? Have

you made the trek, but you can't quite release its hair into the flame so you can redeem the hair with life lessons? Review your Life Story. What suffering in your life is in vain because you haven't yet redeemed it with a lesson that is waiting to be birthed into your life? Mark each event and relationship in which you have become a hero because you climbed the mountain to face your Crescent Moon Bear. (You abided and reckoned with the hardship once you stopped coping with it by hiding, pretending, running away, or blaming others.)

5. What do you think is the destiny you were born to fulfill? What do you need to do to redeem that destiny?

Letting the Crescent Moon Bear Awaken Heroic Qualities

Sometimes I feel inept in convincing others of the value of abiding and reckoning. People want to learn yet they resist. The principles are simple, and yet they are difficult to apply. It's an inward journey of change that requires honesty, courage, and humility; most of us don't want to change. We say we want to meet our Crescent Moon Bear, but we don't want to prepare ourselves to do so. At the same time, most of us have already been able to abide and reckon with difficulties in our lives. Think about a hardship in your own life that you have truly healed: an abusive childhood, an addiction, loss of health, financial collapse, death of someone significant, a divorce or other kind of loss. Initially, you probably coped by avoiding, hiding, or running from the difficulty, living in the illusion that everything was okay, and when it wasn't okay you "rose above it" by disconnecting from the part of self that was having a distressing feeling. For healing to occur, you had to let go of coping and open up to reckoning with the situation, person, or memory and the distressing feelings it caused. This process wasn't easy and didn't happen overnight. It required some struggle to accomplish. It may have necessitated getting help. After it was done, however, your suffering was redeemed with honesty, courage, and humility. You traded knowledge for wisdom and experienced healing. Your suffering changed because you developed a different relationship with it once the suffering was redeemed with a lesson. You are a hero in this aspect of your life, and you now inhabit yourself more completely because of your achievement. Awakening deeper dimensions so you could inhabit yourself more completely was no easy deed.

The next story demonstrates the hero's journey. It shows us how to abide with other people by opening our hearts to experience their joys and sufferings vicariously, which encourages them to do so as well. It demonstrates how to support another person's reckoning journey by helping them change their relationship with their problematic situation, not by avoiding or pretending it away, but rather by encountering it. Just as important is that it reveals how we have to use the process to change ourselves before we can be an effective change agent with others.

I had often urged a nurse on our unit, Lorraine Acompora, to practice the abiding and reckoning process with our patients. She resisted. I confronted her with some situations on the unit. She not only responded, but also became a hero to the rest of us. I asked her to write down the journey she had taken so others could learn from her experience. Here is what Lorraine wrote:

I had resisted learning the principles of abiding and reckoning even though I'd been working on the Hospice and Palliative Care unit for several years. I watched how these principles changed other peoples' lives so that they could behold peace and hope for a different future. What I didn't realize was how this process would change *my* life.

[Lorraine Coping]

I had closed my heart to a volunteer on our unit. He reminded me of my ex-husband. The volunteer would sometimes make wise cracks about me in a joking manner but after awhile, I didn't find his humor funny. I gradually started to resent him. Deborah noticed.

"I feel hurt and embarrassed to see a valued volunteer – a Vietnam veteran – treated in the ways I've seen you treat him," Deborah told me. "If you need to say something to him, say it. If a boundary needs to be set, set it. But it doesn't need to be done meanly and it shouldn't be done covertly."

I couldn't believe what Deborah was saying. I didn't want to hear it. I became angry with her. For days, I didn't speak to her. I got mad at others too. I stopped going to lunch with anyone.

[Lorraine Abiding her Angry Self]

The next day was a scheduled day off from work. I kept thinking about the way I had treated some of the patients, volunteers, and other staff. I'd already spent a week running from my pain, guilt, and anger. Maybe I should try abiding my suffering. Maybe I should reckon with my stuff instead.

[Lorraine Reckoning with Herself]

I decided to write a letter to my soul. I started by writing down my thoughts and feelings about the events of the past several days. I forced myself to be honest and not hide or pretend away my hurt, anger, and guilt. As I wrote, I realized how I had exiled myself from people I cared about and from people who cared about me. I wrote for hours.

When I finished, I could feel my heart open. The spear that had been piercing it was gone. The next day I went to work, toting my letter with me. I had some apologies to make, and I thought the best way to do it was openly and honestly. I'd seen others do it. I could do it too.

I called my seven teammates together and read my eight-page "soul letter" to them, closing with my apology: "It is with sincere humility, coming from a heart that is now willing to suffer, that I ask your forgiveness."

[Lorraine Beholding Personal Healing]

Afterward, I sat beholding my teammates' love and forgiveness. I came away thinking about how much power I had on those around me. I hadn't realized how much harm I'd caused others with my anger, guilt, and pain. I hadn't realized the healing influence I could have on others by abiding and reckoning with that anger, guilt, and pain.

I also found the volunteer I'd hurt, asking to speak to him privately.

"I owe you a huge apology. I'm so sorry for being mean to you. I have no excuse for it. Please forgive me."

He easily forgave me, adding something that surprised me. "I was afraid of you," he said.

Once again, I was brought up short about how intimidating a closed heart can be and about the power I have to influence people around me when I'm willing to abide and reckon.

With my new perspective, I went to care for Mr. Coleman. He was a very contrary, paranoid patient whose sarcasm and put-downs had previously made me close my heart and grumble under my breath each time I cared for him. I did what I had to do and got out of the room as fast as I could. I immediately noticed how differently I now felt toward him. I didn't want to walk away when he spouted his crude and abrasive remarks. I wanted to be open.

"What can I do for you to make you more comfortable, Mr. Coleman?" I asked.

[Patient Coping. Lorraine Abiding]

"Get lost. Get out of here. I don't need you," he retorted. In the past, I would have just walked away mumbling "Screw you" under my breath. This time I asked God to change my heart and stay open.

"Okay. But if you need something, don't hesitate to ask me," I said.

The next day, I asked him if I could sit with him while I had my morning coffee. "Do whatever you want," he grunted.

As I relaxed and sipped my coffee, he started opening up. He told me about a younger sister who committed suicide. He told me about a son who died of cancer and another son who died from an overdose of drugs.

I sat quietly, abiding his pain.

Mr. Coleman also asked me to contact a priest. He said he hadn't been to church in 45 years and had "45 years of sins to confess."

I called the priest.

The next day, I was tucking Mr. Coleman into bed. I turned off his light and kissed him lightly on the forehead.

"What'd you do that for?" he asked.

"Because I care about you," I told him.

"Do it to someone who gives a damn," he retorted.

"Oh Norman, you're not as tough as you want me to think you are," I said to him light-heartedly. He just waved me out of his room.

A roommate was placed in Mr. Coleman's room. Mr. Coleman irritatedly greeted him with, "I really enjoyed having this room to myself before you showed up." He promptly asked me to pull the curtain between them. The roommate died a few days later. I wanted Mr. Coleman to see how reverently we treat our veterans after they die. After placing an American flag quilt over the body, I wheeled the morgue cart slowly past the foot of Mr. Coleman's bed. He saluted.

A few days later, I heard Mr. Coleman shouting for help. When I entered his room, I could clearly see his distress, but I wasn't sure what was causing it.

"Are you having pain?"

"What the hell do you think?" he said angrily.

"Where are you hurting?" I inquired.

"Oh my God! Stop asking questions. You people don't know what you're doing. You're all just a bunch of idiots." He went on to say that he couldn't urinate. I explained that a catheter would drain the urine from his bladder, and he would feel better right away. Reluctantly, he agreed to its insertion. I prayed that the catheter would go in without any problem. Much to my relief (and his) it did. Unfortunately, his anxiety was not relieved as easily as his bladder was.

"Oh my God! You've got to do something," he shouted. "I can't stand this. I can't do this. Help me, please. I need more air. I can't breathe." He was getting more and more anxious. We gave him multiple doses of medications, but nothing had any lasting effect.

I asked Deborah to see him. Afterward, she told me, "He's going to die soon. He's miserable. You need to stay with him at all times until you can gain a sense of what's *causing* his distress."

So I went back, sitting quietly with him. I realized he was literally scared to death, yet he didn't want me to touch him in any consoling way. "Keep your hands off me," he growled. "I don't need you to hold my hand."

I sat quietly with my hand on the bed. I let him reach for it but I didn't offer it. Every once in awhile, he would pat my hand to make sure I was still there.

"Is there anything else I can do for you?" I asked him after awhile.

[Patient Abiding. Lorraine Abiding and
Facilitating Patient's Reckoning]

"I'll have to take it with me to my grave," he said fearfully.

"Is there something on your heart you want to talk about?" I asked timidly.

"I can't say," he said desperately over and over again.

I wasn't sure what to do. I consulted Deborah again. "Ask him if he confessed it to the priest the other day," she said. "If he did, then it's a matter of self-forgiveness; if he didn't, then encourage him to confess it to God and offer to call the priest back."

I returned to the room and sat quietly. "Norman, God knows your heart. If there is something you need forgiveness for and you are truly sorry, then God will forgive you."

"Do you really think so? I'd like to believe that."

"I remember that you told me you used to be an altar boy."

"That was a long time ago," he said dismissively.

"Do you remember how you believed in God back then?"

Norman nodded.

"He's still the same God you served on the altar."

[Patient Reckoning. Lorraine Facilitating his Reckoning]

Without saying a word, Norman put his hands together on top of his chest in prayer. He looked like that innocent altar boy. As he prayed, tears streamed down his cheeks. Afterward, he made the sign of the cross. I wiped away his tears with a tissue. As I leaned over him, I gently whispered in his ear, "God has forgiven you, Norman."

Later, I learned Norman had been a bodyguard in the Mafia, and I shuddered as I imagined what his prayer contained.

[Patient Beholding. Lorraine Beholding]

Norman settled into a peaceful sleep for the first time. Norman's wife came into the room. She sat quietly saying her rosary. I left the room. When I returned, his wife said he had awakened and wondered where I had been. "I've never seen him grateful for anything. What in the world did you do?" she asked.

I stood there for a moment before I could answer her. Finally, I said, "I just loved him."

Norman died that evening. I felt privileged to have witnessed the redeeming of a tortured soul, and I realized that in a very important way my own soul had also been redeemed.

Lessons Worth Beholding

- Our weaknesses and faults are not the abominations that we imagine. They are not the things that set us apart, but rather the things that unite us in our humanity. Finding meaning in our abominations so we can learn and grow is often precipitated when an aspect of self that had previously been slain into unconsciousness becomes integrated. When that happens, we experience wholeness, also known as healing. When this healing happens, we are no longer alone, but rather we are able to be with all the world.
- Beholding is experiencing a newfound peace with the circumstance because the relationship to the problem has shifted. Once this inward shift has occurred, we receive energy from

our deeper selves and our integrity is restored. People often verbalize the shift of energy by saying something like, "A load was lifted off my shoulders."

- We gain real power when we let go of pride and will power and allow ourselves to be broken open so that we can acknowledge our needs and ask for help. As a result, we're able to inhabit ourselves more completely.

- Problems challenge us to birth honesty, courage, and humility within ourselves so we can effectively respond to the situation. If we fail to do this, then our suffering is wasted, and it will likely be perpetuated until we let go of our fear and open up to the changes that we need to make. Once we make these changes, we are able to behold a future filled with hope; peace replaces chaos and pain.

- Beholding seems like a passive process, but it's not. To recognize, acknowledge, and appreciate life-giving moments is an active process that creates space for more of them to occur.

- The hero within is the place inside ourselves that touches God.

- The *Crescent Moon Bear* and other myths provide a map for personally accessing the hero within.

- Suffering is not a tragedy. The tragedy is not redeeming the suffering. Beholding experiences occur with people who view suffering as a doorway to awakening. The primary difference between ordinary people and heroes is that heroes don't waste their suffering.

Chapter Five

Energy:
The Power of
Healing

Suffering ceases to be suffering the moment it finds a meaning.
Suffering has meaning if it changes you for the better.
An exceptionally difficult situation
gives man the opportunity to grow spiritually beyond himself.[1,2,3]
-Viktor Frankl

When we abide and reckon with hardships in a way that changes us for the better, we behold healing. In order to change for the better, we have to grow spiritually beyond ourselves because the energy of the spiritual dimension is necessary to achieve healing. As we become active participants in the healing process, we can then use this energy to tackle other problematic areas in our lives so that we continually strive to live from a dimension of integrity. Many people would say that this energy is found in the spiritual dimension. I'm not sure how to describe the "energy;" neither do I know how to describe the "spiritual dimension." I'm not even sure where the topic of spirituality belongs, yet I know this book would be incomplete without addressing it.

A word that might capture the spirit of energy is "vitality." When I stop denying feelings and instead open up to them, I experience vitality; I become more alive. When I reckon with hardships rather than cope with them, I become *vitally* alive; my spirit is engaged. This spiritual self is important because it's the most true and enduring part of me.

The *National Consensus Project Guidelines* for the spiritual domain defines spirituality as "the aspect of humanity that refers to the way individuals seek and express meaning and purpose and the way they experience their connectedness to the moment, to self, to others, to nature, and to the significant or sacred."[4] Teilhard de Chardin offers another perspective: "We are all spiritual beings here for a human experience."[5] These definitions capture the nature of our inward beingness where energy and vitality are generated.

It's easy to confuse religion and spirituality. Sometimes I conceptualize that their relationship is like trees and forests. Religion is the trees of beliefs that we create to understand the spiritual forest of our existence. We all live our religion (the values and beliefs that underlie our actions); even atheists live out their "religion." Beliefs, however, sometimes interfere with understanding existence because "we can't see the forest for the trees." Many people discount the value of religion because of this distortion of perspective. Yet, forests can't exist without trees; and the quality of the forest is dependent on each tree's contribution. Forests and trees are not mutually exclusive; in fact, they might be mutually inclusive. I learned this from a rabbi on National Public Radio. He was on a panel of religious leaders of different faiths discussing religion and spirituality. All of them agreed that not all spirituality is religious. Almost all panelists agreed that all religions are spiritual. A rabbi disagreed. He said that any religion that teaches exclusivity is *not* spiritual because spirituality is based on humility not arrogance.

So even though I am unable to provide exact definitions, my hope is that the stories on these pages will provide a context for readers to sense the meaning and value of "energy" and "spirit" because as death approaches, people start contemplating deeper issues. Their perspectives shift, and frequently they undertake a spiritual quest.

"Tell me how you are doing spiritually," I'll say to a patient.

Often the response is, "Oh, I don't go to church."

"Sounds like you're not a *religious* person, but I'm wondering if *spirituality* has any meaning to you," I'll reply. "Do you receive strength or comfort from a source of energy or power beyond your own?"

Many will say they believe in God; others talk about nature or their family; some say spirituality has no relevance in their lives. I distinguish between religion and spirituality because I want patients to know I have no interest in trying to convert them to a religion, impose my personal beliefs, or urge them toward any specific beliefs at all. My attitude is important because many patients have had experiences where others had an agenda to change or impose religious ideas; sometimes this kind of imposition was done in a manner that did not respect the patient's personal beliefs or his or her need to doubt and question.

I usually try to provide nonreligious spiritual care. It takes time to assess a person's beliefs, time I don't usually have. Also, there are many different faiths, even divisions within the same faith. It requires time to discern the particular meaning of a patient's religion. Instead, I provide open-ended "generic" spirituality so the patient can infuse his *own* personal meanings. I let the patient lead and I follow. I'm secure enough in my own religion that I don't worry about differing beliefs sabotaging my own. Neither do I think it's my business to convince them of my beliefs. Sometimes, we explore spiritual ideas together. I proceed cautiously though, always mindful that the patient could be vulnerable to my authority as the healthcare provider. I'm also aware that I might unconsciously want him to think like me.

I've learned a lot by watching other people provide religious and spiritual care. Shaku, one of the nurses on our Hospice unit, is Hindu, a religion not shared by many of our patients. She has learned prayers and practices of other religions so she can respond to patients' varying needs. It's not unusual to hear her reciting the Lord's Prayer or the rosary with patients. Patients frequently tell me what a comfort Shaku is to them.

I had an encounter with a nursing assistant who reminded me of Shaku when I, myself, was a patient. I had abdominal surgery and afterwards a small artery began bleeding. I lost many pints of blood, and all my clotting factors were consumed. I not only needed several blood transfusions but also a second surgery to control the bleeding. I was left weak and debilitated. I also had severe diarrhea. Too weak to quickly get to the bathroom, I was incontinent. Embarrassedly, I activated my call light. When the nursing assistant came to the room, I told her apologetically about the mess awaiting her under the sheets.

"Oh, that's okay. That's why I'm here," she said cheerfully. "You don't worry about a thing. Your job is to just let me help you."

Long after she left, I thought about this woman who made me feel like there was nothing more she wanted than to have the opportunity to clean up my stinky mess. She gave me graciousness, and that was a gift of the spirit that remains with me to this day. God was never mentioned, but she helped me realize that tenderly emptying a bedpan for a patient is one of the most spiritual things I can do.

This nursing assistant's act made me reflect on an adage that sometimes circulates in healthcare circles: "Nursing assistants aspire to be nurses; nurses aspire to be physicians; and physicians aspire to be God." I sometimes ask myself, "To what role in a hospital does God aspire?" I wonder if the answer is that God aspires to be a patient whose suffering is redeemed through the love of a compassionate care provider like that nursing assistant who cared for me.

Once I recognized the spiritual nature of the care I was providing, I focused on providing it more consciously. Providing prayer for patients, however, was another matter, a difficult matter. I had always considered prayer to be private, but as I started realizing how important prayer was for many patients, I decided that my discomfort mattered less than their needs. I bought a small book of reflections and kept it in my pocket. I coded each page with words that cued me to its content: hope, comfort, strength, courage. When I met with patients, I'd use the readings rather than prayer. After a few years, I was finally able to personally provide prayer when patients wanted it. I've even provided prayers at public events. Appendix E highlights some of these prayers.

At the heart of all prayer is intention. Flowery words have no spiritual significance if they aren't congruent with what our heart is singing. For example, I was going to pray with a patient, Mike. As I often do, I asked Mike what he wanted me to pray for. "Pray that the

Buccaneers win their game this weekend."

I was a bit nonplussed. His intention didn't match my own beliefs about prayer. Not wanting to be hypocritical, I tried to negotiate integrity of intention. I offered an alternative approach that might still hold some relevance to Mike. Tony Dungy, the Tampa Bay Buccaneer's football coach the previous year, had been fired and was now coaching in Indianapolis. He had been a well-respected member of our community, and we were still grieving his loss. "I'm not quite comfortable asking God to intercede with a football game," I tentatively began. "How about if we pray for Tony Dungy? He's starting his new season with the Colts. Maybe we could ask God for his blessing on Tony's transition there. Maybe we can ask that Tony be able to touch the people of Indianapolis the way he touched us."

"That'd be good," Mike said sincerely. And so we prayed.

Spirituality Extends Beyond Religious Boundaries

As noted with Mike, providing spiritual care can be difficult to determine. Some patients' religious and spiritual needs are clear and predictable; they have a specific faith and need the prayers and rituals of that faith. There are times, however, when there's nothing to prepare you for what their needs turn out to be. Hannah was one of these perplexing patients. She was 48 years old, and a veteran of the Persian Gulf War, spending 22 years in the military. Twice divorced, she had two sons, ages 12 and 21. Hannah's relationship with her parents was strained. Indeed, the first words I heard from her were, "Where are my parents?" She had just arrived on the Hospice unit from the emergency room where her parents had brought her. One of the nurses went to look for her mom and dad, only to discover that they had left without waiting to see how Hannah had settled into the unit. There were no goodbyes; it was a symptom of the angry and ambivalent relationship they had with their daughter. They had been estranged until Hannah had moved into their house six months earlier because she had become incapacitated by her three-year battle with pancreatic cancer. Their relationship was as conflict-ridden as it had been when she was a rebellious teenager. "They never approved of anything I did," Hannah told me.

The strains of caretaking exacerbated the tension. Hannah's parents were tired and angry. When they later came to visit, they warned staff, "Be careful. She'll try to pull something with you."

Over the next six weeks, her parents visited occasionally, but they would remain distant and cold. Pets are allowed on the unit, and her parents usually brought Hannah's dog, Romeo, with them. It eased the tension between them, shifting the focus away from the family issues and onto the dog. A little white fluff of fur, Romeo seemed to know that Hannah was sick and would lie quietly with her when she napped.

Military life had exposed Hannah to many ideas from around the world. She had explored different philosophies and considered death and afterlife from various perspectives. The first week on the unit, she remained aloof; then slowly, she opened up a bit. When we asked about her religion, she told us that she wanted us to honor Buddhist rituals when she died. Specifically, she asked that no one touch her head after her death and that she be taken to the morgue dressed and sitting upright. We looked up Buddhist rituals, but we found nothing about such death practices. Still, we agreed to do what she wanted us to do.

Luminous crystals lined Hannah's windowsill. She became upset if anyone moved one of them. They could only be effective, she insisted, if they were facing a certain direction and placed in a specific order. She also kept a foul-smelling concoction of shark cartilage by her bedside and was upset when a nurse accidentally spilled some of it. The shark cartilage, she told us, had kept her cancer in check since her diagnosis. We apologized for the accident and promised to be more careful in the future.

Hannah demonstrated remarkable ability to control her pain through relaxation and meditation and, in spite of her eccentricities or maybe because of them, she exuded an air of tranquility. In fact, her most striking feature was her dignity in the face of indignities. She took in stride the frequent abdominal taps needed to relieve accumulated fluid. Sometimes the fluid leaked and a collection bag had to be placed on her abdomen; still, she maintained her composure. Her long, black hair (a reminder, she said, of her "hippie days") now gave her a dignified look. Always neat and well-groomed, she diligently brushed her hair each day. Although her energies were flagging and the long strokes left her exhausted, she allowed no one to help her.

She was always courteous, but she never confided in any of us and accepted help only when it was absolutely necessary. Eventually though, she began to confide in Suzanne, one of our nursing assistants. Hannah's independence charmed Suzanne. "You remind me of my teenage daughter," Suzanne told her, elaborating on her daughter's most recent rebellious exploits. Hannah laughed in delight. "I think I understand your daughter," she grinned. From then on, Hannah and Suzanne were the best of pals.

Hannah's two sons and her brother visited frequently. Her oldest son, Ryan, was nearing graduation at Georgetown University. She was immensely proud of him. His father, her first husband, was African-American; Hannah was Caucasian. Hannah cherished Ryan's ability to embrace both aspects of his heritage. Her younger son, Landon, was still growing up and her primary concern related to his welfare after she died.

Hannah's brother, Aaron, came from Chicago to visit her. They had remained close over the years. Their love for each other was evident. Not wanting to waste a precious minute even during the night, he slept on a cot at her side. It was Aaron who clued us in about Hannah's religion. I asked if he too was a Buddhist. He laughingly responded, "Nope, and neither is Hannah. She just got tired of every hospital wanting to code a religion for her. One day, out of exasperation, she told them 'Buddhism.' She thought it would keep them off her back." I burst out laughing. So this explained the odd "Buddhist customs" she had told us about!

Hannah helped our team create a metaphorical mural on the wall of our Hospice unit. The mural depicted the hero's journey of abiding and reckoning with the brokenness in this life. A rainbow symbolized the act of beholding. When the staff encountered difficulties with creating the rainbow, Hannah had the solution. She wheeled back to her room and returned with some dental floss. "Now go get a tack and use my floss to draw the arc," she directed.

The next morning, Hannah asked a nurse to take her out to view the finished product. At first Hannah just grinned at it, but then something moved her. Suddenly, years of uncried tears erupted into sobs. It was the first and only time Hannah surrendered to the pain of her experience. No one spoke. We sat with her as she cried, and when she looked back at us, her smile was peaceful.

Hannah's condition gradually worsened. We knew her death was approaching when she suddenly asked Suzanne to freshen her hair, the first and last time she surrendered her brush. She talked about making peace with her parents and working out things with her ex-husband to assure Landon's care. Her hair now done, she asked Suzanne for a hug.

Hannah died quietly the next day. She had tested us repeatedly by making absurd requests and watching our reactions as if daring us to accept her regardless of what she did. We had passed her tests.

Three months went by. A package from Aaron arrived on the unit along with a note that read: "I found this when I was going through Hannah's belongings. I thought you should have it." Inside was a small statue of Buddha! It was a perfect addition to the cross, rosary beads, Mormon Bible, Menorah, Hindu Om symbol, Islamic prayer rug and Qur'an in the Hospice chapel. Hannah, the make-believe Buddhist, had gotten us again!

"There Are No Atheists in a Foxhole"

This famous military adage is sometimes quoted by veterans when they're admitted to the Hospice unit. Hospice is a type of foxhole that often stimulates spiritual questing. Some feel hypocritical in beginning such a quest at this time in their lives. Some have told me that they've turned their back on God for many years. "What right do I have to come forward so I can know God now?" they'll ask.

Many appreciate an open invitation to simply explore beliefs unbounded by formalized religion. Others express a desire to become reacquainted with childhood religions. Such was the case with Scot, a 61-year-old man with an open cancerous wound on his knee that had spread to his lungs. With only a few weeks to live, he was anxious, putting on his call light frequently to request that staff remain in the room to talk. A widower with no children, his only source of support was a friend who visited frequently.

I introduced myself to Scot, explaining I was concerned about how he was dealing with all that was happening with him. Unlike many veterans, Scot readily acknowledged his fear as well as feelings of bitterness that related to a missed diagnosis a year before. However, he had a hard time acknowledging anger.

"I'd be angry if that happened to me," I said. Although he denied it initially, he was able to verbalize his anger with some encouragement. I then helped him explore his feelings about the many losses he had sustained. "I would guess you might feel sad to suffer all the changes you've had to go through." He nodded and a tear escaped. I waited, bowing my head to give him emotional privacy. "What's the hardest thing for you to face right now?" I asked at last.

"Leaving all this," he replied. "I enjoy my life. I don't want to leave it."

"Tell me about that. What has been important to you over your lifetime?" As we did his life review, it was obvious Scot had led a gentle, loving life filled with joy, despite many hardships and much pain. He expressed strong spiritual values with a Christian orientation, but he did not attend church. He had an innocent, childlike demeanor that was unusual for a man his age.

"You said you felt fearful about what's happening to you. Many people tell me they worry about what dying is like. Do you ever wonder about things like that?"

He nodded.

"I've been with hundreds of people as they've died. Would it help if I told you what I've seen?" I proceeded to describe what happens physically, allaying his fears of pain, which can usually be well managed with appropriate medications. I described the peacefulness that often comes when people confront their fears and losses. I could see Scot's anxiety diminishing as I spoke. Then he interrupted me with a question.

"How long do you think I have to live?"

"That's hard to say," I told him. "A few weeks, a few months maybe. No matter how long you have, it's time to prepare for death so that whenever it comes you'll be ready. Your new job is to get ready for your death."

"Really?" he asked incredulously. "How do I get ready?"

"You're doing it right now. You're telling me how you feel. You're letting yourself feel your pain. You're letting yourself cry when you feel sad. You're being honest with who and how you are. These kinds of actions tell God that your intention is to get ready for your death. Then, he will send you what you need to get ready."

He thought about that for awhile and then he said, "He sent me you, didn't he?"

I laughed. "Yes. I guess he did. And there are lots of other people like me who will walk the path with you. You're not alone. Let us know what you need. We want to help."

I then asked him a question I ask most of my patients: "Pretend like you died today. What would be left unsaid or undone?"

Most patients take some time to reflect on the question, but Scot answered promptly. "Going to church. I haven't been to church since I was 12."

Based on how he'd lived his life, I was surprised this weighed on him so heavily. "Really? What happened when you were 12?"

"I was in church with my buddies," he said. "The preacher said, 'Everyone who loves Jesus come to the altar'." His buddies went, but Scot stayed behind. "I'm the kind of person who wants to do something because I want to, not because someone tells me to." He was making up his mind about what he wanted to do, when the preacher said, "Scot Connolly, if you don't come down here, you're going straight to hell." This statement prompted Scot into action. "I got up and walked out of the church. On my way out, I said over my shoulder, 'Well, I'll see you there, preacher'!"

It was a great story, and I burst out laughing. Scot was surprised at my amusement. "Personally, I'd say the preacher deserved that," I told him. I realized I was now imposing my own meaning on his action. Yet I continued: "How did you ever have the presence of mind to say those words, especially when you were only 12? I'm really impressed with your courage."

Scot answered, "I don't know. But ever since that day, I've never set foot in a church. I'm afraid Jesus won't know me."

"It sounds to me like Jesus knows you well," I said. "I can see how much you love him. I can see how generous you have been helping others with your time and money. You told me you have prayed and praised Jesus every day of your life. You've told me he has worked miracles in your life. I would guess Jesus is eager to welcome you home as your life changes from this world to the next." Recognizing I was now trying to talk him out of his guilt rather than responding to it, I asked him what he thought would help Jesus know him better.

"I was never baptized. I should have been baptized," he said.

"We can do that," I replied.

"How? I can't go home. I can't even get out of bed." He was wide-eyed with questions.

"We'll do it right here. We'll bring the chaplain and baptismal water here."

"Really? You can do that? You would do that for *me?*" he asked.

I laughed. "We would *love* to do that for you," I replied. We planned the celebration for the next day and closed our time together with a prayer and a hug.

The next day, Chaplain Dan conducted the ceremony at Scot's bedside with many staff in attendance. The baptismal ritual was filled with oils and water, rich symbols of cleansing and transitioning into a future without his physical body. We also sang and prayed using symbols of spiritual identity. Scot seemed to take great comfort in all these actions. Then he announced it was his turn to speak.

"Last week I felt all alone," he said, looking down at his hands that were as white as the sheets on his bed. Then he lifted his head and looked around the room slowly. His eyes were tearful but twinkling as he deliberately looked at each one of us. "And this week?" he continued. "Well, look around," gesturing around the room. "I have a room full of friends."

Becoming More Alive as Death Approaches

Christopher was a patient who, like Scot, called upon childhood religious practices as he faced death, although it took awhile before he decided that these practices were important to him. I visited Chris in the community living center at our medical facility. Introducing myself, I told him I worked with the Hospice and Palliative Care team.

"I'm not going to die," he responded immediately.

Although his tongue cancer would probably not threaten his life for several months, Chris still needed palliative care. His pain was out of control even though he was receiving large doses of analgesic medication. He rated his pain a 10 on a scale from 0-10.

"How about if you come to the Palliative Care Unit for two weeks, get your pain under control, and come back to your same bed here in the nursing home," I asked him. With the assurance of return, Chris agreed to admission.

Our Hospice and Palliative Care team enjoyed Chris. Some described his personality as "vinegary" while others noted a sparkle in his eyes "like a kid at Christmas time." He was sketchy about his spiritual beliefs; he said that prayer held no relevance for him. He enjoyed the attention he received from the staff during team meetings with him. He enjoyed old Western movies on the DVD player rolled to his bedside. As Chris relaxed into the environment, his pain receded to a zero on the 0-10 scale, and he asked to extend his stay on the unit.

Chris got a roommate who died a few days after admission. Immediately, Chris asked to be transferred back to the community living center. "Give this bed to someone who *really* needs it," he said. He was transferred back that day.

Several months later, I was again consulted for Chris's out-of-control pain. He was also weaker. However, he was reluctant to come back to the unit. "I'm afraid I won't get out this time," he told me.

"Maybe," I said. I added that he could also die in the community living center; the location wasn't going to affect the time of his death. "At least on the Hospice and Palliative Care Unit, you'll be surrounded by people whose expertise is providing comfort to you." Then I realized I was trying to *convince* Chris to come back to the unit, so I backed off, reminding him that it was his decision. Once I retreated, he seemed more willing to rethink his choice.

"Okay. I guess I'll come," he said. "But remember, I don't want any prayer." I assured him I remembered that prayer was private for him and that his request would be honored.

Chris's ambivalence continued after he came to the unit. His suffering continued, but it was difficult to determine its source. We suspected his physical pain might be an expression of his emotional suffering. Nevertheless, we aggressively treated the pain. Pain brings people to their knees; it can be overwhelming. Left untreated, discovery of emotional and spiritual dimensions isn't possible. A whirlpool bath provided temporary relief; ice packs and hot packs had some effect. The staff provided massage, but Chris's descriptions of the pain remained vague. We couldn't abandon him by not treating his physical pain. However, we knew that treating his nonphysical pain with medication or other physical modalities was also a form of abandonment.

"Point to your pain," Dr. Hull told Chris in a team meeting. Chris pointed straight in front of him, as if the pain were outside himself. "He's telling us his pain isn't in his body," Dr. Hull said to the staff. "No amount of medication's going to fix it. We've got to look to other dimensions. He's got anxiety that people often misinterpret as pain."

So we tried to find out what was happening to Chris beneath

the surface. "What makes life worth living Chris?" I asked him. "What makes you want to wake up each day?"

"My daughters," he said. "I don't want to leave them, and I don't want them to be bothered with my death." His answer seemed enigmatic. His daughters lived out of state, and he hadn't seen them in years; an occasional phone call was their only contact. From his description, the relationships lacked much depth or intimacy. However, he was vague, and so we couldn't be certain that his daughters were the source of his suffering.

As we had promised, we didn't pray for Chris, at least not formally. *Intention* is at the heart of prayer. "Let's be quiet together," I would say, and he would nod. As the chatter of the world fell away, we created spaces for togetherness. Trust emerged, and slowly death lost some of its threat.

Chris's need for deeper relationships with his daughters also emerged. In a moment of confusion, Chris mistook one of the nursing staff for his daughter, Kim. He grabbed her hand and pulled her toward him, apologizing for some of his past actions. We teleconferenced Kim and her sister, Gretchen, into the next team meeting. When I encouraged him to voice his apology, he did. Years of drinking that had eclipsed their love were washed away with Chris's acknowledgement of the pain he had caused them.

Kim then revealed her own alcoholism. She told us she had stopped drinking abruptly one night when a fight with her husband frightened their six-month-old baby. "My baby's silent stare reminded me of my own pain as a child when Mom and Dad fought over Dad's drinking," Kim told us. She had gotten help and had been sober since that day.

Because Chris had been a World War II veteran, we weren't sure if Chris's drinking had been a way of self-medicating against traumatic war memories. "I never thought about that," Gretchen said. "But it makes sense. Daddy never would tell us what happened in the war. He said we wouldn't understand."[6] Chris shrugged as if there had been nothing more he could have done.

Chris's attitude about prayer changed after this meeting with his daughters. He now actively sought religious support. He had been raised Catholic, and now the Rosary, the Lord's Prayer, and the sacraments brought him solace. He also became affectionate. "That's the Dad I remember before he started drinking," Gretchen said when we described his new behavior.

Gretchen and Kim now began phoning Chris daily. They were discovering new things about their father, "Positive things, unlike what our mother told us," Gretchen said. Then she asked for advice about whether she should start preparing for his death by telling him goodbye.

"Your Dad told me a few weeks ago that what is keeping him here is you. He said he didn't want to burden you with his death."

Gretchen began to cry softly as she realized the meaning and love in her father's statement, saying, "Then I've got to tell him that it's okay to go."

I transferred the call to Chris's room, holding the receiver to his ear so he could hear Gretchen's tender message of release.

Chris became more peaceful with the freedom that spiritual growth often provides. Softness now eroded his furled brow. He started seeing his mother and wife, both long dead, only to wake up with a startled, "Oh I'm still alive."

In many ways, Chris was more alive now than he'd been for many years, maybe even his entire life.

SELF-AWARENESS EXERCISE
Encountering Our Spiritual Dimension

This exercise helps animate vitality.
- Mark your Life Story with activities that have engaged your spirit, i.e., things that gave you passion, generated vitality, helped you feel more you.
- Review your Life Story again. Are you currently involved with enough activities that feed your soul? Are there any activities from your youth that you need to develop or reinvest in now? If you're not taking care of yourself by nurturing your spirit, what does that mean about the relationship that you are keeping with yourself?

- Review your Life Story again. Mark the people and events that fill you with gratitude. Do you need to add any other people or events you're grateful for?
- Pretend like you died today. What would be left unsaid or undone?

A Suffering Team That Responds to Distress

Our team developed a format of weekly Quality of Life (QOL) meetings with the patient and family where we gather at the bedside. The idea for the QOL meetings evolved from a conversation I had with my colleagues. "Doesn't it seem odd that no hospital in this country has a suffering team?" My boss thought so too when I mentioned it to her.[7] Next thing I knew, I was designated to start one throughout the hospital.

Quickly I realized that neither patients nor staff would easily accept a "Suffering Team" on their unit; it just wasn't good public relations. A patient suggested that we call ourselves the Quality of Life Team. "That's really what you are doing," he said. "You are helping us improve the quality of our lives." The name stuck and for the next several years, staff throughout the hospital were trained in providing this quality-of-life service. The "QOL," as it has come to be known, is one of the primary ways through which we provide spiritual care. Appendix F provides guidelines for facilitating QOL gatherings.

At the start of the QOL gathering, we reintroduce ourselves to the patient and family. The patients have met many people since they were first admitted, and we want to make sure they know the roles we play in providing their care. Then we explain the purpose of the meeting: "We're here to listen to what might be on your mind or heart. We know this time can be difficult, and we want to listen carefully as you tell us what you are experiencing so we can respond to your needs." Both patients and their family members usually respond easily to this open invitation to share their suffering.

We sometimes inquire about physical pain and symptoms to make sure we're providing adequate treatment, but pain and symptom management is not the goal of hospice and palliative care; pain management is only the vehicle to the goal; the goal is healing. I've seen people cured of illness without experiencing any deeper healing. Likewise, I daily witness people who experience healing even though their disease cannot be cured. We explore the emotional and spiritual aspects of their illness during the meeting. Our job is to vicariously experience whatever the patient says, abiding with whatever feelings arise and to connect with the part of the patient that is generating the feeling. We elicit stories so we can gain a sense of the patient's past, their current struggles, and their hopes for a peaceful death. It's often a time filled with laughter, tears, and cherished memories. We provide guidance about ways they can reckon with their illness. We explore the spiritual dimension so we can understand how to provide spiritual or religious care that is congruent with their beliefs. We ask if there's anything we need to do differently to make things better. Not only does the question help us improve care, but the patient sees we're open and willing to change; they feel free to speak about their needs. We also help them explore the impact of their military history so we are better able to identify its relevance to unfinished business or ways in which it might influence their death. We express our appreciation for their military service by thanking them and ceremonially pinning them with an "Honored Veteran" pin. We also thank their families for the impact the military had on family members and pin them with a military angel.

We offer choices for how to close the QOL session: "We can provide a spiritual reflection or prayer; each of us can offer you a hope for the day; we can tell a joke; we can sing a song; we can each tell you how your story has impacted our own lives; or we can just say good-bye. What would be meaningful to you?"

We've found this format to be invaluable for everyone who participates, including the staff. I asked Percy, a patient who had experienced five of these meetings, how he would describe the QOL gatherings. He said: "These meetings are God, man, and staff coming together to help patients feel happier and more comfortable. It helps assure that the patient's goals are the staff's goals. In the process, the whole organization becomes better and stronger."[8]

Pat, our bereavement coordinator, has a teenage son, Morgan, who volunteered at the hospital one summer. He attended QOL meetings with patients. He witnessed the transformations patients often experience during their spiritual questing, and he called them "miracles." Now, when his mother comes home from work, Morgan asks her, "What miracles did you see today?" His mother responds with stories of suffering she saw redeemed. She tells him stories of patients awakening to their interior hero.

I think our QOL meetings are like a story in the book, *Kitchen Table Wisdom,* by physician Rachel Naomi Remen.[9] Remen attended a workshop for physicians by mythologist Joseph Campbell, in which he displayed a slide of Shiva. "Shiva is the Hindu name for the masculine aspect of God," Remen writes. She explains that the picture shows Shiva dancing in a ring of flames while his hands hold symbols of the abundance of spiritual life. One of his feet is supported on the back of a little man crouched down in the dust, giving all his attention to a leaf the man is holding between his hands.

"Despite the great beauty of the dancing god," Remen continues, "all of us physicians had focused on the little man and the leaf, and we asked Joseph Campbell about him. Campbell began to laugh. Still laughing, he told us that the little man is a person so caught up in the study of the material world that he doesn't even know that the living god is dancing on his back."

In the midst of all the diagnostic and treatment modalities that permeate a hospital culture, we can likewise find ourselves studying leaves and missing the living god dancing on our backs and on our patients' backs. The time we spend in QOL meetings with patients helps us create room for gods to dance.

Spirituality Encompasses Compassion

Compassion is an important component of the QOL experience. The derivation of the word "com-passion" means "with suffering." Sometimes the QOL format has to be adjusted to compassionately join a patient in his suffering. Mr. Moore illustrates a case of com-passionately joining a patient in his suffering. "We can't do QOL with Mr. Moore. He's too confused," said one of the nurses. "He doesn't even know where he is."

Once an engineer, Mr. Moore now had dementia and wandered the hallways aimlessly, picking up books and writing his name on the pages as if to leave his mark so others would know he was still a per-son bearing a name. Although he often smiled, his eyes looked fear-ful and searching. Our team rolled in with our chairs as we normal-ly do for QOL sessions; however, the regular interactive format would need to be modified. We deleted the usual explanation of the QOL; fancy words would only cause more confusion, further sepa-rating us from him.

I sat down on the bed beside him, placing my arm around his shoulder. "We're just here to be with you," I said quietly. He looked at me momentarily with confusion; then he slowly laid his head on my shoulder. His eyes suspiciously surveyed the rest of the team before he relaxed contentedly. He held a hymnal from our hospice chapel in his hands. It was opened to "How Great Thou Art." The team tentatively started singing its melody. Mr. Moore joined in, not tentatively but with a rich, deep, resonant voice. His conversations may have been sketchy, but his singing wasn't.

We sang more hymns. During one of the lulls, I commented on his signatures on the pages. "I see you've written your name in the hymnal there."

He nodded, thumbing through the pages.

Not wanting him to feel scolded, I added, "That's good. It helps us know who you are. Larry Moore is important to us. We're going to remember you for a long time," I said while silently thinking about all the other patients who would be picking up our books and wondering why the name "Larry Moore" was written on so many pages.

Mr. Moore had a different response. He stopped thumbing, becoming still. I couldn't see his face because his head was still on my shoulder. I was surprised when a staff member leaned forward to hand him a tissue for his tears. "I didn't know I was important anymore," he said.

People with dementia often lose their self-esteem and their cognitive abilities like Mr. Moore did, but their spirit remains intact. Rachel Naomi Remen tells a story about Tim, a cardiologist colleague of hers, whose father had dementia so severe that he had neither recognized anyone nor spoken for 10 years. Autopsy subsequently revealed that his brain had been almost entirely destroyed. Moments prior to his death, however, a strange thing occurred. As his father collapsed and Tim went to call 911, his father's voice interceded. "Don't call 911, son. Tell your mother that I love her. Tell her that I am all right." Then he died.

Tim told his physician colleagues, "For many years, I have asked myself, 'Who spoke?' I have never found even the slightest help from any medical textbook. I am no closer to knowing this now than I was then, but carrying this question with me reminds me of something important, something I do not want to forget. Much of life can never be explained but only witnessed."[10]

Witnessing the mystery of life is an important aspect of providing spiritual care. While religions seek to explain this mystery, spiritual awe often revels in the unexplainable. This distinction is important when providing care to professed atheists. Spiritual care must be done sensitively without any religious context. Jane was a patient who called religion a "crutch" that kept people from exerting their individuality. Culturally Jewish, Jane was a firm atheist. She looked at us warily when we came to her room for her first QOL meeting and asked about her spiritual beliefs. "You're not going to hassle me about religion, are you? I get enough of that from my nieces. I tell them if their God makes them happy, they can keep him. Just don't try to force him on me."

Jane was strong and spirited. She had served in World War II. She had been a pioneering woman in an era when women were *dis-couraged* from exerting personal power outside the home. So it was not surprising that she was independent in her beliefs about religion. At the end of her 86 years, Jane prepared herself to die on our Hospice unit. She approached death as she had approached everything: matter-of-factly, with few words, and a calm acceptance.

Jane wanted to see the plot where she would soon be buried, so Chaplain Dan and I took her to the nearby national cemetery. We chatted with her and listened to her concerns about dying. It was the beginning of her friendship with Chaplain Dan. Dan was not a proselytizer, and once Jane saw this, she became comfortable with him. They were both open-minded people who accepted the differences in their beliefs.

Jane was a typical vet. She didn't want any medication; she didn't want any oxygen; she didn't want to talk much. The nurses accepted her attitude, and her primary nurse, Marlene, found other ways to soothe Jane's discomfort. Marlene provided extra pillows and proper positioning rather than morphine. She never pushed or probed to make Jane talk. Instead, she just sat with Jane, letting a quiet peacefulness engulf them. There was an intimacy in their silences that would have been lost with cheery chatter or unwanted questions.

As with many of our patients, we offered a ceremony to Jane that would celebrate her life. Appendix G provides the forms and an example of a typical ceremony. Jane, as well as her family and friends, willingly completed the forms. On the day of the ceremony, everyone joined together sharing their reminiscences that highlighted the value and meaning of Jane's life. When the service was over and the last strains of Frank Sinatra's *I Did It My Way* faded, Jane's well-meaning traditionalist nieces gathered at her side to make one more appeal for her to reconsider her stance about God.

Jane smiled at her nieces tolerantly, then looked at each member of the Hospice team. "Well girls," she replied. "I still don't believe in God, but I do believe in angels. I have to. I'm looking at a room full of them."

Lessons on the Dimension Where Healing Occurs

- An exceptionally difficult situation gives us the opportunity to grow spiritually beyond ourselves. When we open ourselves to grow into the situation, the suffering ceases because it changes *us* for the better.
- In order to change in a way that discovers the unique meaning or the imprinted destiny, a person has to go into the spiritual dimension of himself. In this dimension, we are able to behold healing if we are willing to abide and reckon with the source of our suffering.
- We are all spiritual beings here for a human experience.
- It's important to distinguish between religion and spirituality because people need to know that we have no interest in trying to convert them to a religion, impose personal beliefs, or urge them toward any specific beliefs at all.
- At the heart of all prayer is intention. Flowery words have no spiritual significance if they aren't congruent with what our heart is singing.
- Hospice is a type of foxhole that often stimulates spiritual questing. Questing should be *en-couraged* as a natural way of

preparing for death.

- Pain and symptom management is not the goal of hospice and palliative care; pain management is an essential vehicle to the goal. The goal is healing. Dying people are fertile ground for healing.
- People who are dying often become more alive than they have been previously if they allow themselves to be broken open so that their suffering can be redeemed with the love of others and God.
- It's easy to get so caught up in the material world that we forget that the living god is dancing on our backs.
- While religions seek to explain mystery, spiritual awe often revels in the unexplainable, bearing witness to it.

Chapter Six

Forgiveness: A Reckoning Process That Restores Wholeness

If we have no peace,
it is because we have forgotten
that we belong to each other.[1]
-Mother Teresa

I've come to appreciate how healing and forgiveness are inextricably intertwined, even in small ordinary ways. I have to forgive every disappointment and interruption that interferes with my experience of the moment. Every time I am told, "No" by God, another person, or life itself, I have to actively forgive the world for things not going the way I had hoped. Then I can reencounter the ever-present now; I reestablish peace in my world.

One time, I asked my mother, "Who is your best friend?" She replied, "Whomever I'm with at the moment." I liked that answer. I hope I can live out that wisdom. Similarly, I hope that I can answer the question, "What's your favorite thing to do?" with "Whatever I'm doing right now." Then, I'll know that I'm living in the now, and the key for doing so is forgiveness; I will be able to forgive the world for everything that is not "now."

Forgiveness can have very practical applications. I jog along a two-mile rural road. Trash litters the edge of the road, corrupting its beauty. I frequently complained about the litter with a tightness in my jaw and neck as I did so. Then I realized that I had a choice: I could forgive the litter for being there and enjoy the landscape anyway, or I could pick up the litter. I decided on the latter. My garbage

bag in hand, I picked up each can and wrapper. Initially, I was thinking mean thoughts about the litterers. Then, I realized that I was lit-
tering my mind with resentment, robbing me of *now-ness*. I switched
to blessing each litterer, and actually had great fun on the rest of my
clean-up adventure. Forgiveness is like that; it transforms moments
so I can live in the vitality of the now.

Desmond is a Vietnam veteran who knew how to maintain
peace in the now. During a QOL meeting with him, our team
acknowledged his military service, which he appreciated. "'Nam vets
never got their due," he told us. We offered an apology for the way
he had been treated when he returned from the war. When asked
how he was doing spiritually, he told us, "I'm good in that department because I always keep my feet wiped." He explained that some
people don't keep their "feet wiped" on a daily basis. Instead, dirt
accumulates, surfacing as they approach death, which was the case
with Jim.

Jim was a World War II vet. He was weak with a cancer that
would take his life in a few days. After I introduced myself and we
spoke quietly for several minutes about hospice care, I asked him if
there was anything from the war that might still be troubling him.
He said there was, but he was too ashamed to say it out loud.
Motioning me to come down close to him, he whispered, "Do you
have any idea how many men I've killed?"

I shook my head, remaining silent, steadily meeting his gaze
with my own. He continued.

"Do you have any idea how many throats I've slit?"

Again I shook my head. The image was grim, and I felt my eyes
begin to tear. Jim was tearful too. We sat silently together, sharing his
suffering. No words needed to be said. This was a sacred moment
that words would only corrupt.

After several minutes, I asked, "Would it be meaningful if I said
a prayer asking for forgiveness?"

He nodded. I placed my hand on Jim's chest, anchoring his
flighty, anxious energy with the security of my relaxed palm. My
prayer, like any praying I do with patients, reflected no particular

religion. "Dear God: This man comes before you acknowledging the pain he has caused others. He has killed; he has maimed. He hurts with the pain of knowing what he did. He hurts with the pain of humanity. He comes before you now asking for forgiveness. He needs your mercy to restore his integrity. He comes before you saying, 'Forgive me for the wrongs I have committed.' Dear God, help him feel your saving grace. Restore this man to wholeness so he can come home to you soon. Amen."

Jim kept his eyes closed for a moment, tears streaming down from unopened lids. Then he opened his eyes and smiled gratefully; his new sense of peace was almost palpable. It was a reminder to me of just how heavy guilt weighs.

The reason I prayed for Jim with my hand on his chest is because anxious energy usually rises. Think about when you get excited. Your voice usually gets higher; energy gets flighty. You might place your hand on your chest or near your throat, unconsciously anchoring yourself. A calm, centered person's energy usually resides lower and deeper. If a calm person places his or her hand on an upset person's sternum, it can often help this person feel secure, more weighted, less anxious. I often sit with my dying patients with my hand on their chest. I teach their loved ones to do the same.

It's tempting to try to soothe guilt away with rationalizations: "That was a long time ago" or "You were just obeying orders." This kind of rationalization doesn't help, however. These veterans know when and why they killed, and whether it violates their deepest-held moral beliefs. They need to have the guilt acknowledged and accepted so that finally they can forgive themselves.

Victims sometimes feel guilty. Their guilt might be irrational because the perpetrators have manipulated the victim to feel ashamed of the abuse. Jack was a hospice patient who sheepishly told me that he was worried about dying "because I pissed on a priest's grave."

"You did what?" I asked him, not sure I'd heard him right.

"You heard me. I pissed on a priest's grave."

"I'm guessing you had a good reason for doing that," I replied with curiosity.

"He molested me when I was a boy," he said.

I could still see the pain in Jack's eyes from those long-ago days that had filled him with anger and shame. I leaned forward and looked deeply into his eyes. "I'm glad you pissed on his grave, Jack. He deserved that."

"Do you really mean that?" he asked suspiciously.

"I do. I'm really glad you did that."

Jack relaxed, and said he felt relieved. I could only breathe deeply and let go of the outrage I felt toward the man who had violated him.

Responding to Guilt and Shame

If someone is unable to achieve forgiveness, they might arrive at the end of life filled with bitterness. Stockpiling transgressions of others (blame) or self (shame) is the recipe for making bitterness. Bitterness is a poison that contaminates even the most innocent heart. It is a venom for the soul.

I believe forgiveness is essential because it brings peace with the past. Although it is true that we cannot change the past, we can change *our relationship to* the past, and forgiveness is the means to that end. In fact, I heard Oprah Winfrey say that forgiveness is "giving up the hope that the past can be any different than what it was."

The dictionary defines the word forgive as "to give up resentment against or the desire to punish."[2] For me, forgiveness is simply being willing to open my heart again to a person, a situation, or myself. A closed heart blocks the energy of my larger self. Blocked energy is a significant loss for two reasons: (1) the person who slighted me now controls my heart and its ability to love, and (2) I've shut myself off from the energy of the spiritual dimension where solutions for resolving the trouble in the relationship can occur. In this context, I can now understand the Biblical admonition to "Love your enemies and pray for those who persecute you."[3] I no longer see this as a selfless act, but rather as a means of staying connected with my own vitality. This does not mean that I don't stand up for myself, set boundaries, or keep the person from controlling me. Rather, praying for someone who has hurt me (that is, keeping my heart open to them) keeps me from losing my own self; it keeps the other person from controlling my heart and its ability to love fully. I can then set boundaries with an open heart.

Sometimes people resist doing the work of forgiveness because they think it will then condone what was done to them. "What happened is still wrong. It will never be okay," I tell them. "But until you achieve forgiveness, that act – as awful as it is – is still controlling you. You are locking up the part of you that is hurting, and that part of you desperately wants to come home." I also explain how forgiveness is a process that has to be done incrementally over time. "It doesn't just happen," I caution, snapping my fingers.

I explain how the process starts with a *willingness* to forgive and develops into an intention to do so; this step is the most crucial and also the one most vulnerable to omission because of self-deception. People say they want to forgive, but their actions may belie their stated motive; their intention is to maintain the grudge. If the person has a spiritual orientation, I often simply ask them to start the process by praying for a willingness to forgive. If spirituality has no meaning or if the word "forgive" has an unwanted religious connotation, I usually speak in terms of holding onto something versus letting it go. Often I assign a simple homework assignment. "Write down, 'I am *willing* to forgive _____ (myself or name of someone or a situation), and I intend to do it.' Then tape this to a mirror and say it each day." This act helps people change their minds about their intention to let go of a hurt or disappointment so the forgiveness process can begin.

When someone persistently fails to forgive in spite of attempts to do so, I explore the purpose the lack of forgiveness serves and the role it may be playing in sabotaging their efforts. This role might include receiving sympathy for the victim role or staying safely stuck in powerlessness so no risk is taken to assume responsibility for their needs or to ask for their needs to be met.[4]

Asking people to consider forgiveness without pressuring them is important. There is no need to be pushed into the forgiveness process. Demanding forgiveness is seldom effective; it's more a matter of staying open to the possibility. This is not as easy as it sounds. Because I've seen peace come to people when they do the work of forgiveness, I've developed a bias toward wanting everyone to do it. I have to resist imposing my bias on others, remembering that people may not be able, ready, or willing to forgive. I not only need to accept their decision, but also I need to *understand and respect* it. My job is to *en-courage* them to consider forgiveness, but I have to be careful that I do not judge them if they decline. When I don't completely respect their decision, small inflections in my voice or changes in my posture give me away; the person experiences my judgmental attitude and withdraws. As a result, opportunities to help them consider forgiveness at some future time are lost. This loss is significant. I might open the door to forgiveness, and the patient declines to enter. This reaction doesn't mean they don't want to forgive; it often means they are not yet ready. When I initially see patients to discuss forgiveness, they might not be interested. As death approaches, however, I remind them about the possibility of forgiveness and, often, they are then ready, willing, and able.

It's also important not to rush people into forgiveness prematurely. "Forgiveness should not come until guilt has moved us into remorse. Remorse is realizing how our action hurt others," I heard a presenter at a hospice conference say.[5] "Otherwise, forgiveness is just a self-indulgent, guilt-relieving device that does not lead toward compassion." The presenter was right; I've had the same experience. I do something wrong, and rather than abide my guilt so I can use it to meet the part of myself that committed the wrong, I ask for forgiveness so that I don't have to reckon with the part of myself that caused me to wrongly act in the first place. Premature forgiveness gets me off the hook of remorse so I don't feel the pain of my actions. As a result, I miss an opportunity to grow in humility.

Forgiveness does not require reconciliation; in fact, reconciliation should sometimes be avoided. For example, an abused wife still needs to forgive her husband, but she should not reconcile with him to be abused again. Unfortunately, premature forgiveness often plays a role in abuse cycles. "Believe your eyes, not your ears," I tell people who keep reconciling with an abuser. "I'm sorry doesn't count until you see their actions change for good, and their actions aren't going to change unless they are getting help. Until then, you need to focus on loving and taking care of *the part of you* that is hurt and wounded by them." This sounds simple, but it's not. It's easier to believe the illusion that the unhealthy person will change than it is to do the work of meeting our own inner hero who awaits permission to love the broken part of us back home into psychological health.

Physician M. Scott Peck writes about guilt in his book, *The Road Less Traveled*.[6] He identifies a "disorders of responsibility" spectrum. People on one end of the spectrum don't assume enough responsibility for hurtful actions. When there's conflict in their relationships, it's the other person's fault. They often feel that they don't need to apologize for anything. Statements such as, "What you see is what you get" or "That's just how I am," are their way of saying they have no intention of changing, accommodating, or apologizing. Relieving them of guilt without exploring it means that they never develop a sense of remorse, and they miss the gift of guilt. To tell such people, "You were doing the best you could" or "It's not your fault," when something goes awry only reinforces their reluctance to accept responsibility. Instead, guiding people toward realizing the impact of their actions on others can birth compassion, generating apology and forgiveness.

Eric was such a patient. He assumed too little responsibility for his actions. His health was failing, and he was scared he might die. We were having a QOL meeting with Eric, exploring his fears. He revealed that he had belonged to a motorcycle gang. "I watched lots of women get gang-raped," he told us.

I was struck by Eric's lack of emotion. I asked him about the effect these acts had on the women. He didn't know, remaining more focused on his guilt than on their pain. He showed little remorse, so he was unable to elaborate. When we closed the meeting, the patient requested a hope for the day. When my turn came, I fought to abide in my nonjudgmental self so I could sincerely appeal to a sense of compassion that Eric seemed to lack. Telling us what he did indicated that he might be ready to take responsibility for his actions. He couldn't feel the pain of what he'd done, but if I stayed open and connected to him, maybe I could feel his pain for him. Later, he could feel that pain for himself. With emotion, I offered, "My hope for you this day is that you reflect on what you did to the women you watched getting raped so you can understand the pain you caused by witnessing their harm without stopping it. My hope is that you will let yourself feel the pain of those women, not for their sakes, but for your own so you can sincerely feel remorse and ask for forgiveness." I then offered that at some point he could think about doing something especially nice for a woman so that those raped women's suffering would not have been in vain. Eric looked me in the eyes, gave me a slight nod of his head, and said, "Thank you." I'm not naïve enough to think that what I said produced an "aha" moment for this man; neither am I cynical enough to think that my words had no impact.

Self-Forgiveness

Unlike Eric who assumed too little responsibility, some people assume too much; they are on the other end of Peck's "disorders of responsibility" spectrum. When there is conflict in their world, they not only shoulder their own guilt, but also everyone else's. When something goes wrong, they assume they're at fault. They drown in remorse, or more accurately, "false remorse," taking on guilt that isn't theirs. They need encouragement to let go of inappropriate guilt, and they need to practice self-forgiveness.

Peck's "disorders of responsibility" spectrum is not quite as straightforward as it sounds. I notice that many people, including myself, can be on different ends of the spectrum in varying aspects of their lives. For example, a person may be overly responsible at work, accepting blame for anything that goes wrong in their department, but assume too little responsibility in their personal relationships (or vice versa).

One crucial component of self-forgiveness is learning to distinguish guilt from shame. Guilt is natural and designed to provide feedback so we can learn important lessons; shame is artificially created and designed to punish. Guilt tells us something we did is wrong, guiding us toward more compassionate actions towards others. Shame tells us that we are wrong, filling us with worthlessness, and consuming our self-compassion. Guilt mobilizes us into new behaviors; shame immobilizes us so that we remain stuck. People are often filled with shame. We need to go from shame to guilt before we can get to forgiveness.

"Admit it. Quit it. Forget it," is a good formula to help with self-forgiveness.[7] This formula can also provide clues about a person's orientation on Peck's responsibility spectrum. People who have a hard time accepting responsibility are reluctant to "admit" or "quit" the behavior; whereas, people who take on too much responsibility have a hard time "forgetting." Ed, one of our Hospice volunteers, is a good example of people who take on too much responsibility when something goes wrong. Ed was visibly upset when he asked to speak with me. "I've been sitting with Mr. Zielinski. The phone rang, and I went out to answer it. When I came back, he had died." Just talking about what had happened escalated Ed's anxiety.

"Are you saying you knew he was going to die in the few minutes that you stepped away, and so you said to yourself, 'Oh Goodie, here's my chance to let this man die alone?'" I asked.

"No. I didn't know he was going to die right then."

"Good. For a minute, I was starting to think that you thought you were God and that you were omniscient and could have predicted the moment Mr. Zielinski was going to die."

Ed laughed. "No. I don't want to be God."

"Then are you willing to forgive yourself for being human and not being able to predict the future?"

Ed said he was. Then, he smiled and expressed relief.

Helping people like Ed develop an appropriate relationship with guilt is like separating wheat from chaff, sorting out what to hold onto, what to let go, what is realistic and what is unrealistic, what is their business and what is not. As Peck says, "What we are and what we are not responsible for in this life is one of the greatest problems of human existence. It is never completely solved. It requires continual assessment and reassessment."[8]

SELF-AWARENESS EXERCISE
Forgiveness and the "Now"

This exercise helps integrate puzzle pieces so wholeness can be restored. Review your Life Story:

- Is there anyone or anything in your Life Story that you want to change your relationship with so that you can open your heart again? How does forgiveness play a role in this change? (Remember that there is a difference between forgiveness and reconciliation.)
- Are there any ways in which you are being overly forgiving, enabling others in their dysfunction by making excuses for them? (Remember to believe your eyes not your ears. Truly remorseful people change their lives with actions not words.) In what ways are you betraying aspects of your own self by enabling?
- At which end of Peck's "disorders of responsibility" spectrum do you tend to perceive the world (i.e., not assuming enough responsibility for hurtful actions or assuming too much responsibility)? What is your guilt or your lack of guilt saying to you? What adjustments do you need to make so that guilt can open you to your larger self?
- In what areas of your life have you practiced "false forgiveness" for hurts you have sustained? In what ways is false forgiveness now perpetuating the original abuse to the aspect of yourself that has been hurt or shamed? What steps do you need to take to reintegrate an aspect of self that has been hurt so that then forgiveness can be extended?
- Henry David Thoreau said, "To regret deeply is to live afresh."

Review Appendix H. What do you need to do so you can "live afresh?" What have you not forgiven yourself for? What do you need to do so you can open your heart again to the part of yourself that is left exiled?

Forgiveness Pitfalls: Enabling and False Forgiveness

Enabling is a passive process that fails to hold someone accountable for how their actions impact us. Rather than acknowledge how we've been hurt, we avoid our feelings by letting the transgressor off the hook. Being *overly* "forgiving" of others keeps the hurt aspect of self exiled, reinforcing the original betrayal. An opportunity for the transgressor to grow is also averted. For example, parents who don't require their children to be respectful and responsible "forgive" their child's actions too easily; forgiveness turns into enabling, perpetuating the child's behaviors. Meanwhile, the parent ignores their own feelings of anger, hurt, and disappointment.

Forgiveness can, unknowingly, be faked. A person might say, "I let that go a long time ago" or "It's over and forgotten." Sometimes, that's true. At other times, it's a way to fool ourselves so we can side-step the work of forgiveness. I know, because I'm guilty of practicing "false forgiveness" myself. It's a convenient way of lying to myself.

The most common mistake that leads to "false forgiveness" is that *the wrong part* of the self is trying to do the forgiveness work! For example, we can think of ourselves as having a core self that is whole and healthy. If someone is abused, a part of the self is torn away from the core self. *It is the part of self that has been torn away* that needs to do the forgiving, and it can't do that if it's left split off from consciousness. Disconnected from the core self, the abused self is left exiled in hurt, anger, and shame. It is *the exiled part of self* that has been transgressed. The forgiveness process begins by *reintegrating the exiled self* back into the conscious self. *Then,* forgiveness can be extended. Unfortunately, people often mistakenly omit this step. The conscious self does not feel the hurt, anger, and shame that the vio-lated self feels, so it's understandable that people can easily deceive themselves into thinking, "I let that go." Doing forgiveness work, however, without first integrating the wounded self is especially damaging because *it leaves the wounded self exiled.* It leaves the wounded self saying, "Wait a minute. I'm the one who was damaged. I'm the one who is left hurt and angry. You can't speak for me unless I'm present. You can't speak for me until you re-own me and wel-come me back home." Thus, the conscious self lacks the authority to offer forgiveness unless it first opens up to the pain and anger of the part of self that was betrayed and split off. It is only the betrayed self's voice that has the authority to extend true forgiveness. If left exiled by the conscious self, the wounded self is forced to seek atten-tion *unconsciously,* which is a more arduous, lengthy, and less effec-tive path toward wholeness that can be filled with pitfalls.

When I counsel adult children whose parent beat or sexually abused them, I never accept at face value that they have "forgiven" the offender. I explore the basis for forgiveness, and I often find a façade that hides the abused self. When I confront the façade, unwanted feelings of pain, anger, and shame often surface as the exiled self gains voice. Sometimes a list of excuses condones the abuse so the façade can be maintained: "My Mom was abused when she was little too. She didn't know any better." Sadly, the abused person now perpetuates the original betrayal by silencing the aspect of his or her self that was hurt. This kind of toxic relationship sacrifices healthy personal growth to protect the parent.

The work that I do with adult children is to *en-courage* them to touch their anger and hurt, and coax it out of hiding so it can be used to take a stand with the parent. This healthy stand allows the adult child to develop his or her own personhood. Taking a stand is important because it allows the person to develop their own internal parent who can love and protect them. (The process for this is detailed in Chapters Seven and Eight.) The abuser may then respond by accusing the child of being "selfish" or "self-centered" as a means of controlling the relationship so it can return to its former toxicity. Ironically, just the opposite is occurring; the adult child is becoming *self-ful,* full of self. Once they grow into themselves, guilt-inducing accusations can no longer control them. Once the hurt self is reintegrated into the conscious self, *then* the abused child can forgive the abuser. Once forgiveness occurs, the abuser no longer controls the abused.

Never Too Late to Forgive

To withhold forgiveness means to cut myself off from a compelling force deep in the soul that seeks it. If that forgiving force is denied, vitality and peace remain elusive. Forgiveness restores wholeness; it gives us back the part of self that has suffered the transgression. Although some people have powerful defense mechanisms to resist forgiveness, most just need a little *en-courage-ment.* Such was the case with the family of a 38-year-old patient, Kevin.

"I just can't sit by and watch him die," Kevin's mother told our team as we gathered at his bedside for a QOL meeting. "I just can't," she repeatedly protested as if to convince herself.

Meanwhile, Kevin's father babbled mechanically about anything except that his son was dying. Instead, his father told us that the weather was going to change and that there was a new movie coming out.

"We're on a very short timeline," I said to focus the discussion. I explained the value of preparing for Kevin's death and ways they might participate. At first, they resisted. His father continued to talk about the weather. With some coaxing, however, his mother gradually started letting go of the illusion that Kevin wasn't going to die and opened up to the reality that he was.

"His sister wants to come," his mother said. "But, they've been estranged for 15 years. She doesn't even know why. He doesn't want to see her. Should we tell her to come?"

I polled the team for their opinions. Everyone had a different answer, and we weren't sure what to do. Kevin's condition was deteriorating so we knew an answer could not wait. Finally, we told them to have the sister come, and we would have a nurse in attendance. If Kevin showed any sign of agitation or desire not to see his sister, she would have to leave.

Our team struggled with the decision. How do we measure the needs of the brother against those of the sister? How do we measure the rights of the dying against the rights of the living? How do we measure the patient's verbalized desire to maintain walls of isolation when experience tells us that he might need reconciliation to achieve peace? How do we measure what is our agenda as both professionals and human beings against the patient's agenda that had been explicitly stated? Were we violating Kevin's rights by letting his sister visit? Were we dishonoring his need for control and self-determination?

When Kevin's sister came that evening, one of the nurses, Sherie, accompanied her. "Your sister is here," Sherie whispered in his ear. Although he had been unconscious for a few days, his eyes opened. He smiled, holding out his hand to his sister. Then he lapsed back into unconsciousness and died peacefully an hour later.

Helping Kevin and his family let go of the fears that kept them holding on and then helping them open up to saying their goodbyes and doing the work of forgiveness brought them peace. To facilitate this process, we have to let go of the assumption that the person always knows best and open up to our experiences that have taught us what helps. Otherwise, others don't gain the benefit of our experience. At the same time, we have to let go of our presumption that we know what's best for others and open up to ways that we don't. It's tempting to think that because this story had a good ending that we acted correctly. The truth is, I don't know; I can only hope so.

Often there is no way to know if a decision was correct. By letting go of my need to be right and opening up to ways I make mistakes, I become more teachable. However, I often resist learning the errors of my ways. Sometimes I push too hard, and sometimes not enough. I try to remain sensitive to my weaknesses and stay aware of how they interfere with my judgment.

I went to see a patient whose wife, Emily, wanted to be present when I met with her husband, Adam. I was told that she didn't want the word "hospice" used with Adam because she didn't want him to know he was dying. I deal with these kinds of situations often, and I have found that it's usually better for the patient to know so I disregarded Emily's warning. Emily was not at the bedside so I met with Adam alone and initiated a discussion about his approaching death. He told me he was relieved to be able to talk about death. I left smugly patting myself on the back for proceeding without Emily's "interference."

The next time I visited Adam, Emily was present. I introduced myself, and she stiffened. "Please leave now," she snapped. "And don't come talk to me or my husband again." There was no bridging the gap I had created by disregarding her previous desire to protect her husband. Whatever benefit Adam got from our discussion, it was undone by the pain I caused his wife. Eventually Adam came to the Hospice and Palliative Care unit and died; I had to remain outside his circle of care.

A few months later, I saw Emily again, this time at the hospital's memorial service we hold for the families of patients who die at our hospital. She saw me too and glared from her fourth row seat in the auditorium. When I took the microphone to welcome people to the service, I could feel her piercing gaze. After a few opening remarks, I spoke about how we strive to serve and how we sometimes fail. I then looked directly at Emily. "Mrs. Mann," I said. "I know I made a mistake in not listening to your desires for your husband. I realize my action increased the suffering you were already feeling. I just want you to know I'm very sorry for having done that to you." She hesitated for a moment, then nodded her head and uncrossed her arms.

Seeking forgiveness with Emily followed a rather ordinary course of events. Sometimes, however, circumstances surrounding forgiveness can be downright bizarre. Such was the case with a patient who was a minister. He asked us to call him "Reverend." He said it made him feel part of the team, allowing him to keep his identity. Reverend and his wife, Libby, were devoted to each other as, together, they faced his death on our Hospice and Palliative Care unit.

After a lifetime of church ministry, Reverend maintained his desire to serve others. One day his roommate died; the roommate's wife was crying softly nearby. The nurse asked Reverend if he would like to leave the room. "No," he said. "I'm right where I'm supposed to be." He then offered solace to the wife.

Reverend was a man of modesty and dignity. He wanted prayer when he awakened. He enjoyed leading prayer during QOL meetings at his bedside. Reverend was able to chide us and do so openly. A nurse, Pat, told him, "I'll be back in a minute." When she returned an hour later, he lightly asked, "Do you know the six most common words said in a hospital?"

Pat acknowledged she didn't.

"'I'll be back in a minute'," he said. "Hospital minutes are the longest minutes in the world." They both laughed, and Pat apologized for its truism.

Reverend's son was a music director at a church. We borrowed a keyboard so he could play at his Dad's bedside; they sang hymns together. The son's voice had a richness that filled the unit with heavenly sounds.

Although things seemed to be going well, Reverend and his family had ambivalent feelings about receiving care from the VA. A few years previously, he had suffered a serious complication that occurred during surgery. Reverend had demanded an investigation. A feeling of distrust understandably tainted our team's relationship.

One evening, a surgeon, Dr. McChesney, came to the unit to see a patient. She heard Reverend's son playing the keyboard and singing with Reverend. Dr. McChesney later told me they sounded like angels, and so she went into the room to check it out. I can only imagine Dr. McChesney's shock when she came face to face with the man who had been her accuser just a few years before. Not knowing what to do and at a loss for words, Dr. McChesney later told me that she stood there immobilized. Libby came to her side, and Dr. McChesney braced herself for an assault. Instead, she got a warm greeting.

"I've been praying for you to come," Reverend called from his bed.

Dr. McChesney apologized for what had happened to Reverend as a result of her action.

"I'm so glad you came," Reverend told her. "I wanted you to know that it wasn't entirely your fault."

Dr. McChesney was still tearful when she came back to the nurses' station, telling me what happened. "It's a miracle," she said. "I haven't been on this unit for years. I came to see a different patient. I just went in there to see where the beautiful music was coming from." She kept shaking her head in disbelief. "You have no idea how this has weighed on my mind."

"It sounds like it doesn't need to weigh there any longer," I responded. She smiled with obvious relief.

The next morning, the QOL team gathered at Reverend's bedside with his family. It was fascinating to hear them recount the events of the previous evening. "I had been praying for the past two weeks for Dr. McChesney to come," Reverend said. "I knew I needed to release her spiritually from the investigation. I wasn't sure how to get in touch with her, but I just knew she'd come."

"It's a testament to the power of a dying man's prayer," I

responded. "It's a testament to the power of accusing someone and yet staying open to her. Your 'bad' experience didn't close you off from her goodness. I'm not sure I could do that. I'm going to let you inspire me."

Reverend self-effacedly brushed my comment off.

I continued, "Actually, I don't know who to admire more: you and your courage to forgive or Dr. McChesney and her humility in wanting to be forgiven."

"Healing requires both," the son interjected. He expressed gratitude to the team for the healing environment that had been created. "The love and care here have erased all the past mistakes made with us," he said.[9]

Reverend, his family, and Dr. McChesney helped me understand that forgiveness may be one of the most difficult things we do, and not doing it might be the most foolish.

Lessons in Forgiveness

- Forgiveness is the secret for living in the now. Every time I am told, "No" by God, another person, or life itself, I have to actively forgive the world for things not going the way I had hoped. Then I can reencounter the ever-present now; I reestablish peace in my world.
- "Keeping our feet wiped" on a daily basis helps us live and die healed.
- Though it is true that we cannot change the past, we can change our relationship to the past, and forgiveness is the means whereby we do that.
- Forgiveness is being willing to open my heart again to a person, a situation, or myself. A closed heart blocks the energy of my larger self. Boundaries can be set with an open heart.
- It's important to assess where someone is on Peck's disorders of responsibility spectrum, which ranges from no guilt to excessive guilt. We need to respond differently depending on which end of the spectrum the person is on.

- Don't take people away from their guilt. Help expose the guilt so it can be examined to see if the person needs to assume more responsibility for righting their wrong or, conversely, to let the guilt go if it's irrational.
- *Willingness* to forgive is an essential, often forgotten, element of forgiveness. Affirmation or prayer can help achieve this. "I am willing to forgive _____, and I intend to do so."
- "Believe your eyes, not your ears." Saying, "I'm sorry" doesn't count until actions change. Until then, focus on loving and taking care of that part of you that is hurt and wounded.
- Forgiveness can turn into enabling if care is not exerted.
- Abused people need to touch their anger and hurt, and coax them out of hiding so a stand can be taken with their abuser.
- Being *overly* "forgiving" of others sometimes keeps hurt aspects of self exiled, reinforcing the original betrayal. Only when we reintegrate the exiled aspect of self, do we achieve forgiveness. Once forgiveness occurs, the abuser no longer controls the abused.
- Stockpiling transgressions of others (blame) or self (shame) is the recipe for making bitterness. Bitterness is a poison that contaminates even the most innocent heart. It is venom for the soul.
- Forgiveness may be the simplest and hardest thing each of us are asked to do; not forgiving may be the most foolish because then the person or situation is still controlling our ability to love.

Chapter Seven

Integrative Letter-Writing: Cultivating Honesty, Courage and Humility

Maybe it's exactly the experience of loneliness
that allows me to describe the tentative lines of solitude.
Maybe it is precisely the shocking confrontations with my hostile self
that give me words to speak about hospitality as a real option.
And maybe I'll be courageous enough to speak about prayer as a human vocation
without the disturbing discovery of my own illusions.[1]
-Henri Nouwen

It is difficult to abide and reckon with all aspects of our selves, especially those aspects we don't like and those we don't even know. We all experience loneliness, yet we often don't recognize and even deny its existence. We run from loneliness by turning on the television, calling a friend, shopping, surfing the internet, eating comfort foods, indulging in alcohol, and countless other distractions to disguise its presence in our lives. Developing the honesty to identify loneliness and then use it as a passport into solitude where we find unity with our soul seems unthinkable. Hostility fares no better. All of us are hostile, yet we have a hard time owning our hostility because it doesn't fit with the self image of being a hospitable person. When we can't own our hostility, however, we will blame others for hostility when a conflict arises. We lie to ourselves about our role in the conflict because we're afraid to be ourselves, which includes a hostile self. We talk to other people about the person who angered us, unaware of the hostile act we're committing by doing so; meanwhile, we fail to recognize or accept responsibility for our hostile self. Developing the courage to confront our own illusions about who we are and who we are not is the first step toward being willing to be ourselves. Once we are able to live from the integrity of our deeper selves, we become prayer itself.

Integrative letter-writing is one of the most effective tools I've found to abide and reckon with all aspects of self so we can achieve a deeper level of integrity. I often use letter-writing with my patients and their families, as well as with myself. The goal of integrative letter-writing is to create a more peaceful relationship with the person or situation that is causing distress; it can also be used to address personal aspects of self that are causing loss of vitality. Creating a peaceful relationship is not done by segregating the person, situation, or aspect of self into unconsciousness; rather, the person, situation, or self aspect is *consciously integrated* into personal experience. Segregating the part of me experiencing distress traps some of my vitality, squeezing some of me out of myself; the smaller I become the more suffering I experience. Opening up to the part of self in distress creates more of me because I have to grow into a deeper part of myself in order to hear, acknowledge, and love this part of me.

Much of my work with letter-writing involves helping dying people find peace with the unfinished business that has collected over a lifetime. "That's in the past. Nothing I can do about that now," a person will say wistfully, describing a broken relationship or an unfulfilled dream. Although it's true that the facts of the past can't be changed, one's relationship to those facts can. Letter-writing is one way to facilitate that change. When change is done with a willingness to abide and reckon with sources of suffering, people gain new meanings from old issues, and their suffering becomes redeemed with peace and healing.

When death approaches, motivation for learning is accelerated. Perspectives shift when death is near. Things that seemed important yesterday fade in priority today; things that weren't previously important now seem urgent to complete. Regrets surface; opportunities for healing emerge. A hospice patient may ruefully think about his long-since divorced wife or yearn for the estranged child who hasn't phoned in several years. Sometimes the military war that was supposedly over years ago comes forth unbidden.

Writing a healing letter spans time. A letter can reach into the past, bringing new perspective and understanding. It also preserves the present moment so the healing intention that was summoned to create the letter continues to be useful in the future when healing might be needed by the letter recipient. Letters can even reach into the future to heal problems that have not yet arrived, but can be anticipated, such as the letters John wrote to his son in Chapter One.

Letters Touch Dark Places

Letters need not be written to people who will be able to read them. In these situations, the primary purpose of the letter is to help the writer; it often helps them address unfinished business in a relationship. Drew, the writer of the next letter, reckons with some issues with his father. Drew was surprised to discover anger toward him. As Drew brought his angry self into consciousness, he was able to hear what this previously-ignored self had to say. Then he was able to integrate this aspect of self back into his conscious self. His letter inspires each of us to heal the anger and brokenness in our own lives.

> Dear Dad,
> Thank you for being my dad. Thank you for the wonderful family vacations to Atlantic City and Miami Beach. Thank you for getting me my first job and for coming to support me when I played high school sports. Remember when I joined the Army? You were proud because you also served in the Army. The day came when I was shipped to Vietnam. I could see the concern in your eyes. I promised you I would be okay and that I would be careful. You wrote to me daily and sent me packages from home filled with great food. When I returned home you were there with open arms and tears.
> Dad, I never told you, but there were times when I wished you were not my dad. The times you came home drunk, falling down swearing and yelling. The times you hit Mom and some-

times me. When you divorced Mom and married another woman, you asked me to attend your wedding. I said yes even though I didn't want to. I lied to Mom telling her I didn't attend even though I knew she would find out.

Dad, you died very suddenly with a heart attack. When I arrived at the hospital you weren't there yet. When the ambulance arrived and they opened the door, I knew it was too late.

I carried these memories for many years and I probably should have told you before you died, but Dad I forgive you. I also miss you a great deal. Until we meet again...

Your loving son, Drew

After writing this letter, Drew stated he felt a burden lift from his shoulders, a common experience when an exiled part of self returns. "I was close to my Dad, but I kept these things hidden. Maybe I was afraid," he said. "Now, I'm cleansed and free." Drew said he shared his letter with his sister so she could do the same. He also said that some of his walled-off anger, guilt, and pain had unconsciously sabotaged some of his other relationships. Writing the letter released the energy that had been attached to the feelings, increasing love not only for his father, but for others in his life as well.

Letters to Retrieve Wounded Pieces of Self

This letter is written by Lauren, a physician who had been abused by her mother. It demonstrates how to develop the interior mother to provide the nurturance her mother had been unable to provide. Lauren had a teenage daughter, Anna, who sometimes yelled at her. Lauren realized that her yelling daughter had assumed the role that her mother had previously occupied. To change the relationship with her daughter, she had to change the relationship with the part of herself that was generating angry, hurtful, fearful, and guilty feelings. Here is the letter that helped her re-own those parts of herself:

Dear Adult Self:
I don't like being yelled at. I feel afraid. I feel scared for my life.

When Anna yells at me, it feels like Mom yelling at me. When something happens at work, I'm afraid of being yelled at. When you yell at me, I not only feel scared and lonely, I feel hopeless, empty, abandoned, and near death.

I need your help to know that my life is safe. My Mom tried to kill me. She was too drunk to succeed, but I see her face; I smell her cigarettes and alcohol. God, I hate that smell. It's only recently with the help of a therapist that I can recognize some of these early feelings.

I'm so small when I feel these things. I'm thrown back in time and space. I become an animal myself. I want to yell. I want to hit and scream and run away or run in circles. I panic. I pace. I get a tightness in my chest that cuts off my breath.

Sometimes my reactions aren't so big. That's when I whimper. I ball up and cry inside. I pray. I say, "Stop!" Mostly, I just turn everything off.

You try to help me. You shut me down because you know these aren't effective ways to express myself. But sometimes you can't stop me, so I yell. I'm sorry for not listening to you.

Sometimes you stop me, but then you say mean things to me or to Anna or to anyone else who will listen. I forgive you for hurting me.

Sometimes you stop me and comfort me, telling me it's okay to feel whatever I feel and that you'll be with me. Thank you. I need more of that. I need less violence and more love. I need to know that I'm safe.

Because of you, I am learning that I can't catch it, and I didn't cause it. I love you for that, and because of you I now have more love.

With love,
The part of you that hates being yelled at

After writing this letter, Lauren told me she felt "exultant." Exultant feelings do not emanate from simply ventilating emotions. Exultation comes from welcoming home the part of self generating the emotion. It's like the Prodigal Son in the Bible. The son leaves home, and the father awaits the son's return for many years. When the son finally comes back home, the father welcomes him with a celebration saying, "We must rejoice because your brother was dead and has come to life again; he was lost and has been found."[2] Each time we do the work to reintegrate another piece of fractured self back into our conscious self, we are like that father rejoicing that a piece of himself, his son, has come home. We celebrate that what was lost and dead can now become vitally alive. We become more fully our true self so that we can redeem the destiny we were born to fulfill.

───────── ── ─────────

The author of the next letter, Linda, writes a letter that claims the hero within. This is important because if we don't recognize this part of self, it can get neglected. This type of letter can be especially helpful with people who emphasize their inadequacies or have excessive guilt.

> Dear Self,
>   I just wanted to write you because sometimes you focus on the minor things you do wrong and miss the overall picture, which is really pretty good. The last three years since the divorce have been more difficult than you anticipated. Finances and having more responsibility in raising the kids surprised you. I'm writing to say not only do I forgive you for your screw-ups, but to tell you that I think you've done pretty okay. I wish I could come right out and say you've done well, but you know I've had a tough time saying that.
>   Anyway, the kids are flourishing. They are far from perfect, but overall they are energetic, happy, and friendly. You have kept them your number one priority, which pleases me. You had gotten out of the habit of their regular dental visits, but you got everyone back on track with that. You even have them in orthodontics! You're also working on your own health. Good for you!
>   One of your biggest accomplishments is your fashioning a friendly, working relationship with your ex-husband. You did it for the kids. I don't think anyone, certainly not your ex-husband, knows the financial sacrifices and biting of your tongue you did and continue to do to keep this relationship. I know it bugs you

when people give him most of the credit for this relationship. I'm proud that you usually smile and agree with them when that is said. It will pay off in the end for the kids.

So once more I say to you, "Way to go!" You have worked hard, and the outcomes have made it worth it. Keep up the good work. Now go floss! Linda

Successfully suffering a divorce can grow a person into their larger self just as unsuccessfully suffering divorce can reduce a person into smallness that hardens and embitters their heart with fear and pain for themselves and their children. Linda used her divorce as a passport into her larger self. Though she suffers some lack of acknowledgement from others for her efforts, she finds meaning for her suffering because her children benefit from her sacrifice.

Letters Don't Have to Be Between People

Objects and situations can be the subject of letters. This next letter expresses the anger a woman felt toward her body. Jenny was referred to me because she felt bitter. She had suffered amputations of both legs, and she felt victimized. However, Jenny didn't recognize her feelings. Instead, she said she felt "numb." Jenny's husband was exhausted from caring for her physical and emotional needs. Her future held little promise, appearing bleak and uninviting.

After a few sessions together, I asked Jenny to write a letter to each leg so she could hear the part of her self that felt angry and betrayed. After she wrote these letters, we discussed the need to develop a different relationship with her missing legs. We outlined how differently her future would be if she were able to make this shift. Here is one of the letters that she wrote:

Dear Right Leg:
When I lost your partner, I was ready to die. But God had other plans for me. First of all, I have to apologize for abusing and ignoring you. I know you tried your best, and I was not fair to you. The doctor wanted to do surgery on you, but I wasn't up to

it. You struggled 10 more years to keep up with my whims. I begged for a bypass. He finally gave in, but the surgery site had to stay open for two months and got infected. When I got to the doctor, he sent me straight to the hospital. You were cut off the next day. I was devastated because I realized that I had put you through 10 years of misery for nothing; you still had to come off. You were such a champ. I know how much you hurt with the grueling therapy you went through so I could learn to walk with a prosthesis. I just want you to know that I'm able to do much better now without you. I wish I would have realized how much better I could function before I put you through all that torture.

I also want you to know that I'm going to learn how to appreciate life around me more fully. Rather than feeling sorry for myself, I'm going to start using my suffering to help others. I'm going to volunteer here at the hospital. I'm very sorry, and I'm ready to join you and your partner whenever God is ready for me to leave this life. Then we'll all be together again.

Jenny did, indeed, become a volunteer at the hospital. About a year later, she suffered a stroke that left her right side paralyzed. This did not even deter her! With the use of only one arm, she maneuvered her motorized wheelchair down the halls visiting patients. She was an inspiration to behold that left many patients filled with hope.

Letters Bring Peace to Chaos

Steve was struggling with end-of-life issues that left him feeling depressed and anxious. After listening to his life story, I understood why. He had lived a chaotic life that left him feeling empty. I listened carefully as he forlornly spoke, searching out meanings in his life story. He hadn't seen his two sons since they were children more than 30 years earlier. His alcoholism had destroyed his marriage. He felt constant shame for not supporting his sons. Within months of his death, he now longed to experience this final chapter of his life in a more complete way. He agreed to risk contacting his sons with a letter. I pushed him outside in his wheelchair under a tall oak tree. He smoked a cigarette and spoke. I listened, occasionally jotting down a word or two to capture the essence of what he was saying, and I asked questions that I thought would lead toward healing. I focused not so much on his words, but on the meaning beyond the words. The following letter is the final draft:

Dear Taylor and Sam,

What can I say after all these years? Somehow, words can't express the many feelings I have. Our last day together is one of the worst memories of my life. Your mother and I were at a hateful impasse. I was locked out of my house and ended up in jail for 30 days with a restraining order. She got the two loves of my life: you boys. I felt like I had to leave the hatred. I thought that trying to see you boys would lead to more trouble. I figured I didn't stand a chance, and so I left. I figured it was the best thing for you. Now I wonder if I wasn't just being a coward.

I always was a coward. I hid out in the bottle. The bottle was my best friend. I know you remember how much I drank. What you don't know is that each night after work, I would say to myself, "I'm just going to stop at the bar and have one drink." And do you know each night at 2 A.M. I'd still be there? Did you know that with the booze in me, I was quite a comedian? Pretty soon everyone in the bar would be gathered around, and I would be entertaining them. I thought I had a pretty good thing going. Now, I realize it was just one big drunk that lasted 30 years. I didn't have the courage to stop and face the mess of my life. I didn't have the courage to face the shame I felt. Instead, I kept hiding in the bottle. Well, I don't want to hide anymore. Alcohol robbed me of everything that was important to me. I'm not going to let it rob me of this last bit of life I have.

I want you to know that a day has not gone by that I have not thought of you two and missed you. My heart has hurt with the pain. Holidays have been the hardest. I just keep thinking I should have been there for you. You needed a father, and instead, you got nothing. All these years, I just kept shaking my head and asking myself how I could have done that to you, and then I'd take another drink.

I have sometimes worried you may have blamed yourselves, but I want you to know that it was not your fault. You were innocent bystanders. I am sorry for leaving you, and I ask your forgiveness. I know I hurt you boys a lot, and that hurts me, especially now that I'm sober. It's funny; I used to think I was a good father. Now, I realize I couldn't have been. Good fathers don't drink. Good fathers don't abandon their children. Good fathers aren't cowards.

I do have happy memories with you fellows: the fishing trips, the driving around in the car, the animals on the farm. I think about what you might look like. These memories are what I have clung to so I could stay close to you.

I haven't had a drink now for four months. It took a diagnosis of cancer to get me to stop. It's God's love that is keeping me from picking up a bottle. You see, I hid from God all these years, too. Oh, I had the fundamentals of religion as a child, but fundamentals don't mix with alcohol. So, God was lost to me while I was lost in the booze. Without the booze, and with the help of loving people, I'm finding my way back to God. I don't feel worthy of His love, but I do feel like a different person now.

I want you to know that if you don't want to see me, I understand. I'm also sure you are probably angry with me, and I can understand that. This letter is my way of trying to heal some of the brokenness I have created in your lives, but I don't want you to feel like you have to do anything to respond. I want to leave it up to you. Know that I understand and respect any decision you will make. Dad

The power of the letter comes from Steve's humility: his honesty in abiding and reckoning with who he was and who he was not.

I mailed the letter to his sons in Virginia. Two weeks later, his sons showed up in a van with a mattress and several oxygen tanks. They took their Dad to Virginia so he could die in their home. Instead of feeling isolated and lonely, Steve died feeling loved and connected. Though the facts of the past couldn't be changed, the boys' *relationship* to the past did change. I think about the gap in Taylor and Sam's lives that would still be gaping if the letter had not been written.

Elements of a Therapeutic Letter

A therapeutic letter's ability to precipitate healing is largely dependent on the writer's willingness to change. The writer has to be ready to abide and reckon with difficult issues that he or she may not have previously faced. Once the writer is ready, a new future filled with hope can then be birthed.

Therapeutic letters often incorporate elements of forgiveness. To be effective, however, specific apologies must be made. For example, a global statement such as, "Forgive me for things I might have done to hurt you," is far less powerful than Steve's specific references to what he had done: drinking, being a coward, and abandoning his sons. The acknowledgement of behaviors communicates insight, honesty, and a willingness to accept responsibility.

Steve's humility required some guidance so he could develop insight. He had initially told me he had been a good father, which went against what he had just told me. He readily responded, however, to my questions, which led him to a different perspective:

"I'm not sure I understand," I had said. "I thought you drank all the time. I would guess that interfered with your being a 'good' father?" I asked this question without judgment, trying to understand his perspective and to help him own less-than-"good" behaviors so that he could reckon with their aftermath.

"I loved them. I always wanted the best for them," Steve explained.

"That's nice, but kids need more than that. I'm thinking good fathers would not have been drinking the way you did; sometimes alcohol causes fathers to emotionally abandon their children."

"Yeah. I did that for sure."

"What you're telling your sons is that you hid out in the bottle. Rather than facing the issues, you ran from them," I said quietly, offering perspective.

"I was just a coward, wasn't I?"

"Yes. I'd say that's good insight. And being able to recognize that, say it, and apologize for it is very courageous."

This kind of coaching is often needed to enable someone to

assume more responsibility. When they wholeheartedly embrace an alternative perspective, then the perspective I've offered is included in their letter. If they only halfheartedly agree with what I am saying, I don't include it because the letter will become contrived and lose its authenticity. When I suggested to Steve that thinking about his children every day was not enough to qualify him as a good father, this allowed him to own the ways he had let his sons down. He agreed readily enough so I included my perspective as if it had been his own thought. When I offer alternative perspectives, I'm careful to do it without judgment or blame. To do it without blame means that I've similarly reckoned with ways that *I've* let others down.

I've acquired radar for recognizing when letter-writing will be effective. Guilt, anger, fear, sadness, and resentment are useful markers as are estranged relationships. Sometimes there has been no contact with a family member for many years. In these situations, I suggest that contact may still be possible. It's surprising how many people want reconciliation. Sometimes reconciliation doesn't happen, but writing the letter is still useful because it can help the person forgive himself and the other person.

Logistics of Integrative Letter-Writing

When I first realized the healing power of integrative letter-writing, I often suggested its use to patients; they seldom did it. Then I realized that sick people don't have the energy for such a task. Writing a letter seems overwhelming. Even dictating it is daunting; patients worry about saying things exactly right.

Now I try to keep the focus off the letter. I don't want them to worry about what they are going to say. Instead, I get them to talk about the relationship and memories, inconspicuously jotting down an occasional phrase that allows me adequate prompts for later composition at my computer. Phrases that are particularly graphic, metaphorical, or vernacular bring out the person's personality and increase the letter's power and effectiveness. Steve's "lost in the booze" phrase provides a clear, metaphorical, personal image. Preserving the meaning of the person's intent and keeping vernacular or metaphorical phrases intact is more important than exact wording.

I also offer my knowledge and experience with healing elements by asking leading questions. Realizing that children sometimes blame themselves for a parent's leaving, I offered Steve the opportunity to provide reassurance to his sons that they had done nothing to contribute to his abandoning them: "Kids often blame themselves when parents leave. Even after they grow up, they may not have resolved these feelings. I wonder if Taylor and Sam might feel that way?"

"Yeah that's possible," Steve had said.

Effective letters generally include the "gray" of people and relationships. People may need prompting to provide this balanced perspective. Steve didn't initially offer positive memories for the creation of his letter. Guilt overshadowed pleasantry. I probed his recollection with questions. His statement, "We had some good times together" had to be drawn into a clearer picture of fishing, driving the car, and farm life.

This kind of balanced perspective is also important when people try to compartmentalize people into all-good or all-bad characterizations. Including some negative and positive experiences provide a more complete composite. When we idealize people, we are blind to their struggles and failings. We erase that person's reality. This idealization is commonly done after a person dies; it's called "canonized by death." Similarly, demonizing a person without acknowledging any redeeming qualities misses the complete person. Confronting the truth – the wholeness – of a person promotes healing.

Effective letters usually include seven healing elements: Forgive me, I forgive you, I love you, thank you, good-bye, let go, and open up.[3] Sincerely communicating the first four elements requires honesty, courage, and humility. The last three elements are part of the reckoning process whereby the person is shifting their relationship to the person or situation by letting go of something that has been causing problems and opening up to new possibilities. For example, Steve implemented these elements by letting go of his pride, cowardice, and control so that he could open up to humility, courage and uncertainty, which became his passport for externalizing his internal destiny.

Negotiating how the letter will be handled and preparing the person for possible responses is crucial. When Steve decided to mail his letter to his sons, I prepared him for the possibility that they might reject him. It would help if he could see the letter more as an unconditional gift with no expectation for return. I helped him see how the letter might be healing for his sons at some point in the future, even if they weren't at a point in their lives where they could presently respond. This approach gave Steve comfort so that if his letter met no response, he still would have the fulfillment that unconditional giving provides.

Letters don't have to be sent to be healing. Writing the letter frees the writer, clarifies issues, and promotes expression of hidden or unconfronted aspects of self. The person to whom the letter is being written doesn't even have to be alive. In these cases, rituals can be enacted to add power to the letter-writing. I've had people read the letter at graveside, send the letter on the tail of a helium balloon, or ignite the letter so it goes up in flames. These are just some of the many possible rituals that can add further symbolic value; rituals can reach into the unconscious for deeper healing. Appendix I provides information on how to design a therapeutic ritual that incorporates the three stages of change.

Even when the people involved are alive and can be contacted, it might not be the wisest choice. Bruce, whose history was nearly parallel to Steve's, decided not to send his letters to his five sons, feeling he had no right to ask for their sympathy after so many years of estrangement. When he died, only one of Bruce's sons attended the funeral. I gave the letters to the son and told him that when he and his siblings were ready, they could read them. Thus, the letters not only met a dying man's need for peace, but had the potential to help his children's eventual healing if they so chose.

Avoiding Pitfalls

Jeff was estranged from his daughter, Teresa. He had abused alcohol and drugs much of her life. He had a stroke several years before I met him on our Hospice unit. Jeff would cry whenever Teresa's name was mentioned.

"It's my ex-wife's fault. I know that's why Teresa won't talk to me," he told Sarah, a Hospice volunteer.

Sarah suggested that he write his daughter a letter to try to bridge the gap. Jeff was eager to do so.

Sarah helped Jeff write a letter to Teresa. It was filled with declarations about his love for her.

"This won't help," I said to Sarah when she showed me the letter.

"Why not?" she asked, disappointment in her eyes and voice.

"Because he's not owning anything he did to contribute to the problems in the relationship. His drinking and drugging had to have hurt Teresa. She's probably angry with him."

I went with Sarah when she met with Jeff again. We talked about how much Jeff loved Teresa. Then, I tried to open a space that offered hope for redemption of the brokenness in their relationship.

"You know, Jeff, we all do things to let each other down. It's just part of the human condition. Tell me about a way in which you have let Teresa down just a little bit."

"I could *never* let that girl down," Jeff said. "I *wouldn't*," he added fiercely.

"I know you didn't *want* to let her down. But, you're not God. You're not perfect. You're like the rest of us. We sometimes disappoint the people we love."

"Nope. Not me. I never let that girl down." His intensity broadcast the unapproachability of the topic. Strokes often arrest insight development. Alcohol and drugs can also numb the brain. His own guilt and anger could be preventing ability to own his behaviors. Whatever the cause, giving Teresa a letter that only proclaimed his love for her would probably increase the estrangement because Teresa would be left, again, without an apology or some sense that her father understood how he had hurt her.

"Since he doesn't know what he did, maybe he could just say that he's sorry for anything he might have done to hurt her," Sarah said.

"That will only make things worse," I replied. "Teresa will say, 'Anything you *might* have done. Don't you get yet what your alcohol and drugs did to me?' Then, she'll stomp off and never see her dad again. Sometimes, it is what it is. This situation requires that Jeff change; I don't think he's capable."

"But maybe we could explain to Teresa that his stroke has impaired his ability to apologize," Sarah said, reluctant to accept that reconciliation may not be possible.

"Our job is to create safe emotional environments so that people can change. However, reckoning is *their* job. We can't do the work for them."

"Ah. I get that," Sarah said, satisfied that she could do no more with the letter. We then used a different approach that might bridge the gap. Sarah helped Jeff complete a Life Tribute form (Appendix G) about Teresa so that some of their stories could be captured.

Because people sometimes need support growing into ownership of conflicted relationships, I usually work with people on drafts of letters rather than encouraging them to write a letter on their own and then mailing it without my review. Giving someone "a piece of my mind" is seldom received amicably and often perpetuates hostility. Although it's important to vent the anger so the writer can acknowledge it and set boundaries, anger often covers up more vulnerable feelings like grief, fear, or rejection. Until the aspects of self generating the underlying feelings are abided and reckoned with, integrity is not gained. One way of bypassing this problem is to delude ourselves into thinking we have forgiven someone when we haven't; it spares us having to do the work of abiding with hurt feelings and reckoning with the changes we need to make in order to reintegrate our hurt self. Appendix J provides a sample of draft-development to cultivate the skill of coaxing a person's anger, blame, and fear into increased self responsibility.

To facilitate letter-writing, I often give people the relevant letters in Appendix K to review. It gives them ideas for issues they may want to write about. It also helps them know that other people have struggled with similar issues; they are not alone.

I have helped many clinicians facilitate therapeutic letter-writing with their patients. One was a physician, Amy McDonald.[4] She e-mailed me the result: "We did our first therapeutic letter with a vet. He decided to write to his estranged granddaughter that his ex-wife was raising. His ex-wife said she would bring the granddaughter to visit him. It blew our minds and his! Now I know what you mean when you talk about 'dying healed.' In the past, we were just managing symptoms, but when it came to emotional suffering, I felt I could offer nothing. This is better than any drug!"

SELF-AWARENESS ASSIGNMENT
Integrative Letter-Writing

Review your Life Story for people and situations with whom you want to create a more peaceful relationship. Read the letters in Appendix K to give you ideas about possibilities. Take several days to let their content incubate. Then, write a letter to someone, to some situation, or to yourself. (Alternatively, you can make an audio or video recording.) The letter should abide and reckon with a difficulty preventing you from becoming whole. As you identify aspects of yourself that are not whole, ask that part of self, "What do you need to heal, feel nurtured, and cared for?"

Choose only one issue to address. Seek help from others, if necessary, in order to engage in the abiding and reckoning process. Share the contents of the letter with someone who is trustworthy; this approach can heighten the impact because it provides witness to the healing effects of integrating forsaken fragments of self into the whole.

Better Than Any Drug

Relationships are complex, and letters can't completely redeem the suffering that relationships have created. Healing is a process that sometimes only happens partially, if at all. This was the case for David.

"I'm at the end of my rope," David kept repeating, shaking his head as he was wheeled onto our Hospice and Palliative Care unit for admission. At 88, with a diagnosis of end-stage cardiac disease, David's "rope end" focused primarily on constipation. His bowels consumed him.

"Can't you do something to get him to stop with the bowels? That's all he talks about," complained his wife, Natalie, in her New York accent.

The staff amusedly listened to their post-BM dialogue: "Come here and look at it," David would demand.

"No, I won't," Natalie would retort defiantly. Natalie was not even spared the details when she went home. Sitting on the bedside commode with phone in hand, David would offer the current details she was missing.

Rather than try to distract him from his bowels, the nurses decided to get obsessed with them too, hoping attention and interventions would provide reassurance that his needs were taken seriously. Laxatives and enemas, BM descriptions, and explanations became the order of the day. Sometimes David became exhausted with the ordeals; his family was exhausted just listening.

When he wasn't talking about his bowels, David was acting out the ambivalence he felt about dying. One minute he would frantically declare, "I don't know why I'm here. I'm not dying," and the next minute he would mumble, "Just give me a pill so I can get this over with" or "I just want God to take me."

I quietly sat with David to understand his perspective, abiding his dilemma. Finally, I asked him gently about his father's death. "It was nothing like this," he said. "He died when he was 44. Came home from work one night, said he had a headache, laid down, and died of a brain aneurysm when I was 13 years old. I wish I could go like that."

It was not the dying, but this "in-between" state that was making David anxious. We discussed how difficult it was to exist in this kind of limbo. As we spoke, his frenzy eased. I assured him that talking about death would not make it happen nor did it mean that he was thinking negatively or giving up hope.

"You know," I told him, "this can actually be a very precious time. It's a time to reflect on your life, reach out to family, reconcile differences, and discover new things about yourself and God." He seemed intrigued, though not quite convinced. The mention of God seemed to resonate with him.

He explained he had not followed in his parent's footsteps as a practicing Jew. I suggested that he might want to look at the difference between religion and spirituality, and asked him what role he wanted spirituality to play in his life now. He readily acknowledged a desire to "make up for lost time."

I wanted to give him time for his ideas to incubate, so I gave him the *Waiting Book* to read. It's a collection of our patients' personal writings about living in limbo. "I've found that many people have a difficult time waiting for death, David. Some have said this is a time of straddling the world of the living and the world of the dying. You can't live the way you used to and yet you're not dead. You're just sort of stuck. Maybe reading what other patients have written can help you."

Later, I brought a Life Review form for David to complete. (Appendix G has an example of a Life Review form and an accompanying ritual for enacting it.) The form gave me an opportunity for discovering more clues into the barriers keeping him from experiencing peace. He seemed less anxious than the day before and readily responded to my interest in his life story.

I discovered that David was born to a poor family in Poland. The family immigrated to the United States in the 1940s when David was 13. Soon after that, his father died. David joined the military at age 16: "I lied about my age so I could go fight the war."

"You probably saw a lot of ugly things during those years. Is there anything about that war that might still be troubling you a little bit?" I asked.

He shook his head. "Not really. I had to learn how to survive, but I had already learned survival skills when my father died. I had to grow up overnight in a strange land. I had to become the man of the house. Going to Italy to fight a war wasn't that much different. You just do what you have to do." I listened carefully, realizing his "I can handle it" stoic pride, independence, and control were well ingrained before entering the military.

When the war ended, David worked various jobs, eventually becoming a New York City taxi driver. He had many taxi tales that ranged from driving Sigmund Freud's daughter to getting robbed a few times. He married Natalie. They had four children, including a set of twin girls, Gail and Fran. He worked 14-hour days, leaving him little time for his family.

In part because of his schedule, his relationships with his wife and children had been difficult and sometimes hostile. One or the other of the four children always seemed in conflict with one of their parents. There was no family picture because "There was no time when all of us got along at the same time so a picture could be taken."

What bothered David most now was his relationship with Gail. Now an adult, she lived 2,000 miles away. He had not seen her in eight years. Gail sometimes came to see her sisters, but when David and Natalie tried to see her, she would go in a bedroom and refuse to come out. If either of them reached her by phone, she cursed them and hung up. David didn't understand why.

As he was telling me about Gail, David began to get chest pain. I was tempted to stop the discussion, but instead I gave him a nitroglycerin tablet and *en-couraged* an "anti-flighting" response by asking him to relax and breathe. We discussed the meaning of his chest pain. David said it was his "broken heart" over Gail.

I gently prodded, "I'm wondering how Gail has come to be so angry? She must really be hurting somehow." David seemed at a loss to explain her behavior and was surprised at the suggestion that her anger could be masking pain. "If you had to guess, what do you think it might be about?" I pressed.

Reluctantly he answered, "Maybe it's because she knew I loved Fran best." He said he had never hidden his favoritism.

"That's pretty hurtful for the unfavored child," I responded.

"But that happened so long ago. She's got to let bygones be bygones," he said.

"It doesn't sound all that 'bygone' to me," I said. "Have you talked about it with her?"

He shook his head.

"Maybe wanting this to be a bygone is your way of avoiding reckoning with the situation," I tentatively suggested. "It takes courage to step up to the plate and accept responsibility for difficulties."

To these words, he readily agreed. I explained how he might help by offering an apology for the wrongs his favoritism had caused. "I've already told her that," he said. "I told her I was sorry for anything I might have done."

"General apologies aren't good enough," I responded. "In fact, they can make things worse." I offered more specific suggestions. "Are you sorry now you didn't realize how rejected she felt when you kept letting everyone know Fran was your favorite twin? Do you wish now you would have realized how important your love was to her? Do you wish now you would have kept your feelings for Fran to yourself?"

To each question, he readily agreed. We were moving into a place that held promise of healing, at least on David's part. Because of the extent of Gail's actions, I suspected it might take time for her to be able to look at the pain her father had caused. In these situations, a letter can be more effective; it allows a person to carefully construct the message that needs to be communicated. If Gail remained angry and accusing, then a verbal interaction could be threatening to David. If he then assumed a defensive posture, it could make things worse for Gail and increase her sense of victimization. With a letter, however, when Gail was ready, the letter would be waiting. David readily agreed to have me help with a letter.

The next day, with paper in hand, I asked David about his memories of Gail. I jotted down things occasionally. This would be a letter I would construct later from the content he was providing. It was important not to make him feel he was dictating a letter. I just needed to understand the essence of his story, hold onto a few phrases that exactly captured his meaning, and guide his dialogue to places that offered potential for healing the troubled relationship by asking carefully crafted questions.

Consumed with Gail's hostility toward him, David was too hurt and angry to see the complete picture. "Tell me about some of the happy memories," I said. He couldn't remember any. I persisted. "What were some of the special times you had with Gail?" Slowly a few images were coaxed from his memory: a day at the beach, giving her pennies.

We discussed how his long work hours combined with his fawning over Fran might have made Gail feel abandoned. Since he was not readily forthcoming with insight into aspects of how his behavior had adversely affected her, I offered some possibilities, jotting down those for which he readily took responsibility. "Do you think your long hours at your business may have caused Gail some difficulties?" (Yes, he thought it had). "Working 14-hour days kept you away from your family. Is that a regret you now have?" (Yes, if he had to do it over, he would have made his family more a priority). "Did you sometimes come home tired and grumpy?" (He hadn't thought of it at the time, but now he acknowledged he had). "Do you regret you were insensitive to how hard it was to be a twin?" (He had never considered this perspective. I enlightened him on some of the difficulties Gail probably endured. He readily acknowledged these difficulties had occurred).

David's journey from blame to guilt to remorse was obvious. His anger toward Gail turned to guilt as he realized how self-absorbed he'd been. His guilt turned to remorse and then compassion as he realized the hurt his actions caused his family, especially Gail.

I returned the next day with a draft of the letter for David's approval. I had worked carefully to capture the meaning beyond his words, using his own phrases as much as possible. I read the letter slowly so he could absorb its message, realizing that hearing his own words constructed in an integrative manner, in and of itself, could bring healing to him. (See Appendix L for the actual letter.)

"It's perfect," David said after I finished reading it. He sat quietly for several minutes staring out the window while tears ran down his cheeks; he didn't bother to wipe them away.

David shared the letter with his family, and they were enthusiastic and hopeful for reconciliation with Gail. I cautioned them about expecting reconciliation: "There's a difference between forgiveness and reconciliation," I said. "Forgiveness is a one-way street. Reconciliation is a two-way street. Forgiveness is under your control. I believe we are all required to do the work of forgiveness, no matter what we've done to others or they've done to us. You are doing that, but reconciliation is beyond our control. Forgiveness is required. Reconciliation is a choice. If someone murdered my child, I'd be required to forgive him or I'll remain in bondage. It doesn't mean I'm required to reconcile with the murderer though." David agreed, saying the distinction made sense.

Days passed and still Gail didn't respond to his letter. Daily, David told us that she was certain to answer him soon. I cautioned him to simply view his letter as his gift to her. It would be there when she was ready to accept it, which might be many years.

"But I could be dead by then!" he protested. "I'm going to call her." Not wanting Gail to feel pressured and realizing his impatience could interfere with healing, I persuaded him to delay making the phone call.

"Maybe your final gift to her can be giving her enough space to let her accept your words when she is ready and not pushing her to act on your timetable. That's a very loving and respectful gesture. Someday, that might mean a lot to her."

Slowly, he realized the significance of sacrificing his own needs for Gail's after the years in which he had ignored her needs. "I guess I've done all I can do. The rest is up to her."

Over the next several weeks, there was a definite change in David's demeanor. Although he still occasionally became anxious, the emotion had lost its desperate quality. He was now able to openly speak about his dying. He spoke about his continued hope that Gail would respond to his letter, but it remained a hope rather than a demand. His bowel fixation disappeared to the point that on a few occasions he was surprised when staff started bowel interventions for lack of movement.

With his distress eased, we could now focus on his wife's needs. Natalie had a quiet strength about her that defied the surrounding turmoil. She had endured many hardships over her lifetime, including the lack of a fulfilling marriage: "We've been married 53 years, but after the first three years, it was over." Natalie had mourned the death of her marriage long ago. Although dependent and admitting to no self-confidence, she seemed surprisingly independent. Although she had always been surrounded by family, she had little support from them. Through it all, she marched on "doing what I have to do."

Natalie had been a private person in whom image had been all important. She said she was surprised she aired her "dirty laundry" with us, but acknowledged that it felt liberating not to feel the need to keep up appearances any longer. One day she startled herself by gustily proclaiming, "I don't care what anybody else thinks!" followed by "I don't believe I just said that!" Then, she stood up to her full 4-foot 9-inch height, and exclaimed more loudly and strongly, "I don't give a *damn* what other people think!" She became tickled with her new-found freedom and giggled like a schoolgirl discovering adulthood. The cadence of her march might falter over the days ahead, but there was little doubt her march would continue.

David asked the team to pray for him, which we did. He not only accepted our prayers, but also started participating in the prayers and songs intended for his roommates, even when they didn't share his religion. Sometimes, the roommates' prayers or songs were Christian-oriented, and David would join in. "It's all the same God. We all pray and sing to the same God," he'd say when we commented on the religious discrepancy.

David also began using metaphorical language commonly used by people nearing the end of their lives. The night nurse, Audrey, found him gazing off.

"What are you seeing?" Audrey asked.

"A band playing," he responded.

"What kind of band is it?"

"It's a band I like. People are getting in line," David said.

"What's the line for?"

"It's a line that ends at 4 P.M. That's when I'm going to die."

So it was no surprise, yet it surprised everyone, when a few days later, David ate his dinner, got into bed, and peacefully quit breathing. Natalie was at his bedside, seemingly by coincidence. Their daughter, Fran, had been unable to pick her up as planned, leaving Natalie angry and complaining. Maybe David decided he just didn't have enough "chutzpah" left in him for one more argument.

Integrative Letter-writing Lessons

- Developing the honesty to identify loneliness and then use it as a passport into solitude with the unity of our soul helps us inhabit ourselves more completely. We can similarly use our hostility to encounter hospitality. Developing the courage to confront our own illusions about who we are and who we are not is the first step in becoming ourselves.
- The difference between segregating a situation into unconsciousness versus integrating it into consciousness is "you." The former squeezes some of "you" out while the latter creates more "you." Suffering occurs when you become less "you."
- The goal of integrative letter-writing is to create a more peaceful relationship with a person, situation, or an aspect of self that is causing distress or loss of vitality.

- Therapeutic letters usually incorporate the seven tasks of living and dying healed: Forgive me, I forgive you, I love you, Thank you, Good bye, Let go, Open up. (To be effective, however, apologies and gratitudes should be specific.)
- Guilt, anger, jealousy, resentment, grief, fear, uncertainty, loneliness, and estranged relationships are useful markers that suggest implementation of integrative letter-writing.
- Give people the letters in Appendix K. It gives them ideas for issues they may want to write about. It also helps them know that other people have struggled with similar issues; they are not alone.
- Keep the focus *off* the letter. Preserve the meaning of the patient's intent and keep vernacular or metaphorical phrases intact. Offer knowledge and experience with healing elements by asking leading questions. Negotiate how the letter will be handled and prepare the person for possible responses. Consider developing a ritual that can add further symbolic value, especially if the letter recipient is no longer alive. Study Appendix J; it will help you facilitate effective letter-writing with others, as well as yourself.

Chapter Eight

Healing Communities: Heroes Among Us

Never doubt that a small group
of thoughtful, committed people
can change the world.
Indeed, it is the only thing that ever has.[1]
-Margaret Mead, Anthropologist

I use this last story to summarize the abiding, reckoning, and beholding processes so the reader can appreciate how the interior hero is
gradually birthed into a person's life. Peering into another person's
life story, we peer into our own. Witnessing someone integrating
unconscious aspects of self into consciousness allows us to practice the healing process for ourselves as we observe how lessons
cultivate the qualities of honesty, courage, and humility. In this
way, the hero within expands – in each of us and within our communities.

Rob, a 43-year-old man with cancer of his lymph system, was
struggling with existential issues that his disease and its treatment
were precipitating. At our first meeting, Rob told me, "I keep waiting for some kind of epiphany like Lance Armstrong had. Why can't
I feel the way he did? I can't find anything positive about this experience. All I feel is sick."

Rob worked in the office of a landscaping company, and he hated
his job. He had a girlfriend, Tracey, for three years, but the relationship lacked emotional intimacy so it wasn't very fulfilling. He was
Catholic and became "very religious" in recent years, but since getting
cancer, Rob said, "Religion feels more like a burden than a comfort."

His mother abandoned Rob when he was two years old. His father was a Vietnam War veteran who was alcoholic and unable to care for himself, much less a young son. His father remarried, and Rob had a half-sister and half-brother from that relationship. He was able to live a fairly stable life in his new family for a few years until his father divorced again. After the divorce, his father was unable to care for him, so Rob was in and out of foster care for the rest of his adolescent years.

As a teen, Rob tried to find his mother only to discover that she had died. He did, however, locate his mother's mother who lived in Germany. He contacted her, and they started corresponding. His grandmother did not speak English, so Rob learned German. Their relationship developed, and he started spending summers with her in Germany while he was in high school.

His father died when Rob was a young adult, devastating Rob: "My life is divided into the years before my father died and the years after he died." He had infrequent, though regular, contact with his half-sister who lived in Ohio and half-brother who lived in California.

After high school, Rob joined the Army for four years. He loved his time in the service: "It gave me structure, stability, identity, and belonging, something I'd never experienced before. It was also my first taste of success. I achieved things I hadn't known I could do." After discharge from military service, he graduated from college with a degree in criminal justice and joined the police force for 10 years before leaving because of his unsuitability for the job. He worked in the banking industry for several years, but quit when his grandmother's health required that he go to Germany. When I met him, he was doing sales for a landscaping firm. He had difficulty with emotional intimacy in female relationships. He had two short-lived marriages to a lawyer and then a banker. Both of his marriages ended because of his infidelity.

> *Abiding: Showing up "openheartedly" to all of the emotional dimensions of life: the good, the bad, and the ugly, and more importantly, embracing the part of self that is experiencing that feeling.*

He had a history of depression in which he felt suicidal. He had tried an anti-depressant, but suffered side effects, so he didn't want to take medication again. He had regularly used alcohol and had now started using marijuana to control the nausea he felt with chemotherapy.

My initial session focused on gaining Rob's story. I needed to abide his suffering personally so I could help him abide it. It was easy for me to feel his heartache as I sensed the little boy trapped inside the six-foot man; it wasn't as easy for Rob. The Army veteran and ex-policeman carried a stoic façade that hid the pain of having been abandoned and unloved.

"I can't imagine the pain you must have experienced as a child: your mother leaving you, getting your hopes up for stability with your dad's remarriage only to have them dashed with divorce, your dad unable to care for you, trying to please foster parents so you'd have a roof over you head. That's so sad."

Rob heard the sadness in my voice, and a look of surprise came over his face. A fleeting look of pain crossed his eyes. He wasn't used to someone abiding his feelings. He wasn't sure what to do with it. "Everyone has their sob story," he said. "We all get over it."

I let him escape into his numbness because I knew I would be having more sessions with him; we needed to focus on his cancer and its treatment. For now, it was enough that he knew that I was able and willing to abide his pain.

I asked Rob to tell me about the hardest thing he was going through right now. "Of all the struggles you've experienced with the lymphoma and the chemotherapy, what is most troubling?"

> *Take people INTO their feelings, not away from them.*

"I feel lost. I'm almost afraid for the chemo to be over because then I'll have no excuse for not living my life. I feel numb with all that has happened."

I abided his *lostness*. I did not tell him that my job would be to help him let go of his numbness and open up to feel the pain and his *lostness*.

"It makes sense to me that you would feel lost. Look at all the losses you've sustained in just a few short months. You've lost your

| Validate suffering. |

health with the cancer. You've lost feeling good because of the side effects of the chemotherapy. You've lost your energy, and you're tired all the time. You've lost your hair. You're in a job you don't like. You've lost wages when you can't work. Your self-esteem is in the basement. Meanwhile, you're telling me that this brush with cancer is causing you to think about the deaths of both your parents and is raising 'unanswerable questions' about them. You are shouldering a big load right now."

Rob looked at me speechless. He looked away as tears came. "I don't know why I'm crying."

"Because you have a lot to cry about," I reminded him.

"Everyone keeps telling me that all of this will pass, and I'm going to be fine. And my childhood stuff...that's in the past."

| Create a safe emotional environment for pain and tears. |

"You have gotten a lot of bad advice from well-intentioned people who were trying to comfort you. You have also been filled with scripts from the Army and from the police force that tell you that it's not okay to cry. I'm here to tell you that it's good to see your tears. They are healthy because tears are the normal and natural accompaniment to loss, and you are sustaining more than your fair share right now; you had to bear more than your fair share as a child. You have reason to cry."

Rob dared to look up at me as I was talking. His blue eyes under his furled brow and bald head no longer tried to hide the tears they were creating. "I just don't get it. I eat right, I work out, I go to church, and I pray every day."

"You feel like God betrayed you..."

"Yeah. Cancer wasn't on my map. It's not what I'm supposed to be doing at this time in my life."

| Verbalize the feelings the person isn't identifying. |

"You're right. I'd be angry if it happened to me," I said quietly but strongly.

"It just seems so unfair. I don't know what I've done to deserve this."

I abided his sense of anger, unfairness, and betrayal that he was experiencing. He had experienced a lifetime of neglect and abandonment by his parents; now, he was experiencing it from God. I didn't want to take his feelings away from him the way he hoped I would. I couldn't give him a pill that would magically erase his past or change what he was going through the way he wished I would. What I *could* do was validate the person who had the courage to expose his feelings; I could create a safe environment where he could feel secure amidst all the insecurities he had experienced throughout his life. I could help him create internal resources so he could access the hero within himself.

After each session, I give a homework assignment. I require homework for two reasons. The real work of change and growth comes between sessions rather than during the session. Homework would help Rob realize that the sessions were not going to magically change him. It would also help him see that the goal is for *him* to change; he has to do the work of growing. Secondly, completing homework would indicate how ready and willing he was to participate in his growth. During the process, I'll be committed to him, and I want to ensure that I'm investing my efforts where they'll take root. If he repeatedly doesn't complete the homework, even with modifications that I make to accommodate his needs, then I won't continue as his facilitator. Rather, I'll encourage him to come back later. This approach spares my time and energy, as well as his.

> *Help people change. Change always requires letting "same" go and opening up to "different."*

> *The thing we are running from is, paradoxically, the very thing that will free us.*

The homework I assigned Rob that day was to let himself feel "lost" so he could experience it openly without guilt or anger.

"You want me to feel lost?" Rob asked incredulously when I told him what I wanted him to do.

"I don't want you to feel lost. I want you to let yourself feel whatever you feel. If you keep covering up your *lostness* by pretending it's not there or numbing it with alcohol or filling your time with things that keep you distracted from it, how can you find what you're searching for?"

Rob just looked at me. He hadn't considered using his *lostness* as a guide into the hero within.

"Feeling lost can serve as your passport into something more meaningful to you. Trust it. It's here for a reason. Listen to it."

"I don't like feeling it."

"I know. It's only natural to try to escape uncomfortable feelings, but isn't your lostness with you whether you feel it or not?"

"It's not always there."

"You just told me 20 minutes ago that the hardest thing you are struggling with is

> *Uncover truth. Don't let people minimize their experiences. Help people not be afraid of who they are.*

feeling lost. It's okay to feel lost, Rob. It's even a good thing. It means that if you'll follow that path and seek guideposts, then you'll find a different path."

Rob relaxed, so I continued. "This week, I want you to approach your lostness in a different way. Open up to it. Next week, tell me what you learn about it."

> *Don't stop on the surface. Look for concealed feelings. Let time elapse so the person will dig deeper. Don't rescue their anxiety unless it becomes overwhelming; their anxiety will take them into deeper meanings. If necessary, encourage them to breathe deeply.*

Rob looked at me skeptically, but reluctantly said he'd do it.

He returned the following week, feeling weak. He was still suffering the side effects of chemo, but he seemed more at ease. I asked him about the homework assignment.

"Tell me what you discovered about being lost. What does it feel like?"

"Scary. Very scary because the cancer has changed every aspect of my life.

Nothing is the same anymore. I can't depend on anything anymore."

"How else does it feel?"

"Isn't scary enough?" he asked me a bit annoyed.

"Yes, if that's all there is, but I'm wondering if there might be more…"

Rob sat still and pensive. I didn't say anything. Finally, he said, "It feels lonely. No one can be in my shoes with me. I'm the only one here. I feel really, really lonely right now."

"You've felt really, really lonely and afraid before…"

Rob looked at me without understanding.

"When you were a little boy."

My observation caught Rob off guard. Then the truth of what I said dawned on him, and he relaxed with its recognition.

"Yeah. Now that I think about it, this does feel familiar."

I leaned in close to Rob, peering intently in his eyes. "There's only one thing worse than feeling scared and lonely."

Rob's eyes widened, indicating he wanted to know what that would be.

"It's the fear of feeling scared and lonely."

At first Rob's eyes narrowed in lack of understanding. I didn't rescue him with an explanation. Finally, he started verbally groping his way into insight. "Being *afraid* of fear, makes me more afraid. Being *afraid* of loneliness makes me more alone with it."

> *Fear closes our heart, keeping us from becoming more conscious, keeping us from who we are.*

I nodded my head in affirmation. "Don't be afraid of who you are, Rob. There are aspects of yourself that are scared and lonely right now. Open up to those parts of yourself so they're not alone. The goal is to bring them home and integrate them into your conscious self. Let yourself experience fear and loneliness even though your instincts are to neglect and abandon those parts of you right now."

Rob relaxed with understanding so I proceeded. "Close your eyes. Where do you feel the loneliness?"

"In my chest."

"Describe it. What does it feel like? What color is it? Tell me what loneliness looks like."

"It's a black hole in my chest that can go on forever causing me to panic."

"What does that black hole mean?"

Rob's answer took my breath away. "It means I'm a failure. It means I'm not good enough to be loved."

Affirm the value of "negative" feelings. Use images because they access the unconscious.

I could only sit speechless. There it was: the stark truth. I now understood the pain of his existence, the truth that he was living. He had been honest enough to actually say it. That's the honesty, courage, and humility that would redeem him.

That day, I asked Rob to write a letter from "Robby" (as he was called as a child) to Rob, the adult. I wanted Robby to finally have a voice. His biological parents had not listened to Robby. He had been afraid to let Robby have a voice with his father or his foster parents.

Bring darkness into light. The truth will set you free.

Ironically, Rob had silenced Robby the rest of his life as a way to earn people's approval. Without realizing it, he, too, was silencing Robby. A letter would help him rescue this aspect of self, generating vitality. A letter would also help him learn how to develop a sense of inner security and learn how to count on himself.

Abused or neglected people need to coach their anger and pain out of hiding so they can use the feelings to develop their personhood.

The next week, Rob arrived with the letter that Robby wrote. Slowly and tearfully, he read it to me:

Hello Rob:
Please tell my why. Why did my mom leave me alone? Why didn't she love me? Why didn't she hug me and watch over me? WHAT DID I DO WRONG? I was a beautiful child. Why would she leave me? Why couldn't she give me a chance, a chance to feel loved and cared for? What did I do? How could she leave

me? Look what she left me to. Fear! Alone! I can't even remember one hug. How could she do that? She left me with a dad who
loved me but couldn't even take care of himself. Can someone tell
me why? Why would Dad remarry, give me a home and a mom,
only to rip it away again!?! Why??? I don't understand. Why
couldn't I have friends? Why did I have to sleep on a cot in a hallway? Rob, why didn't I get a chance? Why did I have to go to
other peoples' homes? Rob, please help me! Help me understand
how a mother could abandon her son, how a father could allow
so much fear and terror into a small boy's life. The confusion!
Please help me! I never had a chance. I could barely read and
write because I changed schools so much. I was not stupid! I was
not given a chance. How could my mom leave me? How could
my dad neglect me? I tried so hard for his love, for his approval,
for something that I could never achieve. God, please help this
hurt go away. Rob, please hold me. All I have ever heard was that
life is not fair. Well it has not been fair to me because of other
people. I hate this, and I am angry! WHY DIDN"T I GET A
CHANCE?

When Rob finished reading the letter to me, he looked up to see
my reaction. He saw sadness. "I'm so sorry that you weren't loved,
Robby. I'm so sorry that no one got to know you for who you are.
I'm so sorry that no one cared about what you were feeling. You did-
n't deserve that. You didn't do anything to cause that. You have done
nothing wrong. It was your parents' fault,
not yours."

Robby cried. He wasn't embarrassed
about his tears this time. He let himself
abide the heartache he had lived. Robby's
voice had finally found a home.

Later, Rob told me he felt surprised at
what the letter revealed to him. "I now

> *Validating suffering.*
> *Valuing and appreciating*
> *what one has been*
> *through instills courage to*
> *reintegrate the lost self*
> *into the conscious self.*

realize how much I've been through. I'm a lot stronger than I realized. Even though I have damage and scars, I'm proud of the battle I
went through as a child. I was a good kid and didn't get into trou-

ble." I smiled with his insight; he no longer had a need to hide Robby, to hide who he is.

I validated the honesty, courage, and humility that he exhibited in doing the work that he'd done over the past few weeks. I emphasized the need for him to access the hero inside himself by developing internal parents who could provide him with love and protection.

"For homework this week, each day, even in small ways, you are to make at least one decision based on what you want or don't want to do, rather than on what you think someone else wants or doesn't want you to do."

"That's going to be hard."

"I know, but look at how hard you've worked so far. It's amazing what you've done in just a few short weeks. Robby deserves a place in your life. You need him; you need his vitality. He needs you; he needs your protection. I want you to start standing up for yourself. I want you to start standing up for Robby. Every time you don't, you're doing to him what your parents did to him."

> *Without realizing it, we do to ourselves what others have done to us.*

At the next session, Rob said he had been able to make "a few" decisions based on what he wanted rather than ones based on fear of rejection from those around him. He said that the decisions were hard, but he was beginning to realize how he had been silencing and neglecting Robby the same way that his parents had, perpetuating the abandonment. I validated the courage it took to face his pain and anger. I validated his need to take care of himself by developing an internal "mother" and "father" so he could stop the cycle of neglect. Rob now understood that all the years of telling himself that his past was over were simply not true. Robby was still residing with him, waiting for the attention he deserved but never got.

For homework, I gave Rob a CD on

> *Telling ourselves that we have "risen above" neglect exiles the hurt self who suffered the neglect. Rather than fearing this part of self, we need to integrate it, by opening up to this aspect of self.*

communication; its guided imagery would allow him to continue his dialogue with Robby. This approach would help him let Robby abide with him, so they could become integrated. I also provided a similar CD of guided imagery on self-acceptance. The imagery would help him continue to not only accept Robby but also to feel proud of what he had endured. He could integrate Robby's unconscious energy so he could grow into his conscious self.

After completing the exercises, Rob said, "I didn't realize I was so sensitive to other people's feelings. I'm a lot more empathetic than I thought."

"A gift that Robby's experience gives you. Not even the neglect of your parents was able to erase it," I told him.

The next week, Rob arrived anxious and uncertain. He was awaiting results from his x-ray scans that would reflect the status of his cancer. He was also feeling weary from the effects of the chemotherapy, so I kept the session short and supportive, asking Patty, our volunteer massage therapist, to see him; massage would integrate the tension he was feeling.

Recognize when someone is not able, willing, or ready to do inner work.

Rob's scans showed that his cancer was in remission. Although Rob felt relieved, he still worried about recurrence. "Every time I get a new ache or pain, I'm worried it means the cancer is back." He also developed empathy for other people with cancer: "I cry whenever I see anything on TV about people with cancer. I just feel so sorry for them."

"I want you to write a letter to your cancer."

"You want me to do what?" he asked in disbelief. "I don't think I can do that."

"I want you to summon all your courage and all your honesty and tell your cancer what you are thinking and feeling. I want you to abide your fear and loneliness openly. Don't hide anything. Be real with whatever is." I kept my gaze unwavering so that he knew that I had confidence that he was ready for the task.

At our next session, Rob tentatively, and somewhat sheepishly, gave me his letter. He didn't want to read it aloud. I hesitantly, yet excitedly, unfolded it:

> Dear Cancer,
>
> Fuck you!!! Fuck you! Fuck you! How did you find your way here? Where did you come from? I was doing things right and then you came along. Where did you come from? Did I allow you in? Are you my fault? Did you get handed to me by my family? Are you in my genes? You made me sick. Really, really sick. I had to strap a bag of pee to my leg for months because of you. I had to rethink my entire life because of you. Are you waiting to strike again? Maybe you're waiting until I find happiness to strike again. You fuck!! I hate you, and yet, I have changed and am changing for the better because of you. I don't like that. I don't want you to be a good thing!! I hate to admit that you have revealed many problems in my thinking. I have lost so much and yet I'm better off without those things. You have brought me people who have helped me. I'm getting emotionally stronger because of you. You have made me face issues that I've needed to face for years.
>
> I feel weak now. I'm scared of you, and I never thought I would be scared again. How do I live now? I can't pretend that you don't exist. Four tumors. You fuck! Four!! I want you gone! I want you eradicated. This is my body and you are not allowed! Please don't hurt me again! Please, please, please stop hurting me.
>
> I fucking hate you!! You have made me braver and revealed my weaknesses. Why did you come? Did God send you? Don't' come back. Please leave! Don't hurt me anymore. You have made me see how fragile I am. Leave me alone! I will not let you beat me! You have made me see that I love life, but you've spent more than a year beating me up. Fuck you! Rob

"Wow! I love it!" I told him.

"I was afraid you'd be offended by the language," he replied.

"I love it because I can feel the vitality of your anger. I love it because I can see what's underneath your fear and loneliness. I love it because it's the unvarnished truth of what you are going through right now. I love it because you weren't afraid to be who you are."

Now that Rob could fairly easily abide with the aspects of himself that he had previously been hiding, I turned to the task of reckoning. Although his parents had not helped him do so, I knew it was not too late to redeem the destiny that he was born to fulfill.

I started by telling Rob to write a letter to Robby. My hope was that the letter would further redefine the relationship that he had been keeping with the lost and silenced child. This is the letter he wrote:

My Dearest Robby,

I hear you, and I know your pain. I understand your anger. You are right to be angry. You didn't get a chance, but you made one. I am so very proud of you. You never quit. You never gave up. You were pushed away and your feelings were discounted, but you never stopped trying – trying to be a good and understanding son. My God, look how strong you were! I wish I knew how to make you feel safe. I wish I could comfort you and hold you so tight to my chest. This world sucks. You were too good and caring and sensitive, yet you are a credit to yourself. You should stand proud, young man, and hold your head high because YOU HAVE NOTHING TO BE ASHAMED OF!

I love you. I hope I can learn to show you how much I love you. I hope that together we can learn how to be at peace. As you hide and look at the world with fear, remember that people are sometimes self-centered. The crap handed to you was not a reflection of you, but of self-absorbed people who didn't realize the treasure you were and are. This is so hard for us, but we will overcome.

I love you Robby. Maybe someday you will come to trust that.

Rob.

When Rob looked up to see my reaction, I could only smile. There was nothing to say. We just basked in the moment. Finally, I said, "I'm so proud of you, Rob."

Recovering Robby was an essential

Reckoning: Shifting a person's relationship with the problem is often done through letter-writing and forgiveness.

step in the forgiveness process, a step usually overlooked. Robby was the aspect of self that had been betrayed. It was Robby, not Rob, who had the authority to forgive his parents.

Over our next several weeks together, Rob started reaching out to the few family members he had so he could start growing a sense of belonging and identity that he'd not had previously. He vacationed with his half-sister in Key West. She, too, was abandoned by their father, but she was more forthcoming about this, not minimizing its impact on her life. Her response helped Rob to stop minimizing the neglect he had experienced. He visited his 86-year-old grandmother in Germany. He was, indeed, beginning to manifest the hero inside himself, a hero that yearned for healing and redemption.

> *Only when we reintegrate the exiled aspect of self, do we achieve forgiveness. Only the broken aspect of self has the authority to forgive.*

I was seeing Rob infrequently now because his fears were less crippling. When we did meet, we focused on his relationship with his girlfriend, Tracey. She had not been very responsive to his need for support during cancer and chemo. Although it was a neglect that felt familiar to him, I was hopeful that he could grow into expecting more from a relationship. I was hopeful that he could experience true intimacy. Intimacy would require some reckoning on his part.

"I'm curious why Tracey didn't visit you when you were hospitalized. What was that about?"

"I told her she didn't need to."

"Why'd you tell her that? Didn't you want to see her? Wouldn't she have been a comfort to you? You were really sick."

Rob had many excuses for Tracey: she worked, she had an 11-year-old son, it was a long way to drive.

"She doesn't work in the evening. She can bring her son with her. It's an hour drive to get here. So, tell me again why you didn't ask her to come."

> *Being too "forgiving" fosters enabling.*

Helping people reckon with truth rather than create illusions of how they want someone or something to be.

Rob was at a loss for words.

"Let me take a couple of guesses, and you tell me if any of them ring true. You don't feel worthy of her time or attention? You don't know that it's okay to tell her that you have a need for comfort? You're afraid of the fear and loneliness you would feel if she didn't come when you asked? You're afraid she's not capable of really caring about you and responding to your needs?"

Rob didn't say anything at first, but he was pondering the possibilities. "All of the above. They're all true."

Although I knew that Rob's difficulties with intimacy related to his lack of relationship with his mother and father, I wasn't sure where he was located on the spectrum. Did he have low expectations because he was willing to accept anything as long as he wasn't rejected? Or did his insecurity take him in the opposite direction, making him needy and clingy, searching for the mother he never had? I made a spreadsheet to make the determination, listing the expectations that were reasonable and unreasonable. In doing so, Rob had a tangential insight: he still felt guilty about how he treated his second wife. "I don't know what I was thinking. She really loved me. She made me feel important."

"What did she do that made you feel so important?"

"She always wanted to be with me."

"Wanted to be with you?" I questioned.

"You know. Always calling me. Always telling me how much she loved me."

"How many times a day was she doing this?" I asked suspiciously.

"Ten, twenty times a day."

"That sounds annoying to me. Didn't that interfere with your work?"

"Yeah. I'd be out on patrol in the cruiser, and she'd keep calling me. I'd tell her not to call me, but she'd call anyway."

"That's not love Rob. That's disrespectful and intrusive. I don't condone how you treated your ex-wife. You cheated on her. I'm glad you feel guilty about that. Cheating is probably what made her call and check up on you so much. I don't know if she loved you or not, but you could have gotten in trouble for accepting so many personal phone calls, not to mention that it probably distracted you from your work. I don't want you to mistake possessiveness for love."

> *Before reckoning can occur, determine someone's relationship with the world: they think the world owes them or they think they owe the world. Otherwise, you enable behaviors rather than change them.*

Boundaries. Rob needed them. "For your homework assignment, I want you to recognize a time when you are in need of support. Tell Tracey your need. See how she responds. She might not know what to do at first because she won't be used to your revealing your need. You can tell her what would help; tell her what would comfort you."

Rob said he would try.

"How'd the homework assignment go?" I asked upon his return several weeks later.

"I was really tired. I had to come home from work early because I was so nauseated. I felt really awkward asking Tracey to hold me. I realized that I have a hard time receiving comfort from others."

"I'm not surprised. You never had a parent who knew how to give you comfort. How did Tracey respond?"

"She did it, but she seemed a little annoyed."

"Do you think she's a trustworthy source of comfort?"

"What do you mean?"

"Does she want to be a comfort to you? Has she cared enough about you to figure out what gives you comfort and how to do it?"

"No. She doesn't see any point in talking about feelings. She says that she doesn't like anything sad. She says she sees nothing wrong with our relationship the way it is. She says our relationship is already perfect."

> *Mature mental health includes being vulnerable by stating our needs and asking for help.*

"Doesn't it seem odd to you that she considers your relationship 'perfect' when you are expressing dissatisfaction?"

"I think she means that it's perfect for her."

"That's my point. Does it concern you that you have told her you want a deeper relationship, that you have told her that you are getting counseling so that you can change and learn how to be a different person so that you can have a fulfilling relationship, and she just erases that with 'everything's perfect for me, so nothing needs to change'?"

"I hadn't thought of it that way."

"Sounds like a rather shallow, one-sided relationship. Is that what you want?"

"No. I want to get married. I want to learn how to be a good husband because all I've done so far is screw up both marriages I've had."

"You are doing the first step: changing yourself and becoming trustworthy. The second step will be surrounding yourself with trustworthy people who value who you are. I'm not sure Tracey values you."

"Why do you say that?" he asked.

"When you tell her you want to discuss marriage, she tells you she doesn't care about getting married. You ask her to come here to see me to discuss how things are going with you, and she tells you she's too busy and sees no need for that. You come home sick from the chemo and ask her to hold you and she feels annoyed. You're in the hospital for a week, and she doesn't visit you."

"But I told her she didn't need to come to see me in the hospital," Rob legitimately protested on Tracey's behalf.

"That wouldn't stop someone who loved and understood who you are," I responded.

I let silence reckon the truth I was offering him.

In my motherly voice, I softly reminded him, "You don't ever need to be afraid of who you are, Rob. You are worthy of love. You are worthy of comfort. There are women who are trustworthy of your love now that you are becoming trustworthy, now that you are changing."

Rob's homework was to see the movie, *Alice in Wonderland*. The movie metaphorically depicts the healing process. It would help Rob see how abiding and reckoning would allow him to recover himself so he could face his fears to redeem the destiny he was born to fulfill. He was now becoming capable of redeeming that destiny because of the honesty, courage, and humility he was demonstrating.

> *Preparing for uncertainty.*

Rob saw the movie and enjoyed Alice's antics. He especially related to Alice's crossing the bridge with all her fears terrorizing her. "I loved the scene when Alice said, 'I'll show you who has lost her muchness,' and she went forward determined to find it even when she didn't know what muchness was."

I laughed, remembering the scene and its significance.

"I'm here to recover my muchness," Rob proclaimed with a smile, but he quickly lost his twinkle, shaking his head. I could feel his muchness quickly dissolving. "I want to redefine myself, but I'm tired of the struggle."

"You're getting impatient with how long this takes."

"I just feel like I'm holding on too tightly. Sometimes, I wish I could just become wacky in a store and not be worried about what others would think. The way Alice did. I want to feel free without constraints."

"That'll come. It takes time."

"But how long?"

"Growth is not a smooth, linear, upward trajectory. There are incubation times as you integrate new experiences. I wish you could

> *Metaphors, especially metaphorical images such as movies, are powerful because they access the unconscious.*

just go from A to Z on a steady route, but you're going to have to do it the way the rest of us do: one step at a time, opening up to the setbacks that occur, and reaching out for support when you get disappointed with the process."

"You mean you go through this, too?"

"Of course, but I haven't had to muster the courage that you've had to."

He looked at me without understanding.

"My mother neglected me, but not nearly the way your parents did. Also, I had a grandmother, father, and older sister

> *Providing glimpses of our shared humanity.*

and brother who were able to help fill the gap. So, you can see your journey requires much more courage than mine."

Rob looked surprised.

"What's happening with you and Tracey?" I asked, suspicious that his loss of confidence and increased fear were caused by the threat of loss of their relationship that we had previously broached.

"Nothing. I'm realizing that I really don't want a future with her, but I just don't know how to get disentangled from her."

"Ouch," I responded with the hurt that his statement implied.

"I'm realizing that the main reason I'm staying in the relationship is because of Sean, her son. We get along great. He'll be so hurt if I leave."

"You know what that feels like."

"I do. That's why I don't want him to have to go through it," Rob said, wincing as he said it.

"It'll be hard for him."

"It will. I go to all his ballgames. My dad didn't show up for anything that I did. I know how important that is to a boy his age."

"Do you think there are some things you could do that would prepare him for your leaving?"

We talked about important messages that Sean should receive: The breakup was not Sean's fault; he was important and worthy; his Mom would keep his routines the same to minimize disruptions; she would continue to love and protect him; and it was normal to cry and feel bad for awhile after Rob left.

Over the next several weeks, Rob broke up with Tracey several times. His insecurities would heighten when he was away, and he'd go back.

"You're using Tracey to treat your anxiety and loneliness. That doesn't seem very fair to her."

Rob hadn't thought of it that way.

"What are you doing to get your life on track? What gives you passion? What gives you meaning so you don't have to keep using Tracey as a substitute?"

He identified possible sources of enjoyment: painting, going to the gym, learning how to play the guitar, and rebuilding computers. He said he also had a lifelong dream to visit the Orient. He was rather animatedly talking about his aspirations when he suddenly became quiet and pensive.

"What's going on?" I inquired.

"I don't know," he said. He seemed quite perplexed.

> *Cultivate the animating force: Vitality and Passion.*

"Close your eyes." Rob obediently did so. "Tell me what you're feeling."

"Panic."

I was surprised by his answer, not sure how he'd gotten from pleasure to panic so quickly. I was even more surprised by his description of it. "Tell me what color it is."

"Green."

Green was a color of vitality, life. The last time he had described panic to me, he had told me it was "black."

"I want you to just let yourself go down into your chest. Let yourself become that green panic in your chest," I said slowly. Knowing that his panic often stemmed from his insecurities as a child, I went on: "Imagine that you are Robby, pulsing green in your chest." Tears slowly leaked from Rob's eyes, splashing onto his royal blue polo shirt one drop at a time. I sat quietly not saying anything before I finally resumed. "Now, I want you to breathe green. You are that ball of panicky, green Robby in your chest that is now breathing." I waited. "Now breathe more deeply. Let Robby breathe and grow into every cell of your body. Breathe and grow green

> *Engaging personal, uncontrived images can bypass conscious filters. Our filters fool us into thinking: We don't need to get honest with what we are experiencing. We don't need to summon any courage so we can change. We don't need to be humble so that we can learn.*

out into your arms and hands. Breathe and grow green up into your neck and head, even your hair. Breathe and grow green down into your legs and feet. Even your toes are green. Your feet are heavy with green. Let yourself breathe and grow and turn green." Rob breathed, his tears slowly continuing as he grew into his full self. "When you're ready, you can open your eyes, bringing Robby with you."

"What are you feeling now?" I asked.

His answer intrigued me. "I feel three-dimensional," he said as if he were trying on the experience like a new suit.

"That's the gift that Robby gives to you. He brings you life. He brings you dimension. He brings you vitality."

Rob's poignant answer dropped me in my tracks. "You mean I don't need to be ashamed of who I am anymore?"

I felt proud, and sad, and joyous, and heartbroken all at the same time. "No. You don't ever need to be ashamed of who you are. Not ever again."

"Would you mind hugging me? I need a hug right now," Rob and Robby said.

I don't think I've ever been more proud of anyone than I was at that moment when that boy/man had the courage to ask for his need to be met. I stood up to give him a hug,

> *Traumatized people need grounding because they tend to dissociate from their body. Imagery should focus on the body, ending with the feet.*

saying: "I am the mother inside you who welcomes you home. I am the mother inside you who knows how important and valuable you are. I am your internal mother who hugs and comforts you."

Afterward, Rob and I sat looking at each other. We both knew that something powerful and important for him had just occurred.

"Tell me this is real," Rob said.

"This is real," I assured him.

"Tell me this will last, that it won't go away."

"It will go away. This feeling won't last," I said gently but matter-of-factly.

Rob looked crushed.

"All things pass away. That doesn't mean they're not real; it doesn't mean that you haven't experienced healing. You will be different

> *Beholding: Experiencing a newfound peace with the exiled self because the relationship with the conscious self has opened up. The blocked energy is now free to be integrated into the whole being.*

because of what you have experienced today. You *are* different. There are still going to be ups and downs though. There will still be times of uncertainty, and you are going to feel scared. There will still be times when you question whether you are worthy or important. That is part of our human condition. The difference is that your fear will be less intense, and you will no longer need to close down to those experiences. Or, if you do, you know how to ask for help so you can open your heart to them again."

Rob was disappointed, and he also understood.

"I have a request I want to make," Rob said tentatively.

"Yes…?" I answered expectantly.

"I'm uncomfortable when you called yourself my 'mother'," he said hesitantly.

"Okay. Tell me more about that."

"Mothers can abandon their children and leave them scared and lonely. You are a confidante I can trust. I don't want to think that you are someone who is going to abandon me."

"Point well taken. You got it. Confidante, not mother," I said beaming.

"I was afraid I might hurt your feelings telling you that," Rob said with obvious relief.

"That's why I'm happy," I said.

"I don't get it."

"You were able to speak your need, even though you were afraid I might not like it. You were less afraid of hurting my feelings than you were afraid of being you. Now, you are starting to have self-respect. I like that. I respect that. You are gaining your *muchness!*"

Rob laughed with my reference to Alice recovering her *muchness* in Wonderland.

"Before you leave, I want to ask you a question," I said mysteriously.

Rob waited expectantly for me to proceed.

"Forced choice answer: Would you rather die at age 45 feeling like this or live to age 80 the way you were living before you got cancer?"

"I don't want to die, but I do not want to go back to living the flat existence I was living. If I had to choose, I'd choose death now. Everything else is counterfeit."

"Let's imagine your death," I said.

"Why would I want to do that?" Rob said, his eyes widening.

"Because it's the elephant in the middle of the room that neither of us is talking about. It's the fear that's haunting you. We might as well get it out in the open, bring consciousness to it so it doesn't have to stalk you."

By now, Rob was used to my having him open his heart to whatever he was fleeing so it didn't take him long to trust me to do what I was asking.

"Close your eyes. Imagine that today is the day you are going to die. Silently answer the following questions with images in your mind. Where would you be?" I gave him time to create his answers after each question I asked: "What would you be seeing? What would you be hearing? What would you be smelling? Who would be there? What would they be feeling? What would they be saying to you? What would they be saying to each other? What would you be saying to them? What would you be feeling?"

"Take a few deep breaths, bringing this image with you, and then you can open your eyes," I told him gently. "Tell me what happened."

"I'm a little disappointed," he said enigmatically.

"How so?"

"I couldn't quite connect with it. I couldn't experience it the way I did with the other imagery we did together."

"That's okay. This took you right into the center of your fear. Your mind knows how to protect you. You probably would have been overwhelmed if you would have completely connected with it. Where were you dying?"

"Here. On this Hospice unit."

"Who was with you?"

> *Denial is a needed self-protective mechanism that helps the other person and me.*

"You. The chemo nurses. My sister and brother. Some of my close friends. What's more interesting is who wasn't there."

"Who wasn't there?"

"Tracey. Tracey wasn't there."

"You said she doesn't like anything sad. Your death would be sad, so it makes sense that she wouldn't be there. That's good for you to know."

Rob was different and the same after that day. He accepted a friend's offer to come visit him in Bangkok for three weeks. "I have a few fears about going there, but I'm not going to live in fear any more."

"Really?" I tested him.

"I used to think that if I feared something, I had to go charging into it; that's what the military taught me to do."

"Yeah? What are you going to do differently now?"

"I'm open to my fear. I'm going to move forward with my travel plans. I realize now that I can make changes if things come up that I'm afraid of, and I know now that I can handle it."

He also ended his relationship with Tracey. "I did it honestly this time."

"I'm not sure what you mean by that."

"I talked to her about it instead of attacking her so that I'd have an excuse to break up with her. That's what I used to do."

"How does that feel? How does it feel to live from a place of integrity?"

"Different. Very different. I still don't like confrontation, but it's getting less scary."

Rob's breakup with Tracey didn't last though. He needed a few more attempts because each time he left, the loss triggered feelings of anxiety and abandonment. I reassured him this was okay as long as he was honest with her while learning ways to reckon with the discomfort of uncertainty and develop a strategy for the next breakup. I reminded him about the Crescent Moon Bear: "The little wife didn't just charge into the bear's den with the food. She kept patiently feeding the bear and running to safety until she could muster the courage to stand strong even when the bear roared."

Rob laughed with the memory when we had enacted the myth in my office a few weeks before. "I'm glad to hear you say that because I've realized that it's Robby who is feeling so scared when we break up. Now, I talk to him. I have this mantra that really helps: 'Robby, I love you. Robby, I'm here for you. Robby, I won't leave you no matter what'."

Rob also quit his job at the landscaping office. "My friends wanted me to lie to my boss and tell him I had all these aspirations with the company so that he'd pay me more money."

"You didn't do that?"

"I told him that landscaping sales is simply not my passion and that I just wasn't sure that I wanted to continue. I didn't want him to invest in me if I didn't stay on, and yet I felt loyal and grateful to him for all his support through my cancer."

"How'd he respond to that?"

"He said he appreciated my candor. He even said he'd create a different position for me as long as I would provide a six-month commitment."

"So what did you decide to do?"

"I told him I couldn't do it. I told him I needed to invest in myself now. I needed to do something that will make me happy."

Rob visited his brother in California, checking out a job that his brother was willing to look into for him. Rob decided not to take the job. I was proud of his reason: "I have to make sure that I'm not just running away like I've done in the past."

Rob decided to return to the banking industry, accepting a job as a mortgage counselor. He participated in a Healing Community (See page 174.) with other people who had experienced neglectful or abusive childhoods.

> *Integration: Making the unconscious conscious. Living from a place of integrity.*

He embarked on a spiritual quest, exploring various religious denominations. He started reading (a hobby he had long neglected), buying a book by Henri Nouwen, excitedly reading a passage to me: "Stand tall in your feelings of pain, rejection, and fear."[2] He agreed to an evaluation for depression and started on anti-depressant medication, which helped lift his mood. He tentatively started exploring a 12-step recovery program. He's on maintenance chemotherapy for a few years, which makes him tired, but he doesn't have the severe side effects of his initial chemo. He still overdoes it at the gym: "I won't accept any more limitations. The cancer is in remission, and the tough chemo is done. I have to build myself back up and the only way is all the way. Anything less is just excuses."

I still nag him about that attitude. It's my job. "You want to disregard what your body has been through with the chemotherapy? You don't want to listen to what your body needs to gently coax it back into strength?"

"I can't do that. It's all or nothing with me," he responds.

"How does Robby feel about that?"

"I don't understand what you mean," he says quizzically.

"That vital little boy who lives in you, who knows how you feel and knows that your body is still recovering from the chemo. He cries out to you to take care of him. You're not listening to him. You're just going on as if cancer and chemo hadn't happened. I'm not sure that's good self-care. Overdoing your workout sounds a bit compulsive to me."

> *Separating reasons from excuses.*

"I don't know any other way to do it."

"Yes you do," I say steadily. He makes excuses. My job is to hold him accountable.

With his cancer in remission, Rob is looking for a symbol that represents the trek he has made. He wants to have the symbol tattooed on his arm: "I don't know what it's going to be, but I know it needs to be green to reflect my *muchness*," he told me, referring to the vitalizing imagery Robby had provided a few weeks previously. Rob's Healing Community also celebrated his completion of chemotherapy by enacting a ritual of walking a labyrinth with him. (See the self-awareness assignment in this chapter.) Each person gave him gifts to remind him of his "*muchness*." Music that reflected the three stages of ritual was played. I also conferred a Ph.D. (personal hero degree) upon Rob to acknowledge the heroic efforts he made to cultivate honesty, courage, and humility so he could grow into his larger self.

I didn't forget about Rob's desire to "get wacky in a store." So, along with Patty (our massage therapist), we went to lunch at a near-by restaurant. The three of us donned wacky hats I have in my office to use when some levity is needed. Rob chose a giraffe hat with legs dangling around his shoulders and the long neck arched over his forehead. We drew some attention initially when the three of us walked into the restaurant, but we found a sequestered table where we could talk and laugh together, sharing our stories.

> Getting "wacky" keeps a healthy perspective: a light-hearted relation-ship with our personal liabilities.

A few weeks later, Rob arrived for his scheduled appointment carrying two pic-tures. "This is a drawing I made of my father," he said as he displayed a well-drawn picture of a contemplative man done in detailed pencil.

"I had no idea you had such talent, Rob."

He shrugged off my compliment. After we discussed the details of the drawing, Rob brought out another penciled sketch. "This is a drawing of me." A young boy of about ten stared from the depths of the picture. "My father drew it." The drawing was done well, but in a different style than the previous drawing he had shown me.

"I'm so glad to meet Robby," I said with delight.

> Labyrinths, music, and rituals help integrate the unconscious into the conscious.

"You should be. You're the one who rescued him," Rob said.

"No. No. I was just your guide and cheerleader. You're the one who did the work. You're the one that had to mount the courage to find him. You're the one who had to be willing to feel his pain and anger." Rob slowly recog-nized the truth of what I was saying.

"I'd like you to have it," Rob said earnestly.

I was speechless. Beholding moments often do that to me; my

breath is taken away by the eternal moment. I simultaneously feel humbled and awed.

SELF-AWARENESS EXERCISE
Create a Healing Community

Using this book as the focus, start a Healing Community of two to eight people. Complete the Life Story exercises at the end of each chapter, processing them when you come together. Be creative. You will be amazed at the personal healing and the development of intimate relationships that develop as you grow together. After a few weeks, you might want to name your group as you see what patterns or themes emerge. Appendix M provides guidelines for creating a Healing Community.

Healing Our Lives Together

"To be a healing community, we have to heal our community," Dr. Hull, our Hospice and Palliative Care physician said one day. So we created a ritual to help us heal our community. We gather our chairs in a circle once each month to tell our stories. The process we use is based on a Native American tribal custom. When they come to pow-wow, the natives pass a "talking stick" to everyone gathered within the circle. About a foot long, it is often adorned with beads and feathers. Two rules are observed: Only the person holding the stick at that moment can speak, and everyone else must listen; whatever that person says while holding the stick has to be truthful, with no pretenses or coverups.[3]

I recognized the power of this format to elicit deeper and more meaningful stories that can emanate from the hero within. The format also levels the playing field, equalizing the power for all participants regardless of position; no voice dominates, and no voice is excluded.

At our first meeting, we didn't have a stick. A smooth, black rock was on the table, so we used that. It became our touchstone. I added two rules of my own: "We are free to pass the rock without speaking; no apology needed. Also, we must resist the urge to give advice or philosophize. Instead, we each tell a personal story or experience about the topic."

Monthly sessions usually start by asking if anyone is seeking counsel. Someone identifies a need, and the touchstone is passed. Sessions have included multiple themes. One staff member spoke of a family death, and the rest of us responded with our own stories of recovering from a death or loss. Another time a nurse said she was feeling "lost," which elicited stories when others felt lost and uncertain. One nurse said she was having difficulties with a family member's alcohol usage; the rest of us responded with our own stories of how alcohol had wounded people we loved. An adult son moving back into a parent's home prompted story-telling of lifestyle changes and boundary setting with older children. One session responded to the need of a staff member whose young adult son had stopped any contact with her. All responded with stories of children (sometimes themselves) rebelling against parents. One staff member noted changes in health as she aged, realizing that she might need to consider retirement. The rock was passed to gather stories about our own experiences of aging and illness.

There has been little overstepping of boundaries in the sessions.

Self-controlled disclosure creates an atmosphere for safe and comfortable sharing. I'm thankful that Native Americans understood the
wisdom of this powerful and meaningful forum for connecting and
growing together, drawing out deeper insights from within the participants.

The touchstone has collected hundreds of stories over the years.
Wisdom is found in stories because stories have value beyond facts
or biographical information. "The story is not told to lift you up, to
make you feel better, or to entertain you. The story is meant to take
the spirit into a descent to find something that is lost or missing and
to bring it back to consciousness again," writes Clarissa Pinkola
Estes.[4] She's right. Stories are healing; they restore wholeness to our
fractured selves. They help us find ourselves. There's always room for
each of us in a story, even though it's someone else's story. It reminds
me of something I read: "We comfort others not from the foundation of our superior faith, but from the commonality of our mutual
struggles."[5] A good story almost always has a "mutual struggle" that
connects each of us in the "common-unity" of the community.

Shared struggles foster community. For example, the
Zimbabwe sculpture exhibit in the Atlanta airport depicts the
plight of many of the African people. One sculpture, however,
Conversations, is particularly relevant. The sculptor, Agnes
Nyanhongo, writes: "The three figures represent the importance of
coming together to make things grow and change."[6] She notes that
these kinds of gatherings breed "compassion and silent strength" to
face our mutual struggles.

Nyanhongo is right. A trustworthy community fosters strength
so that growth and change can occur. My hope is that people will
apply the abiding, reckoning, and beholding processes to heal their
lives, using this book as a manual to start small, healing communities. I believe that small groups of people can learn these principles
together without professional facilitation. I have been a participant
in many such groups. I am convinced of their value and feasibility.
Healing groups become hero birthing centers!

It's a challenge to abide with ugly feelings that we don't want to feel and to welcome home the part of self that is feeling those ugly feelings. It's a challenge to reckon with realities that are hidden underneath illusions that help us deny and pretend away our vulnerabilities. By participating in a trustworthy group, we encounter members who can cheer us on and activate the courage required to address the brokenness in our lives. Group participants can provide accountability with each other to facilitate the honesty needed to heal when we are fighting/flighting/freezing our discomforts. As each member abides and reckons with their woundedness, humility is fos-

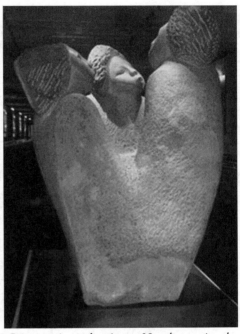

Conversations *by Agnes Nyanhongo in the Atlanta airport*

tered. Others may not have the same story, but each person can relate to some aspect of the story being told and realize they are not alone. There is communion (common union) with one another as community is developed.

As each member shares their Self-Awareness Exercises, I tell the rest of the group that their job is to simply abide with the person: "Open yourselves to him or her. Feel what they feel and help them feel it, especially the feelings from which they're running. This process creates the safety needed for deeper layers of stories to emerge. Then validate the aspect of self that is dealing with the difficulties."

I tell group members that their job is to be an *en-courager* so people will enter the process, especially when they want to "fight or flight" their reality. *En-courage* them to breathe deeply and stay open to the uncertainty and ambiguity that come prior to breaking through their fear and coming to grips with changes." I remind them that these steps, by themselves, are often all that is needed to provide support.

I also remind people that some members of a group are less willing to change than others. Our job is to recognize and respect that choice. I also add a caution: "Just because someone chooses not to abide or reckon with their situation doesn't mean we judge them for not doing so." There are many important reasons why people don't, won't, or can't do the work of healing. Invariably, there will come a point when the person is ready. Usually that turning point is their witness of other group participants who abide and reckon with their Life Stories.

People worry about saying the right thing to another group member. I remind them that they are not responsible for having the right response for someone else. They are responsible for having the willingness to abide the emotional dimension of the person's story. *The individual* is responsible for reckoning with what he or she needs to do to shift the relationship to their dilemma. Abiding is the group's job; reckoning is the individual's job.

Sharing Our Stories: Pathways to Healing

Rob's healing journey began when he was willing to reach out for help, sharing his story with someone who was willing to abide his suffering and help him reckon with scattered pieces of broken self that were seeking integration into his conscious self. I sometimes call this a "belonging process," whereby we become whole by welcoming home all our banished selves. The parts of ourselves that we have exiled no longer need to hide and unconsciously shame and terrorize us; they become "belonged."

Stories, shared in a small community of trustworthy people, remind us that we belong to one another and that we can help each other. Stories connect us to each other and ourselves. Sharing our story opens our hearts and teaches us how to encounter our pain.

Telling our story renders meaning out of chaos so that our suffering is not wasted. Stories preserve memories and help us define who we are. They help us sort out what is significant from what is not. Understanding our story grows us into our larger selves so we can become more conscious. They expand our imagination and stimulate creativity so that new vistas are opened. Stories shared among trusted friends restore hope as possibilities for new passageways are created. Stories help us redeem the destiny we were born to fulfill. Stories show us how to cultivate honesty, courage, and humility so that we can access the hero within. The question is: Am I willing to become the hero I was born to be?

Lessons in Community

- Never doubt that a small group of thoughtful, committed people can change the world. Indeed, it is the only thing that ever has.
- Healing often includes the "belonging process," whereby we become whole by welcoming home all our banished selves. Parts of ourselves that we have exiled no longer need to hide where they can shame and terrorize us; they become "belonged."
- Traumatized people need grounding because they tend to dissociate from their body. Imagery should focus on the body, ending with the feet.
- Labyrinths, imagery, symbols, music, and rituals help integrate the unconscious into the conscious.
- Getting "wacky" keeps a healthy perspective: a light-hearted relationship with our personal liabilities so we don't take ourselves too seriously.
- Stories help us find ourselves; there's always room for each of us in a story, even though it's someone else's story.
- We have to be willing to become the hero we were born to be. Then, the resources from our deeper selves become available to us.

- To be a healing community, we have to heal our community.
- The talking stick format elicits deeper and more meaningful stories from the hero within. The format levels the playing field, equalizing the power for all participants regardless of position; no voice dominates and no voice is excluded.
- Healing Communities develop into hero birthing centers. Appendix M will help with the logistics. Have the courage to start a Healing Community. Sharing the mutual struggle within a small community of trustworthy people fosters honesty, courage, and humility so the abiding and reckoning processes can precipitate healing. The result is worth beholding!

Appendix A

Abiding and Reckoning: A Contrast

This chart compares the processes involved in abiding and reckoning. Both are necessary to accomplish healing.

Abiding	Reckoning
Heart Domain: Abiding includes feeling all our feelings, including uncomfortable feelings that we fear or don't like. More importantly, abiding also includes opening up to the part of self that is generating the feelings. Abiding has two-directional foci: turned inward we abide with ourselves; turned outward, we abide with others.	**Head Domain:** Reckoning includes identifying needs, as well as making a decision to change the relationship to the aspect of self experiencing a problem. To achieve reckoning, we must be willing to cultivate qualities that discover needed lessons: honesty, courage, and humility. Reckoning requires that we be willing to change and ask for help.
Abiding without Reckoning: Abiding our heart without engaging our head so we can change our relationship to a problem causes us to stay stuck in a victim mode. A victim perspective keeps us bitter and powerless (if the feelings relate to guilt, anger, fear, sadness) or irresponsible and cowardly (if the feelings relate solely to maintaining happiness and comfort).	**Reckoning without First Abiding:** Healing is incomplete if abiding is not included in the reckoning process because the change won't be whole-hearted. Will power might accomplish the goal, but it's not heart-felt nor is it long-lasting. The vitality of the emotional dimension is also lost causing us to become less who we are rather than more because the aspect of self generating the emotion is left stranded and silenced.
Requirements: Abiding requires honesty to acknowledge all feelings.	**Requirements:** Reckoning requires honesty to acknowledge problems

It requires courage to feel what we don't want to feel. Humility is needed to allow ourselves to be vulnerable and acknowledge the existence of aspects of self we don't like or want.	and confront distress, rather than "fighting/ flighting/freezing" distress. It requires courage to make a decision to change our relationship to the aspect of self dealing with the problem. Humility is needed so we can ask for help or reach out to others.
Tools: Abiding will not occur unless we value the role that feelings play in generating vitality. Abiding requires us to give ourselves permission to feel. Abiding requires us to acknowledge and value the part of self that is experiencing distress.	**Tools:** Reckoning tools might include: forgiveness (Chapter 6), integrative letter-writing (Chapter 7), joining a Healing Community (Chapter 8), 12-step programs, a good counselor or accountability partner, Post Traumatic Growth Inventory (Appendix D), etc.
Tension during Change: Any time change is occurring, tension will arise. Abiding the tension requires that we develop a willingness to experience uncertainty, loss of control, and helplessness while change is occurring. (Deep breathing helps tolerate the tension while it is occurring). We have to learn how to stay "at home" in our own feeling skin so we don't revert to old comfort zones.	**Tension during Change:** It is crucial that we strategize ways to resist urges to revert to previous habits, comfort zones, or quick fixes. We have to make a decision to tolerate the struggle of change, developing patience and tolerance for the tension that occurs during transitions. We tell ourselves to stay "at home" in our own uncertainty skin, and we make a plan for how to do that.
Abiding with Others: Abiding is my job. I allow myself to vicariously experience whatever the other person is saying; I feel their feelings, and I am changed and touched by them. I also help the other person feel their feelings,	**Reckoning with Others:** Reckoning is the other person's job. We have to resist the urge to give advice, take the struggle away, or fix things for them. Instead, we create safe emotional environments whereby they can ask for help and receive support.

especially ones they are afraid to feel. I help myself let go of their feelings by reminding myself that they are responsible for themselves, that they need to learn the lessons so that they develop their own inner resources, and that God is with them. I remind myself that I do not want to be guilty of enabling.

Remember that there is always going to be tension prior to change; don't rescue them from that unless it becomes overwhelming for them. Help yourself to let go of their problems by reminding yourself that you are responsible for you, that they need to learn the lessons so that they develop their own inner resources, and that God is with them. Otherwise, we become guilty of enabling.

Appendix B

Coping vs. Reckoning

This appendix contrasts coping mechanisms with reckoning processes. The distinction is similar to weeding a garden. You can cut the tops off the weeds and the garden looks good temporarily, or you can pull the weeds out by the roots so that they are less likely to come back to clutter up the beauty. Coping is cutting our weeds, and reckoning is pulling our weeds out by the roots.

On one end of the coping spectrum are people who don't assume enough responsibility for hurtful actions. When there's conflict in their relationships, it's the other person's fault. On the other hand, some people assume too much responsibility. When there is conflict in their world, they not only shoulder their own guilt, but everyone else's as well. When something goes wrong, they assume they're at fault. They drown in "false remorse," taking on guilt that isn't theirs. The goal is to realize what we are and what we are not responsible for, which is a reckoning process.

Coping	Reckoning
• Is like cutting the tops off our weeds.	• Is like pulling our weeds out by the roots.
• Is a passive, automatic process.	• Is an active, conscious process.
• Wastes suffering by not getting needed lessons.	• Uses suffering as a doorway to awakening.
• Either fails to confront others, living in the illusion that this is "keeping the peace," or bullies others.	• Recognizes that confrontation is necessary, which might stir things up so that change can occur.
• Maintaining the status quo is the goal.	• Changing one's self by letting go of same and opening up to different is the goal.
• Focuses on containing and managing.	• Focuses on opening up to the source of distress.
• Breaks a person down.	• Breaks a person open.
• Diminishes consciousness in the situation.	• Inserts consciousness into the situation.

- Criticizes failures in others or self.
- Is defensive with criticism, only wanting to hear compliments.
- Instinct is to cover up deficiencies.
- Has difficulty saying, "I was wrong."
- Does not recognize the consequences of their actions toward a problem.
- Acknowledges problems in generalities.
- Waits for others to resolve a conflict.
- Thinks that either everyone else but themselves needs help or that everyone else is right and only they, personally, need help.
- Is either arrogant or has low self-esteem.
- Is either independent or needy.
- Is self-conscious. Compares self to others.
- Keeps others at arm's length.
- Creates an illusory world generated with wishes, wants, and excuses.
- Desires respectability, protecting their reputation.
- Has difficulty sharing needs with others.
- Strives for comfort, control, and pride.

- Accepts own humanity. Acknowledges faults.
- Receives criticism with an open spirit, opening up to justified criticism.
- Willing to be exposed. Willing to be human.
- Is quick to admit failure and seek forgiveness.
- Recognizes how they've contributed to a problem.
- Acknowledges specific contributions to problems.
- Takes initiative to reconcile a conflict.
- Has a continual need for inner renewal and discernment. Sorts through ways they need to change and ways they don't need to change.
- Esteems others as no better or worse than self.
- Recognizes need for others without demanding it.
- Is not controlled by appearances or need for approval.
- Is willing to risk getting close to others.
- Lives from a place of integrity generated with hopes, intentions, and reasons.
- Is concerned with being real, protecting their integrity.
- Is willing to be open, transparent, and vulnerable.
- Strives for courage, honesty, and humility.

Eulogy for Joseph McCoy

A eulogy that depicts both the triumphs *and* struggles of abiding and reckoning with our humanity can be very powerful because it captures the truth of who we are. Pat McGuire, a nurse caring for Joseph McCoy, was able to effectively capture the meaning of his life by showing how he redeemed his suffering. Here is what she wrote:

> We are so grateful to have participated in the life of Joseph McCoy. When I first met him, he was in incredible pain. His brow was completely furrowed with deep grooves that looked like a road map. He was not receptive to prayer, hugs, or therapeutic touch. He didn't like to talk about his childhood or the painful memories he still suffered. The Hospice team worked with his medication, but his forehead still looked like a road map. Sometimes Joe would cry and let go of a painful memory and ask for a hug. Many of his memories were of times when he had not been the kind of man he wanted to be. As these memories surfaced, he cried and received love and acceptance. He talked of the pain of his divorce, and I cried with him. It helped me heal the pain of my own divorce. I vividly recall the time when Joe prayed aloud asking for forgiveness, and then we sang *Amazing Grace*. He was able to achieve enough self-forgiveness to allow him to feel the love deep inside of him. After that, he spoke of the love he felt for all of you.
>
> Joe was always thrilled when family members came to visit, yet he was afraid no one would come. You came. He began to trust. His sisters spoke of the forgiveness they had been able to achieve. They gave him love and ice cream sundaes. More family came. Their loving support and forgiveness began to penetrate the emotional pain Joe suffered. He began to open up to the support of the staff and allowed us to love him. Slowly, white lines began to appear on Joe's forehead as the furrows relaxed and skin that had not seen sunlight for years began to appear. Joe became a delight to the Hospice team. He drove his electric scooter by

the desk just to smile at us. He accepted hugs and allowed us to pray and hold his hand.

The Hospice team speaks of Joe often. It was an honor to be with a man who blossomed before our eyes. Because of the healing he was able to accomplish, we have placed street signs along the two hallways marked *Forgiveness Street* and *Peace Boulevard.* They will be signposts for others that highlight the work needed to be done. These signposts will act as a lasting tribute to the work Joe did here and the way he inspired us. Truly, it was a privilege and honor to be a part of Joseph McCoy's life.

Appendix D

Post-Traumatic Growth Inventory

This appendix provides a list of factors that the American Psychological Association (APA) uses in their Post-Traumatic Growth Inventory to assess changes sustained after life-altering events. The scale is useful in assessing a person's relationship to any event, even if it's not traumatic. The APA identifies life-altering events as: loss of a loved one, chronic or acute illness, violent or abusive crime, accident or injury, disaster, job loss, financial hardship, career or location change/move, change in family responsibility, divorce, retirement, combat, and other.

After a life-altering event, five categories of change in a person are measured on a 0-5 scale. These categories of change include: relating to others, new possibilities, personal strength, spiritual change, and appreciation of life. These are the statements about possible changes that a person self-evaluates:

- I changed my priorities about what is important in life.
- I have a greater appreciation for the value of my own life.
- I developed new interests.
- I have a greater feeling of self-reliance.
- I have a better understanding of spiritual matters.
- I more clearly see that I can count on people in times of trouble.
- I established a new path for my life.
- I have a greater sense of closeness with others.
- I am more willing to express my emotions.
- I know better that I can handle difficulties.
- I am able to do better things with my life.
- I am better able to accept the way things work out.
- I can better appreciate each day.
- New opportunities are available which wouldn't have been otherwise.
- I have more compassion for others.
- I put more effort into my relationships.

- I am more likely to try to change things which need changing.
- I have a stronger religious faith.
- I discovered that I'm stronger than I thought I was.
- I learned a great deal about how wonderful people are.
- I better accept needing others.

After a traumatic experience, each of the above statements is answered using a 0 to 5 scale:

0 = I did not experience this change as a result of my crisis.

1 = I experienced this change to a very small degree as a result of my crisis.

2 = I experienced this change to a small degree as a result of my crisis.

3 = I experienced this change to a moderate degree as a result of my crisis.

4 = I experienced this change to a great degree as a result of my crisis.

5 = I experienced this change to a very great degree as a result of my crisis.

Appendix E

Prayers for Public Events

I'm often asked to provide prayer for public functions. When I pray, I include the principles of abiding and reckoning. This appendix provides some of the prayers that I have used.

For Clinicians

I ask that we close our eyes and go into that deeper part of ourselves... that place that connects with peace... that place that connects with Love... that place beyond our material selves... to that place that generates vitality.

Take a minute to think about all the patients and families you've cared for in your career... Think about all the patients and families you are caring for now... Take a minute to acknowledge the difficulty of caring for some patients. Silently acknowledge the struggle it sometimes requires to bring kindness to some people who may not be so kindly themselves. Acknowledge how lonely it sometimes feels; how tiring it can be.

Now take a deep breath and let your breath take you to that deeper place within you... that place where there is energy to love the unlovable... energy to touch the untouchable... to heal the unhealable. Acknowledge your need for this energy and your willingness to receive the vitalizing energy from this deeper place within.

Now, think about all the patients and families that you have yet to care for at some point on their future journey... Thank them in advance for the privilege of serving them. In your heart, ask them to let you abide with them... to abide their heartaches and hope... to abide their suffering. Acknowledge the ways in which you might let them down... Be willing to own that (not in a blaming way, but simply letting it be instructive)... Acknowledge the ways in which you, too, are a wounded healer... In your heart, seek to be re-formed by the wisdom of your patients and their families as they redeem their suffering.

As you leave this space, may you go forth with a blessing.

May each of you leave here today with a deeper sense of who you really are.

May you gain a deeper sense of your connection with each other, your patients, and with your deeper self.

May you have a deeper sense of purpose and greater understanding of your mission in life and in the agency where you provide care.

May you have a profound sense of how important you are to your patients, their families, to each other, to me, to your own families, and to the transcendent energy of this universe.

Mainly, I thank each of you here for having a heart that is willing to suffer the brokenness of this world. Your footprints touch my soul, and I am healed.

For a Women's Day Conference
Dear God,

We are grateful we can join together this day – as women, as men, as people who work together – as people who pray together as we are now. Dear God, we are truly grateful that this country and this institution know the value of acknowledging and honoring the spiritual nature of each one of us, and that we can have this opportunity to gather as we are this moment.

Dear God, as women, we sometimes struggle with our roles in society. Sometimes we feel pulled in many different directions at the same time. Sometimes we strive to adopt a male-like image that may not exactly fit us. Sometimes we try to conform to a male-dominated culture that has not yet completely come to understand the gifts we, as women, offer. Sometimes God, we, ourselves, get lulled into forgetting the value of our womanly gifts. Sometimes we get fooled into believing the gifts valued by society are the molds we should try to become rather than the mold *You* would have us become.

God, help each of us guard against trying to be like men – just for the sake of being like men. Help us be able to discern between "equality" and "mimicking" lest we betray the very gifts of womanhood you have given us – the very gifts you need in this world – the very gifts you created to fulfill our soulful natures. God, help us accept those gifts and give us the courage to resist being anything other than the unique woman you have created each of us to be. Help us know and understand our inner beauty – to know and understand our soulfulness – to know and understand You. Amen.

For Nurse Week Ceremonies

Dear Heavenly Father,

We come before you this day as your sons and daughters, united in the spirit of God. We come before you recognizing the suffering in our world. We ask you this day to open us to our deeper selves so that we might learn the lessons you would have for us in our earthly strife.

We come before you this day recognizing the many gifts that you have provided this Medical Center that allows us to do your healing work. Sometimes, though, we struggle with our humanness. Sometimes, God, we feel so alone as we tend your ill and lame. Sometimes, God, we feel burdened when we are needed to carry the load for someone else or face the tragedies we see each day.

Dear God, it is so hard to see your light in some of our patients. We get frustrated. Sometimes we feel unappreciated or even mistreated by them. Sometimes we feel at odds with our coworkers, and we don't get along with each other. Sometimes, God, it is just so darn hard to love one another. Forgive us when we fail to do that. At these times when we cannot see you clearly, guide us into love. For it is your love that heals the unhealable. It is your love that touches the untouchable. It is your love that comforts the uncomforted.

We are often called to be your angels of mercy. Open our hearts to answer that call. Fill us with your presence so that we may know you are with us on the journey. We come before you this day as a health care community. We ask your forgiveness when we forget that we are not the true healer. We ask your forgiveness when we forget our paychecks are not our true reward.

We ask that you break us open, God. Break our hearts of stone that keep us from feeling you in one another. Break our senses that keep us from seeing and hearing you in each other. Break our spirits open when they fail to yield to your will in our lives.

Dear God, we ask you this day to *re-form* us into the healing ministers you call each of us to be. We ask you to *re-form* us into a *community* of healers. *Re-form* the ministry this Medical Center is called to offer. Broken as we are God, bring us together as we are this day. Wounded healers that we are, help us bring you to all those in our midst. Amen.

For Martin Luther King Day Celebration

Dear Heavenly Father,

We gather here today to remember. We gather here today to celebrate and to act.

We pause to remember that each of us here is a person of prejudice. Sometimes we don't like to admit that, God, even to ourselves. But we know that healing is not ours until we can come before you, confess our humanness, and give you the filters of prejudice in each of our minds that keep us from each other and from you.

We pause to remember Martin Luther King, Jr., – a man of courage and vision – a man who responded to your call to help us confront those dark places where injustice lurks. These dark places in our souls seduce us into thinking that the color of our skin or the characteristics of our bodies are what are important to you.

Also, we remember Martin Luther King, Sr., – a man who calls us into holiness by his example of love for you. A man who had every reason to hate and be bitter with the murders of his wife and two sons, yet he refused to hate and be bitter. He chose to love you and your people instead. We remember the healing image of him sitting with George Wallace[1] and George Wallace asking him to pray for him and we remember Martin, Sr. saying lovingly that he would.[2]

And we celebrate, dear God. We celebrate that in the midst of a broken world, you are here. We celebrate that in the midst of injustice, hatred, and violence is justice, love, and peace if we but choose to turn our face from those shadows of our souls into the Light that is you. We celebrate today the gift of Martin Luther King Jr. and his Dad – men who had the courage to be you in our world – men who have been beacons calling us home to you.

Dear God, our prayer to you today is that these gifts you have given us, will call us into action. We pray the sufferings of our past as a people and as individuals are not in vain, but experiences that draw us closer to your love, your peace, your healing. You tell us we are to pray for our enemies, to pray for those who persecute us, to pray for those who hurt us. Those prayers are so hard for us to do, yet that is our prayer today. Each of us here suffer the scars of pain and injustice in our lives. Help us recognize that our pain and our anger are calling us into the action of drawing nearer to you. Our action today is prayer for all the George Wallaces in our homes, work places, and communities. We pray they might experience your healing love. And we pray for the George Wallaces in ourselves God. Those places inside us that lure us into thinking that our view is the right one and that others are not worthy, those places inside us that deceive us into thinking we are better than others because they are different and not worthy of our respect. We give our prejudices to you, God. We give you the injustice of our arrogance and self-righteousness that separate us from others and ask that you transform them with your love and forgiveness into acts of kindness and mercy that we may be lights in the midst of the darkness of a broken world. Amen.

Appendix F

Quality of Life Gatherings: Facilitation Guidelines

The purpose of Quality of Life (QOL) gatherings is to support successful suffering as people encounter difficulties in their lives. Abiding and reckoning are the primary therapeutic processes used. QOL gatherings are especially meaningful when provided during critical transitions in peoples' lives, such as changing jobs, teenage crises, or facing terminal illness. This appendix supplies a basic foundation of information and skills to facilitate the QOL process in an inpatient hospice unit. However, the knowledge can be applied in any setting, situation, or relationship. The most important thing we bring to QOL is openness and willingness to do it.

QOLs are normally done with the team sitting at the patient's bedside; however, they can be done outdoors or in an area that is meaningful to the patient. QOLs should include all the people who are affected by the situation. If people can not be physically present, conference calls that include everyone can be made. The call is then placed on speaker phone so that everyone can participate.

QOLs are often verbally interactive, but they might not be so. With people who are cognitively impaired or comatose, quiet nonverbal presence may be more effective. Touching and singing also bring comfort.

We want to open doors without pushing people through. Pushing can do damage. Not opening the door also does damage. It abandons people and prevents them from talking about important issues no one wants to talk about, issues they may not even know how to talk about. We are often guilty of not opening doors because we fear pushing, which means we are putting our own comfort needs above the patient's needs. It means we are more worried about making a mistake than learning how to respond to difficult needs of others. You have to have courage to make mistakes. When we do, apologize: "I'm sorry. I can see I overstepped. I apologize for not listening more closely."

Opening Introduction

The opening of the QOL needs to acquaint the participants with the purpose of the gathering. It should also establish time boundaries as well as introductions of everyone present. Examples might include:
- "This is a 30-minute session when we come together to hear what might be on your mind and heart, a time for us to listen. We don't have an agenda. This is your time. We'll start by introducing ourselves."
- "Sometimes we get so busy doing things to patients and for patients that we forget how important it is to just quiet ourselves and be with patients, to listen. So, we take these 30 minutes to just be here with you, to see how you are doing. We'll start by introducing ourselves."
- "We call these meetings our Quality of Life meetings. We don't know what quality of life is for you yet. Our job is to take these 30 minutes together to listen so that we will know how to improve your quality of life. We'll start by introducing ourselves so you know who we are and what we do."

Physical Pain

Although we need to make inquiries into physical pain, the QOL should not stay focused on this dimension. If inquiries make you realize that more time needs to be spent assessing and alleviating physical pain, then the clinician can further assess this factor after the meeting is over.

Emotional Pain

Exploring the emotional dimension of suffering is one of the most important aspects of the QOL. Because several clinicians are present, different perspectives can be provided. Because multiple family members and friends are present, alternative pieces of the suffering puzzle often emerge. I usually start out with a general question about change. Most people want certainty and a guarantee that everything will *not* change. Helping people accept uncertainty as part of life's transitions can decrease their fear. At the heart of all fear of change is an unwillingness to let go of same and open up to different, that is, wanting things to go back to the way it used to be. Helping people let go of same and open up to different brings peace. Commenting on all the changes that they have experienced validates their suffering and also gives me an idea of how they are responding to it:

Validate Changes and Uncertainty:

- "Your life has changed a lot lately."
- "I would guess that you are reeling with all the changes you've had to go through."
- "It's not easy to have to go through all the changes that have happened in the past few months."
- "Your world has really shrunk."
- "Now is a time of uncertainty. Learning to be at peace with the uncertainty is hard."
- "What else is difficult about the limbo that you're in?"
- "I know that _____ (staying on top of things, being in charge, being able to take care of your wife, etc.) has been important. Things are changing now though. More changes might be coming. I'm wondering what things are important for you to let go of so things could go more smoothly?
- "Would you consider letting _____ (same) go?" (cooking dinner every night, working 40 hours/week, putting up the Christmas lights, etc.) "What would happen if you let that go?"
- "How would things be different for you if you were able to let that go?"
- "You have given all your life to your family, to your job, to your country. Now is the season of life when it's your job to accept help from others. You're in the cycle of life where it is important for you to learn how to receive." (Then, pin a "Gracious Receiver" button on them. The "Gracious Receiver" button is especially important for people who are stoic.)

Validate Suffering:

- "You've been struggling with a lot lately."
- "You've had a hard go of it."
- "It takes a lot to go through what you've been through."
- "You've endured a lot."
- "I would guess you're pretty weary with all that has happened."
- "Tell us about the difficulties you've been having."
- "Of all these difficulties, what is the hardest for you to deal with?"

Abide Feelings:

Engage the emotional component of the person's experience. Help them to honestly feel whatever it is they are feeling. Take them into their emotions instead of away from them:

- "I know it can be hard for you to express feelings, but now is not a time to pretend like nothing is going on, that nothing has changed."
- "It may be difficult to express the hurt you may be feeling. It may be tempting to try to hide it and act like everything is going on like normal. It takes a lot of energy to pretend."
- "How's your heart today, your inward heart?"
- Empowering silent voices: "If your _____ (anger, fear, cancer, liver, Deeper Self) could speak, what might it say?"
- I can see you are comfortable talking about your feelings. I'm wondering, though, if there are ever times when you let yourself *feel* your feelings?"

Anger

Many people would rather feel angry than experience vulnerable feelings. Anger keeps other feelings away. Anger often covers up hurt, fear, and helplessness, especially in men. On the other hand, many people have been taught that it's "unlady-like" or ungodly to feel angry, in which case they need encouragement to acknowledge their anger. The approach to anger depends on which end of the spectrum the person is on.

Creating space with someone who tends to hide their anger:
- "I think I might feel angry if something like this happened to me."
- "I'm wondering where your anger is?"
- "I'm wondering why you're not feeling angry?"
- "Sounds like you might feel a little bit angry about all that has happened."
- "What else makes you angry?" (This question takes them into a deeper level.)

Creating space with someone who uses anger to hide other feelings:
- "I'm wondering if beyond the anger, might be a bit of hurt. It can be very hurtful when ____ happens."
- "I'd be hurt and sad if something like that happened to me."

Creating space with patients who anger us. Approach patient when you feel calm and centered. (Remember the Samurai warrior never acts out of vengeance, only for cause.) Come bearing kindness:

- "I find myself angry with you sometimes because you treat me disrespectfully. I want our relationship to change, but I don't know what I can do differently. I feel like we're letting you down somehow."

Fear

- "You look worried about something." (Cite your observation.)
- "I would guess that this is a bit frightening for you."
- "What else might be a little bit scary for you?" (takes people to a deeper level)

Emotional Pain

- "You look down today…" (observation)
- "You seem sort of heavy…" (observation)
- "Of course you are crying. This is a sad time."
- "It's good to see your tears."
- "Your mouth is smiling, but your eyes are not."
- "They say that the only bad tears are uncried tears."
- "What else about this situation might hurt a little bit?"
- "On a scale from 0-10 where 0 is perfect serenity and 10 is complete turmoil, where are you right now?" Patient describes what the number is. Get them to describe what this means to them. Then, "What needs to happen for that number to be a ___ ? (Decrease the number that they give you by 1) What would be different?" (They are revealing to you what they need so they can heal.)

Loneliness

- "It's been a lonely road you've had to journey."
- "It takes a lot of courage to let yourself feel lonely."

Guilt

Don't quickly dismiss guilt or minimize it. Give it time and attention. Be

alert to "false forgiveness" which can be a way to avoid doing the work of for-giveness.
- "Sounds like you may feel a bit guilty about that."
- "Sounds like you let her down when you did that."
- "I'm wondering if you've considered asking for forgiveness about that?"
- "I wonder if you have forgiven yourself for having done that?"
- "Would you be interested in learning how to forgive and let that go?" (only after some exploration of the guilt).

Helplessness

Many roles are designed to protect, fix, do. Helplessness threatens all these. The goal is to become at peace with the helplessness.
- "Is there room for dependence on others in your new situation that you are now facing?"
- "Sometimes helplessness can make people feel angry. Is that the case for you?"
- "How difficult is it for you to let go, to relinquish control?"
- "I know you're a doer and a giver. How are you with receiving?"
- "Are you the kind of person who can accept that things are changing and ask for help?"
- "If you don't ask for help and you need help, what do you do?"
- "It can be very humbling to have to depend on others now."
- "How might pride be getting in your way right now?"
- "What else are you feeling helpless about?" (Takes people beyond sur-face answers)

Point out Incongruities

Remember that only 10% of communication is verbal. Nonverbal commu-nication is often more accurate. Stay attuned to it.
- "You're smiling on the outside, but your eyes seem sad."
- "I know you said you feel 'fine,' but you don't sound like you really mean it. I noticed you sighed as you said it." Beware of "fine" in unfine situations. (Fine acronym means **F**reaked out, **I**nsecure, **N**eurotic, **E**mpty)

Facing Death

Make sure you don't just paint half the picture when explaining options to patients. Explain hospice care too so they can truly make an informed decision.

- "You know what medical care is like because that's what you've been receiving. The difficulty is that your needs are changing and medical care can't help as much now. We have other things that can better help. Your quality of life is important. You might choose a more flexible environment of care like hospice. They will get you outside to smoke, get you a beer, let your family stay with you, go home on pass or out to restaurants, let your pets visit, put you on a motorized scooter so you can enjoy the outdoors, those kinds of things. They are experts at pain management and helping you achieve peace." (Follow with a long pause.)
- "Pretend like you died today. What would be left unsaid or undone?"
- "What are your hopes so that you can achieve a peaceful death?"

Include Family Members:

- "Do you all have the kind of relationship where you can speak openly to each other about what's going on or do you all sort of try to protect each other so that the outside always seems fine and on the inside things are not so fine?"
- "You two have shared so much. I'd hate to think you are leaving each other alone and that you'll miss this special time together. I can't think of anything worse than spending the last few weeks lying to each other."
- "It has to be difficult to even think about letting him go."
- "Your world is going to be very different after he dies."

Opening Spaces to Reckon with Grim Futures:

- "I'm sorry. I wish I *could* do that" (when they're asking for futile treatments).
- Sometimes people think we are God, that we can fix anything, do things beyond our abilities."
- "If there were any further medical treatments we could offer that

would help, we would do it."
- "In spite of everything we're doing, your condition is getting worse."
- "I'm worried about whether you're going to be prepared for the end of your life. Tell me a little bit about what thoughts you have about getting ready for your death, whenever it comes."
- "We can't control the quantity of your life. We *can* control the quality."
- "This is a very precious time of life because you might not have many days left. You might want to think about how you want to spend these days, so that no day is wasted doing something you don't want or distracts you away from what might be important."
- "All of us need to be prepared for death so that when it happens nothing is left unsaid or undone. Whether you die today or 10 years from now, it's good to be prepared."
- "Some people worry that if they talk about death then that it will make it happen or it means they are thinking 'negatively.' If something is so fearful that we can't even think or talk about it, then it has a lot of power over us; it occupies a lot of space and energy."

Peacefulness

Ultimately, the goal of QOL is to help people achieve peacefulness in spite of the turmoil and chaos of change that is occurring.
Unfinished business:
- "If you died today, what would be left undone or unsaid?"
- "Pretend like your loved one died today. Would you have any regrets? A year from now, would you look back at this time and wish you'd said or done something differently?"
- "Hopes change. Your hope has been in the physical dimension, hoping your body would get cured. Tell me about your hopes if that doesn't happen – your hopes about the non-physical dimension."
- Relationships: "What would you hope could happen between you?"

Seven Tasks of Living and Dying Healed

Ira Byock provides the first five steps of living and dying healed: forgive me, I forgive you, I love you, thank you, good-bye.[1] I have added two more steps: let go and open up. I believe that the reason you do the first five steps is so you can achieve the last two. At the heart of successfully navigating any

change is the ability to let go of same and open up to different. For palliative care patients, I make sure that the first four steps are addressed; for hospice patients, I cover all seven steps.

"Sometimes people think there's nothing that can be done. It's true that
nothing more can be done for you physically, but there's a lot that can be
done for healing, for emotional wholeness. There are seven things that will
help accomplish healing. All of us have done things to hurt one another.
None of us are saints. Now is a time to reflect on people you may have hurt
and consider asking for forgiveness. Think about those who have hurt you,
and any hurts you may be holding onto. Consider letting them go, offering
forgiveness. Think about whom in your circle of friends and family may benefit from an expression of your love. Think about those people who have
impacted your life who might benefit from an expression of gratitude. The
next step is the hardest, but the most important, and that is to say goodbye.
Say goodbye to all those that you love and want to hold onto. Say goodbye
to this world and everything in it and open up to the next world (however
you conceive that world to be or not be). Say goodbye to all that's been the
same and get ready to say hello to all that is different. After you've done these
five things, then your new job is to relax and let go. Open up to all that is
new and different that is coming your way. If you are willing to do these
things, you will be more peaceful. It's a good way of living healed too. In
fact, I practice this at the end of every day."

Vision for the Future

- "What hopes do you have for your death?"
- "What would a 'good death' look/be like for you?" (…and if that's not
  possible? What else?")
- "What do you need to do to get prepared for your death, whenever it
  comes?"
- "What do you think death is like?"
- "What do you think life after death is like?"

Power of AND

Try to gain both sides of a story. Invite completeness. Avoid either/or dual-
ism.

- "He sounds like a saint. Can you tell me a little bit about his 'not-so-

saintly' ways? (This approach counters the "canonized by death" syndrome.)
- "He sounds like a demon. Can you tell me about one redeeming quality that he may have had?"
- "Sounds like things are going great for you. I'm wondering about the times when things weren't going so great."

Spiritual Pain

Make sure to distinguish between religion and spirituality:
- "Tell me a little bit about your faith life."
- "How are you doing spiritually?"
- "Do you feel ready to meet your Maker?"
- "They say 'there's no atheists in a foxhole.' Is hospice a foxhole experience for you?"
- "This can be a very important and productive time for exploring the spiritual dimension, a time to ask questions and seek answers. It's a time of questing. Would something like that be meaningful to you?"
- "Sometimes religion hasn't been important to people during their adult lives, but as they're nearing the ends of their lives, it becomes more important."
- "Would prayer or a nonreligious inspirational reading be meaningful to you?"
- Offer a hope: "May you have a deep sense of peace and understanding (based on whatever they need) this day."

Exploring Meaning

Find out what a situation or relationship means by asking questions that tell you the meaning it holds for them:
- "What difference did that make for you?"
- "How has that come to be important to you?"
- "What that tells me about you is that you have been _____ (conscientious, irresponsible, a good role model, a disappointment, etc.)

Life Review

Distinguish between reminiscence and life review. Reminiscence therapy simply recalls stories; we recall stories automatically when we meet with old acquaintances. Life review therapy, however, goes beyond sharing memories. It adds the component of evaluating what the experience meant. So invite stories and then figure out how they mattered or how they made a difference.

- "Tell me how the two of you met." After the story, sum up the meaning: "Sounds like he knew what he wanted right away, but you needed a little more time to know what you wanted."
- "Tell me your favorite story about growing up together." After the story, offer a meaning: "Sounds like you really looked up to your big brother, that he was your hero."
- "What's a funny memory that you will always have about _____?" After the story, sum up what it means to them: "Sounds like you had a good sense of humor, that you were able to laugh at yourself."
- Comment on pictures in the environment. "It looks like everyone except that little boy on the side is having fun in that picture. He looks a little worried about something."

Life Affirmation

- "What does _____ especially love or appreciate about you?"
- "How has _____ been important to you?"

Affirming Qualities that Promote Healing: Honesty, Humility, Courage

Counteract pride, independence, and control by helping people value qualities they have which will transform their experience:

- "It takes a lot of courage to open yourself to your emotions and fears. I admire that."
- "I appreciate your honesty with yourself and with me. It's refreshing."
- "You're accepting life on its own terms now rather than trying to impose your own. It's a humbling process. Humility is a good thing, an honorable quality I see in you."

Military History

- "Tell me a little bit about how things went for you in the military."
- "You probably saw a lot of ugly things in that war. Is there anything

that might still be troubling you a little bit now?"
- "Some combat veterans have told me they lost their soul in that war. Did anything like that sort of happen with you?"
- Thank them for serving our country. Honor them with a flag pin.
- If family members have sacrificed because of their loved one's service, honor them with an American flag angel pin.
- If a person is a Vietnam War veteran, have another Vietnam War veteran pin them with the Vietnam War beads (see page   ).

Self-identified Improvements

- "How can I help today?"
- "What can we do today to improve your quality of life?"
- "Is there anything we can do a little bit differently to make things better?" (Implies that we are open to change and willing to let the person tell us his needs.)

Needing to Interrupt

- "I wish I could hear all of that story, but right now I'm wondering about _____."
- "I hate to have to interrupt you, but I need to know about _____ right now".

Closing

- Provide a warning of approaching time limit: "We only have a few minutes left. Is there anything else we need to know that you can briefly tell us?"
- "Is there anything we didn't address that you wish that we did?"
- Offer choices for closing:
  - Prayer: "What would you like us to pray for today?"
  - Hope for the Day: "We can each offer you a different hope for the day. Your job is to just remain silent and absorb our intentions."
  - Joke
  - Song
  - "We can tell you how you have impacted us today."
  - "We can just say good bye."

General Guidelines for Implementing the QOL Format

- Remember, patients have never died before. They may not know how to do it or what their needs are. Our job is to open the door without pushing: to push damages, to not open the door damages. "Patient-centered care" does not mean that we do whatever the patient says and we're not on the playing field. Also, we have to be careful that we don't get prescriptive, thinking we know what this patient needs without their direction and lead. It's a tension that we negotiate and navigate to get the best outcome.
- *Want* to hear him/her, join him/her. Sit down. Lean in. Have his/her affect reflect on your face. They should be able to see their words in your face.
- Share the questions. Don't provide the answer. Make provocative statements and then let the statement hang in the air: "I would think this is pretty scary…"
- Be curious and with wonderment about their experience: "I'm wondering if you're worried a little bit about what's going to happen to you?"
- Couple ambiguous words (maybe, might, little bit, sometimes, guess, wonder, usually, possibly, etc.) with direct words that might be threatening (death, guilt, fear, etc.): "It sounds like you might be feeling a little ashamed about what you did…"
- Remember people usually get lots of affirmation for being positive and feeling happy. There's not always a lot of people to validate their suffering. Validate it!
- Acknowledge any uncomfortableness, awkwardness, hesitancy, distraction that you might be feeling: "I'm a little hesitant to bring this up because I might be pushing into private business, so I don't want you to feel like you have to answer this, but have there been times when you mistreated your children?"
- For patients that you've done several QOLs with, ask them for a question they want us to answer: For example, they might ask us, "What do each of you think about _____?" (life after death, how you would respond if you had to wait for death to come, etc.)
- With threatening topics, keep a solemn but light-hearted tone.
- Always reinforce expression of feelings by affirming the honesty, courage, and humility it takes to do so.

- Silence

    When to use silence:

    - a. Whenever the patient expresses feelings: Stop! Just experience the feeling with him/her.
    - b. After asking a probing question: Real answers take time. Also, a little anxiety in the air helps take the patient deeper into himself. Instead of a superficial answer, a deeper answer often emerges.
    - c. With older or impaired patients where it takes time to think and respond.

When not to use silence:

Don't use silence if it places an expectation on the patient to perform. Try to avoid putting the patient in that kind of situation. For example, you say to a patient, "Do you remember my name?" He might feel embarrassed if he can't recall your name, or he might feel like he didn't pass your test of name recall. Instead, say: "I know you meet many people here and there's no way you can remember all our names. My name's Deborah and I met you last week when you were in the hospital."

Appendix G

Life Review and Life Tribute Ceremony

This appendix provides a Life Review form, an outline of a ceremony that can be used to enact the life review, and a sample ceremony.

I encourage patients to take every opportunity to enhance their precious time together. These forms are one way to do this. The forms also become precious keepsakes after a loved one's death and can provide a meaningful basis for developing a eulogy or other tribute.

I also encourage patients to complete a Life Review form on each young family member so it can be given to them as they grow older. The young person will then know the meaning they had in the dying person's life, and help give them a sense of their history.

The forms can also be used at other times in peoples' lives. Many people have collected Life Review forms from friends and family members to present to someone for their birthday or a holiday event.

The Life Review form has two parts. One is for the patient to complete on his or her own life, although family or friends should assist. I tell people to ask the questions and get the patient talking while the family/friend jots down some of the responses. It's not so much about completing the form; rather, it's about sharing the stories. The other part of the form is for the patient to complete on other family members and for family members to complete on the patient. I encourage them to consider mailing Life Review forms to family members unable to be present.

I encourage people to come together as a group and share what each has written. This meeting can be a very powerful and meaningful time together. It is a time of recalling stories and sharing them with one another, a final gift that often creates tears, laughter, and cherished memories.

Life Review: Self
(Patient will respond with family members writing the responses.)

One of my favorite childhood memories is

_____
_____
_____

Words that describe me include:

_____
_____
_____

One way in which my military service impacted my life is

_____
_____
_____

One of the most difficult things for me to deal with in my lifetime
has been

_____
_____
_____

The reason this experience was so difficult was because

_____
_____
_____

What I have learned because of the burdens I have endured is

_____
_____
_____

One of the things I am most proud of is

_____
_____
_____
_____

One of the things I like best about myself is

_____
_____
_____

If I were to live my life over again, something I would change is

_____
_____
_____

If I were to live my life over again, something I would not change is

_____
_____
_____

One of the ways I think I have touched other peoples' lives is

_____
_____
_____

One of the things I most want to be remembered for is

_____
_____
_____

If I could give one piece of advice to someone it would be

_____
_____
_____

Something that would bring me more peace right now is

_____
_____
_____

Something I want to say to my family/friends is

_____

_____

_____

Life Review
(Patient will complete reviews on others.)
or
(Family/Friends will complete review on patient.)

My favorite story about my loved one is

_____

_____

_____

_____

A memory that will always make me laugh is

_____

_____

_____

A favorite story from my childhood about my loved one is

_____

_____

_____

A meaningful story my loved one told me about his/her childhood is

_____

_____

_____

A story from the military my loved one has told me that I'll never forget is

_____

_____

_____

One of the things I most appreciate about my loved one is

_____

_____

_____

One way in which my loved one has touched my life is

_____

_____

_____

The difference this impact has made in my life is

_____

_____

_____

A virtue that my loved one has that I want to carry on in my own life is

_____

_____

_____

Something I think would bring my loved one more peace right now is

_____

_____

_____

A hope I have for my loved one right now is

_____

_____

_____

Something I want to say to my loved one is

_____

_____

_____

Life Review Ceremony

Designing a ceremony to formalize the Life Review can also be very powerful. The format should follow the three stages of ritual so that it will be maximally effective. (See Appendix I for more information about designing therapeutic rituals.)

Preparing for the Ceremony

A. Preparing the Honoree. Give the honoree a form that reads: Your life has been important. No one else has walked your path so your footprints leave behind unique impressions that mark your earthly journey. Your path has crossed other peoples' paths. Sometimes your presence has been helpful to others; sometimes your presence has been less than helpful. Whatever your path has been, it has not always been easy to fulfill the meaning for your life. This tribute honors the meaning of your life and helps other people gain a deeper sense of the importance of your journey.

　　　The ceremony in which this tribute will be enacted can be profound ly meaningful. We encourage you to invite any friends and family with whom you want to share this experience. Children, of any age, are welcome to attend.

　　　　We want to work with you and your family to create a ceremony that incorporates the values and principles that are important to you. We need your guidance to do this. With the information you provide us, we can combine secular or spiritual music, prayers, or readings into a celebration that brings meaning and unity to your life experience.
Context of Ceremony:
___Secular (no references to God) ___Spiritual ___Religious
　　　(If Religious is checked, religious affiliation: (_____))
_____ Mixed (incorporate both)
_____ No preference
How important is spirituality to you?
___very ___somewhat ___not at all
If you desire a spiritually-based ceremony, choose the word(s) you are most comfortable using:
___God ___Christ ___Heavenly Father ___Higher Power ___Jesus
___Lord ___Buddha ___Mother-Father God Other: _____

Three songs and three readings will be done. We have numerous selections that are suggested or you can provide your own selections.

_____ Staff to provide appropriate music/readings at their discretion.

_____ Please include the following selections. List one to three choices:

_____ Family to provide the personal selections.

_____ Family request assistance from staff in providing the personal selections.

B. Give or mail Life Review forms to family and friends for them to complete. You can then incorporate the information into the tribute, plus you can give the forms to the patient after the ceremony for a cherished keepsake.

C. Have the patient complete a Life Review form on themselves.

D. Have the patient complete a biographical information form providing stories about his/her life story. For example: "In order to provide a meaningful tribute to you, we will tell a story that reflects the path you have walked. We will need some information so your journey can be reconstructed. In addition to the Life Review form, please complete the following information. Include information about your parents, siblings, places you lived, schools you attended, anything that stands out in your memory."

Your Childhood (ages 0-12):

Your Teenage Years:

Young-adult Years:

Career/Occupation Reflections:

Elder Years:

E. Work with the patient and the family in selecting appropriate readings, music, and reflections.

F. Ceremony (Note how the format follows the three stages of therapeutic ritual described in Appendix I.):

1. Preceremonial Music might include the patient's favorite tunes, hymns, or musical traditions.

2. Introduction. Explain why you are gathered and what is going to come so the group knows what to expect. For example: "This is a day of pain and joy as we celebrate the meaning of Edwin Jones's life. We will pay tribute to your story and honor who you are. It is also a day of sorrow, as we anticipate your leaving us and we learn to let you go. Though your remaining days are few on this Earth, your story lives on in the lives of others. I just encourage all of you

to allow yourself to laugh and cry today. Let yourselves feel all of the tumultuous feelings you may be experiencing."

3. Reading (Something that acknowledges the temporariness of life). A Bible reading might include the classic Ecclesiastes 3:1-8. Readings from the *Rubaiyat,* the *Koran,* Marianne Williamson, Kahlil Gibran, etc. are also fitting.

4. Opening Prayer or Inspirational Reflection or Poem. The selection should reflect the temporary quality of life and acknowledge the pain of letting go. (For example: "Dear God, We come before you this day, as your sons and daughters, united in the spirit of God. We come before you, grateful for the life of _____. S/He has walked a path among us, and we have come to know him/her in a way that brings sadness and joy as we gather here today. And so we ask that you gather us in. As we hear _____'s story today, open our ears to hear our own stories. Open our eyes to see the inspiration of his/her life so we can change our own lives. Gather in all of our pain and sorrow. Gather in all of our laughter and love. Make it your own. For we are uncertain about what lies before us, and it hurts to let go of what we have known and loved before. We know that the tears we have for the losses we are feeling are your tears. We know that you feel our pain and our fear. We know you long to comfort us and bring peace to our souls. And so we offer our sorrows to you, knowing that beyond our sorrow is a place that knows no sorrow, a place where our souls are free, a place that dances with the song of our hearts, a place that is you. Amen.")

5. Song of Separation. Selections might include hymns with a theme of the temporary quality of life: "I Come to the Garden," "Shepherd Me Oh Lord," "Gather Us In," Messiah chorales. Secular songs might include "Everything Must Change," "How Can I Help You Say Good-bye," "What a Wonderful World," "Somewhere over the Rainbow," "Turn, Turn, Turn," "Dust in the Wind."

6. Life Story. Read a biography of the patient's life that is a compilation of information provided in the biographical form and the Life Review forms. (See end of this appendix for an example of a Life Story I wrote for my father.)

7. Transition prayer. Preface prayer with: "We all have hurts that

linger in our minds and hearts that need releasing so that forgiveness and healing can enter our lives. At this time, silently bring anything that might be bothering you about _____ (name of honoree) to your mind. (pause) Likewise, _____ (name of honoree) bring anything or anyone you want to release into your mind."

After a pause, provide a prayer, such as: "Dear God, We so thank you for the life of _____. S/He has been a (wo)man of _____ (list characteristics such as: perseverance, courage, persistence, hard work, generosity, graciousness, etc.). S/He has touched the lives of others in ways that only he/she could. It is true that there have been times when s/he has stumbled and fallen. There have been times s/he has hurt others and let them down. We ask your forgiveness for those times when _____(name of honoree) ignored your will in his/her life. (pause) And for any of us here who still hold onto hurts or those who may have places inside that are dark or not completely smiling when they think of _____(name of honoree), we let that go now. Not for _____'s (name of honoree) sake, but for our own. (pause) For anything that anyone here has done that brought hurt or harm to _____ (name of honoree), we ask your forgiveness. We, too, have stumbled along the way and we seek your healing upon these broken places in our hearts. (pause) As your healing love fills our relationships with peace, we feel the comfort that you bring to our lives, and we thank you for the gift of forgiveness. We pray that our wounds might be made holy by becoming a source of understanding and strength to others. Amen"

8. Song of Transition. Hymns might include: "Amazing Grace," "Eagle's Wings," "Be Not Afraid," "Abide with Me." Secular songs might include: "As Time Goes By," "Only an Ocean Away," "Take my Heart to Higher Ground," "Distant Shore," "Let It Be," "Wind beneath my Wings," "Perfect Day," "You'll Never Walk Alone."

9. A Reading. Acknowledging the need for forgiveness and letting go are appropriate themes.

10. Family and Friend's Tribute. Read Life Review forms of people not present and also invite spontaneous affirmation from those

who are in attendance.

11. Song of Integration. This song should be upbeat with a sense that there is hope for renewal. Hymns might include: "Sing a New Song," "I Danced in the Morning," "Awake and Greet the New Morn," "All is Well with my Soul." Secular songs might include: "Spirit in the Sky," "I Believe," "I Hope You Dance," "Love Can Move Mountains."

12. Reading or Prayer of Integration. Close service with a reflective reading or prayer, such as: "Dear God, We thank you for the many feelings that we have experienced here today: joy, pain, faith, sorrow, assurance, fear, love, dread. We honor all of these feelings because we know it is through our humanity that we meet you. In the midst of our despair is your hope. In the midst of our fear is your love. In the midst of our darkness is your light. Thank you for that. Help _____ (name of honoree) know that just as you will care and comfort him/her, so too, you will care and comfort us. For you are the alpha and the omega, the beginning and the end. There is no place we can be that you are not there. As difficult as it may seem at this moment, all is unfolding as it should. We recognize that there is a vision greater than our earthly eyes can see. Thanks be to God. Amen"

13. Stand (military song if a veteran)

14. Salute

15. Hugs

Sample Life Story Tribute

This is the Life Tribute that I wrote for my father's funeral. It is actually what propelled me to initially develop the Life Review forms so that a Tribute could be delivered *before* someone dies. This example will help you see how stories gathered from the biographical information forms plus the Life Review forms can be compiled into a meaningful narrative.

I always pictured your childhood like the adventures of Tom Sawyer and Huckleberry Finn. Maybe it's because I heard how you canoed behind the paddle boats on the Ohio River. Maybe it's because you were such a prankster. There was the time your Mother told you to escort your teenage sister home from work so she wouldn't be scared. You escorted her all right. You hid behind trees making her think someone was following her, and she ran screaming all the way home. There was the time you put the kittens in the butter churn to see if they could save you work by churning the butter for you. There was the time the coal wagon driver told you "Whatever you do, don't touch the mules' heels or they will spook." Little did he know who he was talking to. They say the mules didn't stop until the edge of town. But it was little brother, Morgan, who took the brunt of most of your pranks. There was the time you were walking the train trestle, and you pretended your foot was caught in the switch. You told Morgan, "I guess I'll be here when the train comes. But, you go on. Save yourself." Morgan started crying and stayed there with you, saying, "I won't leave you, Brother." Morgan didn't leave you that day, and he never left you a day after that either.

I didn't hear too much about your high school years except that you only weighed 97 pounds, and you helped the baseball team win the 1937 state championship. You also tried out for the St. Louis Browns. They told you to come back after you gained 40 pounds. Mainly, I heard stories about how you courted a girl named Juanita. Nothing slowed you down in your pursuit. When you broke your ankle and were on crutches, it didn't stop you from walking the mile to her house. When she was quarantined with scarlet fever, you came to see her each day, pushing the crack in her window through so you could touch fingers. You conspired to get Juanita to marry you by hedging your bet: paying a month's rent on an apartment and then asking her to marry you so you wouldn't lose your deposit.

You started working at a paint and varnish company. You started out washing beakers and cleaning the lab. That led to an interest in chemistry and taking classes at the University of Evansville. Your career had begun.

Meanwhile, you and Juanita had bought a little house where you could raise a few chickens and grow a fine garden. Soon you had a baby son and a few years later, a daughter. With your family growing and your job more secure as the manager of the varnish plant, you decided to build a house, a house you would live in until you died. Shortly after you built your home, I was born.

By now, your son was picking up the baseball mitt you had retired and many a summer was filled with your coaching and managing the Little

League and Pony League teams. You won some county championships, and I suppose that was important; but I think you taught the boys more than how to play baseball. There was the time the umpire couldn't see if your boy was tagged out on second base. The ump said since he didn't see it, he would call your boy "safe." But you simply turned to the boy and asked him if he had been tagged and the boy said "yes." You ended up losing that game, and many criticized you because your action changed the call. However, you were like that. The truth was the truth, and that made things pretty simple. In fact, I don't think you ever told a lie in your whole life, leastways in your adult life.

Your children were growing up now. Juanita says you two had always wanted four children, but you just couldn't make up your minds. The years went by, and I guess in your indecision, your fourth child had to make up your mind for you. So in your mid-40s, you were finally blessed with the daughter who completed your family.

There were lots of Sunday morning breakfasts at Lincoln State Park with family and friends. There were Thanksgiving meals and summer reunions in Kankakee at your sister's farm. Then, there was your 50th wedding anniversary at French Lick; there was music, dancing, and snowman-making, hiking, skiing, and much joy and laughter.

You were also a great outdoorsman and naturalist. You knew most of the woods around Evansville and had spent almost all your life hunting squirrel, rabbit, or quail. Sometimes, you went with your birddog, sometimes you went with your brother, sometimes you went with your son, and sometimes you went by yourself. However, you always went with God. You said you always felt close to God when you were out there in the world of nature and beauty. You had a wonderful appreciation for His world and you knew so much about His wonders. You could talk in great detail about most any bird, fish, animal, plant, tree, or natural phenomena. You told me recently it was beyond you how anybody could study the order and beauty of the universe and not know for sure that there was a God.

You also loved to play golf. It wasn't so much the golf, but being outdoors that delighted you. Tee-off time was 6 A.M. Saturdays, and I was usually at your side as your caddy. Then there's the fishing. I remember fishing with you many a morning when I was a little girl. You caught bass, croppy, and blue gill. Then, you discovered saltwater fishing in Florida when I was an adult. Fishermen are known for their patience and persistence. You definitely had persistence, but you had a most impatient style. No matter where the boat was anchored, you were sure the fish were 50 yards in a different direction. Most holes were fished out in 10 minutes if you weren't getting a bite. Hardly a day went by you weren't calculating tides, buying shrimp bait, and plotting weather reports in your quest to outsmart those fish. With great enthusiasm you would tell of your catches: trout, catfish, pin fish, flounder, a few shark, and sting rays. It didn't matter. It was all fun to you. Anything you caught was an adventure.

Actually, almost everything was an adventure to you. You were interested in about everything and that made you interesting. Even food was an adventure. I don't think there was any food you didn't like: pickled pig's feet, Limburger cheese, dandelion greens, morels, raw corn, raw soybeans out of the field. It didn't matter. And then there was your cooking. Ann always said, "Old chemists don't retire, they just move to the kitchen." The kitchen became your new laboratory, and recipes were your new formulas. Unfortunately, you also continued to enjoy your consumption of beer. I say "unfortunately" because by the end of the day, you were sometimes withdrawn and distant, and we missed you.

As I said earlier, you loved kids, and your grandkids were no exception. You loved to be with them, and they loved to be with you. They spent summers and vacations with you and you instilled biology and chemistry lessons in them whether you all were fishing, or hiking, or feeding the squirrels, or setting up feeders for your birds, or building a fire in the fireplace. You weren't much on hugging or cuddling, but you were big on patting and pinching cheeks, and you were very big on making them feel important.

Just like that train trestle, your brother Morgan never left your side. He said it began as hero-worship when he was a child and developed into respect as an adult. You worked at the same paint and varnish company together, golfed, went to the race track, hunted, watched football, and vacationed together. Morgan says that in all these times, he can never remember an argument. He says he's known and loved you all of his 69 years, and he has a hole in his heart that no one else will be able to fill.

Your children share similar sentiments. Jeff will remember that you

were always there for him. He could always count on you for help and support. Sidney says what will always remain with her is that you were a plain-
spoken man who was never impressed with the flashiness of the world
because you knew and lived the truth. Your gifts to Ann have been your
humor and your love as a father and grandfather. You taught her many
things including the importance of responsibility and self-discipline. For
myself, your gift to me was simply that you loved me; you loved my husband; you loved my children; you loved my brother and sisters; you loved
my Mom. By doing that, you made my world a better place for me to live.

I guess the real measure of a man may well be how he loves his wife.
Your love was tested when Mom had her stroke four years ago. Your devotion was beyond words. We were worried about how long you could maintain the energy and effort it took to care for her, but it never seemed to phase
you. You told me: "I love her. I *want* to do it," saying it was not a sacrifice.

So, you can see how hard it is for us to let you go. We hold on to those
things we love and we love you. But, as hard as it is, we let you go today. You
go to join your brother and sister who preceded you, and your Mother and
Father before them. And it will only be a blink of an eye, before the rest of
us here today will join you too. You have lived a good life Edwin Jones, and
as God welcomes you home to His kingdom today, He says to you: "Thank
you for loving my people." We thank you for loving us too.

Appendix H

Forgiveness Inventory

This appendix is an enhancement to the self-awareness exercise in Chapter Six. Forthrightly reviewing these questions can help uncover guilt, shame, and unresolved conflicts. It can also reveal tendencies to be overly forgiving, causing enabling. It can help uncover any wounded aspects of self that are still waiting to be reintegrated into the conscious self so that forgiveness work can begin.

- Is there anyone I harbor resentment toward?
- Are there any relationships that are suffering because I'm still holding onto hurt?
- Is there anyone or anything toward which I'm keeping my heart closed (which means that I'm closing myself off from the source of my own vitality)?
- What aspects of my wounded self are still waiting to be reintegrated into my conscious self?
- In what ways have I utilized "false forgiveness" to avoid reintegrating my wounded self?
- What have I done that I feel guilty about? Is the guilt unreasonable and so I need to let it go? Is the guilt reasonable prompting me into action to make amends?
- In what ways do I need to forgive the world for being like it is?
- In what ways do I need to forgive God for not making the world the way I want it?
- What do I need to forgive my body for?
- Is there any situation from my childhood that I have a sense of regret or unfairness? (genes, poverty, abuse, neglect, sibling rivalry, looks, education, etc.)
- What have I done that I'm unwilling to forgive myself for?
- Is my determination to maintain control related to someone or something that I've not forgiven?
- Is maintaining a façade so that I don't let myself be vulnerable interfering with my ability to forgive someone or something?

- Am I willing to be free of resentment and blame?
- Am I willing to stop being the victim?
- What benefits are there for allowing myself to continue being the victim?
- Do I want to forgive?
- Am I willing to make a decision to forgive?
- Am I willing to do the work of forgiveness?

For these latter three questions, ask yourself how willing you are to do the work of forgiveness. (Unlike desire, intention will manifest itself in actions. You might *want* to forgive, but have no *intention* of doing so. There's no point in fooling yourself by doing forgiveness work if you have no *intention* of changing):

"On a 0-10 scale, how willing am I to change my relationship with this problem?"

"On a 0-10 scale, how motivated am I to do the work of forgiveness?"

"On a 0-10 scale, how willing am I to let go of _____ (bitterness, resentment, denial, resistance, control, etc.)?"

If your intention number is above a 7, you are probably ready to do the work of forgiveness. If your intention number is below 7, then your intention needs to change before doing the work. So tape a piece of paper to a mirror that reads: "I *am willing* to forgive _____ (myself or name of someone or a situation), and I *intend* to do so." Repeat this several times in a mirror for a month and then re-scale your intention. Don't try to force this. You might also ask a few other trusted people to pray that you receive help and insight to increase your willingness to forgive.

Overly Forgiving

Commonly, some people are overly forgiving. They allow others to take advantage or disrespect them. They make excuses for them and fail to hold them accountable. If they do speak up, the offender only has to say some apologetic words and the person believes the actions will not recur. This fosters enabling. It erodes self-respect. It also short-circuits the process for either party to discover their interior hero.

- Is there anyone that I let take advantage of me repeatedly?
- Is there anyone that I let treat me disrespectfully habitually?
- Is there anyone that I tend to believe what they say rather than what they do?

- "On a 0-10 scale, how willing am I to stand up for myself?"
- "On a 0-10 scale, how motivated am I to risk the other person's disapproval or displeasure?"
- "On a 0-10 scale, how willing am I to let go of enabling so that I can meet my interior hero and they can meet their's?

For these latter three questions, ask yourself how willing you are to do the work so you can stop being overly forgiving. (Unlike desire, intention will manifest itself in actions. You might *want* to stop enabling, but have no *intention* of doing so. There's no point in fooling yourself by doing the work if you have no *intention* of changing):

If your intention number is above a 7, you are probably ready to do the work of learning how to stop enabling. If your intention number is below 7, then your intention needs to change before doing the work. So tape a piece of paper to a mirror that reads: "I am *willing* to stop enabling _____ (myself or name of someone or a situation), and I *intend* to do so." Repeat this several times in a mirror for a month and then re-scale your intention. Don't try to force this. You might also ask a few other trusted people to pray that you receive help and insight to increase your willingness to stop enabling.

Appendix I

Therapeutic Rituals: A Forum for Reckoning with Change

For healing to be complete and heartfelt, the unconscious mind must be engaged. Rituals provide access to the energy of the unconscious. This appendix will help readers value the therapeutic role of rituals. Once these rituals are valued, I hope that people will learn how to use them to navigate important changes in their lives. When combined with integrative letter-writing (Chapter Seven), it becomes a powerful tool for abiding hardships and reckoning with the changes needed to create healing.

The Power of Myth,[1] a book by Joseph Campbell, awakened me to the value of myths and rituals and their relationship to the change and recovery process. To my scientific mind, myths were untruths. Yet, here this brilliant professor was showing me how myths spoke *truths* about personhood and humankind. Just as parables (stories that are not "factual") are used because words cannot completely represent truth, so too do myths embody larger truths. Myths use symbols that access the energy of the unconscious. Campbell reminds us that truth is often hidden in symbols, requiring non-physical eyes to see it.

Joseph Campbell spoke similarly about rituals. To me, the word "ritual" meant a habit that was empty of meaning; it meant actions that were robotical, automatic, habitual. However, Campbell writes that the rituals to which he speaks are just the opposite. They are filled with meanings that provide maps for navigating change. They provide order in the midst of chaos, helping things fit together. Their purpose is to transform the experience by bringing congruence to what was initially incongruent. The ritual does not fix the problem but rather opens us up to a deeper interior dimension that allows us to be at peace with the changes that have occurred. Just as myths speak a larger truth of the unconscious, so do rituals.

The term "ritual" often has a negative connotation; people sometime associate it with cults or gangs. Unsavory groups do take advantage of ritualized forums, but they also use forums such as speech and books to disseminate their message. Yet, the rest of us don't stop speaking or reading for fear it might link us to something sinister; neither should we fear rituals. In fact, the more I learned about rituals, the more convinced I became of their therapeutic value. The more I let go of my preconceived ideas about what I thought rituals were, the more I became open to their effectiveness in reckoning with change. I realized that in times of uncertainty, loss, and change, therapeutic rituals provide a format for letting go of the old, integrating the uncertainty of change, and redefining a different, hopeful future. I became so convinced of the value of rituals that I designed my graduate school master's thesis on the relationship between rituals and hope. I embarked carefully upon the study of designing therapeutic rituals that could be used clinically to provide support, guidance, and hope for hospice patients and families as they faced the uncertainty of changes that accompany death.

Creating Therapeutic Rituals of Healing

In my study of therapeutic ritual, I learned the importance of choosing symbols for rituals that have shared meanings for the individual or within the group. I also learned about the three stages of ritual: separation, transition, and integration.

Separation Stage

The purpose of the separation stage is to acknowledge the problems and difficulties that make change necessary and to recognize the need for a person to separate from their former roles or behaviors. During this stage, there is a request to reframe unwanted change into an *intention* to change. For example, military rituals are formatted with highly evocative styles and symbols. Patriotic music and American flags activate unconscious images that motivate new identity and new will. Induction rituals help new recruits separate from civilian identity. Uniforms are issued, and heads are shaved. Recruits are sometimes ridiculed for their former immature, lazy, and civilian ways.

Many religious rituals might begin with a confession of sinfulness, asking for God's help to separate them from their thoughts and actions that interfere with more godly ways. Funeral rites or memorial services start with the acknowledgement of death and the need to face life without the loved one.

This separation stage is crucial in creating an effective ritual. In a grief-denying, "never say good-bye" culture, it's tempting to skip the separation stage so that we don't have to give adequate time and energy to articulating the need for change and separation. For example, modern funeral ceremonies sometimes try to skip this essential stage by proclaiming, "This is a day to celebrate, not grieve." Unfortunately, this eliminates a safe space to grieve, the very thing the participants need. Not only that, if the need for change is not openly expressed, the silence reinforces fear of the problem, heightening the control it unconsciously exerts. The whole point of a therapeutic ritual is to create a safe environment whereby the problem can emerge from hiding so its power can be diminished and the person's empowerment to deal with the problem can be consciously enhanced.

Transition Stage

This stage is often the turning point for acceptance or rejection of the required change. Anxiety or resistance can be anticipated to be highest at this stage. Participants are asked to leave behind the familiar and anticipate a new beginning without knowing what a new beginning will require. Old identities are let go while new identities are not yet secured. Straddling two worlds, people don't feel like they yet belong to either. The transition stage of ceremonies usually focus on educating the participants on ways to navigate toward the desired change.

In the military, the transition stage is used to indoctrinate recruits with a new world view that promotes warrior perspectives during six weeks of basic training. The transition stage in religious rites might include Bible readings and sermons that encourage change and living a more godly life. Funeral rites eulogize the deceased person during this transition stage of the burial ritual.

Integration Stage

The final stage of a therapeutic ritual is the integration or incorporation stage. This stage seeks to instill hope for a future that promises growth. Thus, the ceremony is closed with a sense of renewal and confidence that change can be navigated. A symbol is often given to participants. They are encouraged to let the symbol act as an inspiration to continue with the change, especially when they are tempted to return to old habits.

In the military, the integration phase culminates at the end of basic training with graduation ceremonies that symbolize the new warrior identity. In religious services, this phase might include celebration rites such as communion. In funeral rites, it might include a challenge to let the deceased person's admirable qualities inspire others or assist in filling the gap the person leaves behind, which helps people let go of the world as it has been with their loved one in it. Then, they can open up to a world without their loved one in it.

Rituals to Navigate Unwanted Change

It's tempting to erase a broken past, but the goal of a well-designed ritual is not to remove a painful past because that would only serve to reinforce denial or other "flighting" behaviors. The goal is to develop a different relationship to the past by opening up and integrating the past into the present. Integration instills confidence that the participant(s) can reckon with the past by using it to give their future new meaning. Integration encourages participants to redeem their suffering with new insight from lessons learned. As a result, their destiny is reshaped.

The three stages of ritual also correspond to how we interpret time: past, present, and future. The first stage (separation phase) reflects a new willingness to abide with the past, acknowledging the specific brokenness that has been incurred. The next stage (transition) highlights the present, where a releasing of the past is done and there is a reckoning with the uncertainty and ambiguities of the present. The last stage of integration expresses a willingness to behold hope for a different future.

Campbell's book, *The Hero with a Thousand Faces*,[2] describes how ritualized formats depict the timeless journey all of us are required to make if we are to become heroes in our own lives.

Therapeutic Rituals for Professional Change

I have used rituals professionally when difficult transitions were needed. When our oncology unit developed the hospice program, we didn't anticipate the strife and division it would cause the staff. Creation of new programs with different patients upset the usual pattern of care. Tension and arguments ensued as staff coped with the change. Staff were reluctant to let go of their identity as oncology nurses and expand into the identity of oncology *and* hospice nurses. The new identity was necessary for the unit to function successfully.

I designed a therapeutic ritual to promote the inward changes needed to incorporate the larger identity. During the separation stage of the ritual, each staff member recalled a cherished memory, said good-bye to "the good old days," and acknowledged the difficulty and pain of doing so. Each proclaimed an intention to grow into a new identity that included hospice nursing. Each brought spiritual readings and songs that reflected letting go and saying good-bye. During the transition stage, the anxiety of journeying into unfamiliar territory was acknowledged. Songs and readings that reflected a willingness to stay open to the uncertainty were articulated as well as a willingness to suffer required changes. Each person acknowledged the difficulty of changing and identified something they needed to do to make the transition into hospice nursing. A circle was formed with each person lighting a candle, saying, "A heart that is willing to suffer is a light to the world." The integration stage of the ritual included receiving a small footprints pin with the words, "Know that your journey is sacred and that your footprints are holy." Songs that appealed to the hope of living from our larger selves were sung; a final blessing dispensed.

There were many tears during this ceremony. There was also much change because there was no longer a need to fight or resist. Problems still arose, but they were dealt with openly and with understanding. I subsequently modified the ritual and used it at the conclusion of each "Living and Dying Healed" course I teach.

Therapeutic Rituals Surrounding Illness and Death

Rituals are enacted at time of death on our Hospice unit. These rituals are especially important in our under-ritualized, death-denying, "we-don't-need-a-funeral" culture. A flag quilt replaces the blanket on the bed while family has time with their loved one's body. The body is then transported to the morgue under the flag quilt. As the body passes down the hallway, people often turn toward the passing gurney and pay respect with a salute. The patient is also honored with a rose and footprint with his/her name and date of death placed on the empty bed. The six-inch footprints are made by staff from baked dough. When the dough hardens, it is painted. These footprints honor the veteran and also highlight their separation from us. Other patients see the footprint and anticipate that they, too, will be remembered and treated with respect. This footprint also acts as a trigger in the environment for them to anticipate and prepare for their own deaths. The footprint remains on the bed until another patient comes to occupy it. Then, the footprint is moved to a wall in the hallway that depicts a rainbowed road with the inscription, "Together we walk, one step at a time." The wall with all the collected footprints acts as another trigger in the environment for death preparation. In November, the footprint is moved to a holiday tree and later given back to the family members at a holiday bereavement program.

Another important ritual occurs with the family at time of death. After a loved one's death, an electric candle is lit with the family. The pain they are feeling is acknowledged. The courage to let go is affirmed. Family members are encouraged to tell a few of their favorite stories about their loved one. Each is then asked to write a message to their loved one on the back of the patient's namecard, one more opportunity to address "unfinished business." The card is placed on a stand in front of the candle. A prayer or reading that offers hope and support for continuing without the loved one is provided. Marianne Williamson's book of spiritual prayers, *Illuminata*,[3] is often used. It has one section devoted to prayers for use in therapeutic rituals. A pin with three footprints is then fastened on each person with staff providing a message of hope. "One footprint is yours. One footprint is your loved one's. The third footprint represents all the people who are willing to help you walk this painful part of your journey. May each time you see these footprints, you know you are not alone. May you have the courage to ask for help when you need it." As modern culture continues to devalue grief, as mourning is shortened from months to days, and as funeral services are eliminated, this ritual becomes increasingly valued.

The Grief Recovery group also uses rituals to process grief. Bereaved group members finger paint a picture that reminds them of their loved one. One by one, they light a candle and explain the picture to the group. They also tell their loved one whatever they want them to know or they speak any unfinished business. Then they blow the candle out, while being affirmed that they can meet the challenges of a new world without their loved one in it.

We use ritualized formats that incorporate the three stages of change for several bereavement events. We hold a Memorial service every four months to honor all the veterans who died in the Medical Center. On Memorial Day, we use a ritualized format to provide bereavement care at a picnic. All of these rituals are well attended with more than 200 family members in attendance.

When employees die, especially if it's an unexpected death that leaves unfinished business, I meet with the employees on that unit. A candle is lit, and a memorial card with the person's name and date of death is given to each person. They write their good-byes on it during the opening separation stage. During the transition phase, a picture of the deceased or some other object is passed and each person recalls a story about the deceased person. In the integration phase, each person identifies one quality of the deceased they are willing to let inspire them.

Vietnam War veterans have developed a ritual for honoring one another. Yellow, green, and red are the colors that signify service in Vietnam. Beads of these colors are made by Vietnam War vets and presented to other Vietnam War vets. Only Vietnam War vets can make the beads; only Vietnam War vets can present the beads. Marie Bainbridge, a Vietnam War veteran who works on our unit, presents the beads to our Vietnam vets. She thanks them for their service and welcomes them home from a war that they were often not welcomed home from. The homecoming often takes our breath away when we see the effect the pinning has.

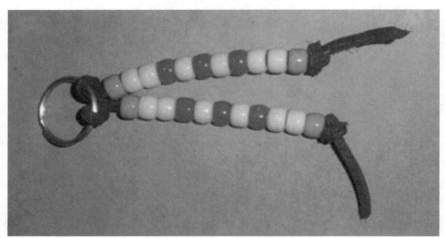

Red, yellow, and green Vietnam War beads

We use a ritualized format for other processes. Quality of Life gatherings include ceremonially presenting veteran certificates and pins, as well as gracious receiver buttons to stoic veterans. Staff support groups utilize the Native American talking-stick[4] ceremony. I often try to ritualize ordinary processes. For example, volunteers make lap blankets; they leave them with the staff to give to the patients. Now, we ask them to write a note about why they made the blanket for them, and we present it to the patient, acknowledging the difficulties they are having, and presenting them with a symbol of care and support. There's a dramatic difference in the impact of the blanket depending on whether the presentation is ritualized.

I use the ritualized format when I do guided imagery with patients. Rather than only visualizing a finished product (for example, an improved relationship), I have patients imagine the process: (1) communicating the problem clearly and without blame (separation from old patterns); (2) opening up to hear the other person and projecting self into the other person imagining how they think, feel, and want to communicate (transitioning into give and take tension of a changing relationship); and (3) imagining accepting the other person's position, whatever it is, without closing off to their personhood so that a new relationship can be born (integration stage).

I also use ritualized formats in counseling sessions and in personal circumstances surrounding loss and change. A loss by death might prompt a written message or letter to give voice to unspoken fears, guilt, anger, and longing. I might encourage the person to read the message at graveside, send the letter on the tail of a helium balloon, or ignite the letter so it goes up in flames. These enactments add further symbolic value that reach into the unconscious for deeper healing.

The end of a marriage might prompt enactment of a ritual surrounding the removal of a wedding ring along with hope for successfully suffering the changes that will be forthcoming. Successfully suffering a divorce can grow a person into their larger self just as unsuccessfully suffering divorce can reduce a person into smallness that hardens and embitters their heart with fear and pain for themselves and their children.

My friends and I have begun birthday ritual adventures that humorously welcome us into "crone-ism." It helps us resist the urge to protest our aging. Instead we open up to its redemptive blessings by valuing the lesson of humility that aging teaches (unless it's bypassed with a facelift). As my 90-year-old mother told me, "It takes a lot of courage to grow old."

Development of Letters to Integrate Difficult Experiences

This appendix provides an example of how to facilitate the letter-writing process. I usually work with people on drafts of letters, rather than encouraging them to send a letter written on their own. Giving someone "a piece of my mind" is seldom received amicably and can even perpetuate hostility. Although it's important to vent anger so the writer can acknowledge it and set boundaries, anger often covers up more vulnerable feelings like grief, fear, or rejection. Until the underlying feelings are abided, integrity is not gained. One way to bypass the experience of feelings, such as grief and rejection, is to delude ourselves into thinking we have forgiven someone when we haven't; it spares us from having to do the work of abiding with hurt feelings and integrating the part of self that is generating those feelings. "False forgiveness" prevents reckoning with the changes we need to make to discover aspects of exiled self that are hurting. This was the case with Lindsay who was estranged from her brother after their father's death. She longed to reconcile their differences and she fooled herself into thinking she had forgiven her brother. Her "forgiveness" covered up feelings of anger, hostility, and arrogance. Here is the first draft of her letter:

Dear Donnie,
    This letter is a long time coming. It comes with much thought and consideration. After decades of hurt feelings and wishing things were better, I have at last come to forgiveness. It's amazing what happens when you come to an understanding of what true forgiveness is.
    I was never the favored one in our family. You were the fair-haired boy and the one most expected to succeed. As much as I tried to win Mom's favor, I was never able to do so. You were it.

Although Dad was my hero, I didn't seem to be his favorite either, although he came to my defense as often as he could. Living under such a suppressive and controlling mother, took most of "me" away. I was just too busy trying to please and receive some sort of positive recognition.

Your attitude toward me was very difficult to accept. I know now you didn't understand my inner struggle to escape the suppression at home. I know you thought me weak, but the everyday struggle to live in the house was not easy. I became successful in my careers, and each time that I achieved a new plateau, I was pushed down by a jealous, controlling mother.

When I finally took a vacation to California with a friend to see you, you completely destroyed the vacation for your own personal gain. That was really a turning point for me with our relationship. It took me a long time to get over the hurt.

Dad appointed me trustee to the estate; he was convinced that I was the better head for business and more competent to manage the estate. Donnie, Dad did not trust you or your wife to be fair with distributions or manage his care. At that point in our lives, I had become more successful than you. I did not say anything to you because I wanted to preserve what little relationship we had as a family. The trust states the reasons I was appointed trustee and the reasons you were not. These are Dad's unsolicited opinions to his attorney not known to me prior to the reading of the will.

Dad was extremely upset by the way you removed him from one home and took him to DeSoto County without his consent or my knowledge. You and your wife, in essence, kidnapped him to try and make your gain. All of the details are stated in the trust. When I went home to sell and clean out the property that he had lived in for 53 years, your complete refusal to help with the exception of a couple of hours was inconceivable. The neighbors were furious with you, Donnie, and Dad was at wit's end. I know you stole items from the house and lied about it because the neighbors told me what you took: the Indian stones from the castle, the tool chest, and the patio set that was Grandma and Grandpa's. I have a letter written by Dad giving me the patio furniture. He did not want you to have the furniture, yet I didn't say anything because I wanted to maintain the peace. I will send you a copy of the trust and the letter if you wish.

Donnie, we are all that is left of our family. I can understand what happened in our family. I am free now in my heart and head. I forgive you for the past and want to move forward from here. I am at last at peace and wish the same for you. Lindsay

I worked with Lindsay to help her see that her anger and resentment remained strong, signals that she had not yet forgiven her brother the way she thought she had. I told her that the letter was important because it helped her see that she had justifiable anger. I encouraged her to use her anger to take a stand with her brother; if she took a stand, she would no longer need the anger. We also examined whether she truly wanted reconciliation with Donnie. It was clear that she did, so I crafted a second draft, leaving some blanks for her to complete. She could then further modify it as she saw fit. I also softened some of her dramatic either/or language ("never," "completely destroyed," "kidnapped," "furious," etc). Note how this draft opens possible perspectives for Donnie and also includes Lindsay's feelings that her anger was hiding, as well as her role in contributing to the conflict in the relationship:

Dear Donnie,

This letter is a long time coming. It comes with much thought and consideration. After decades of hurt feelings, I want to make things better between us. I hardly know where to begin after all this time. I can only tell you how I feel and give you my perspective. My hope is that we can come to understand each other more and maybe start talking.

I always thought that I was not the favored one in our family. You were the fair-haired boy and the one most expected to succeed. As much as I tried to win Mom's favor, I was seldom able to do so. You were it. Although Dad was my hero, I didn't seem to be his favorite either; however, he did come to my defense as often as he could. Even though I knew this situation was not your fault, I couldn't help but feel jealous and angry. No matter what I did, it didn't seem good enough; it seldom got me the attention that you got. This neglect left me feeling sad and inadequate. I thought something was wrong with me. Living under such a suppressive and controlling mother, took most of "me" away. I was just too busy trying to please and receive some sort of positive recognition. In your shadow, I felt like I was a nothing. I know now you didn't understand my inner struggle to escape the suppression at home. I know you thought I was weak, but the everyday struggle to live in the house was not easy for me. My struggle to survive was important at the time. You may not be able to understand my attitude because from my viewpoint, life in our house was not a struggle for you. On the other hand, I realize that you probably had a different set of struggles, and I was just too consumed with my own survival to notice.

I became successful in my careers and each time I achieved a new plateau, I was pushed down by a jealous, controlling mother. (How? Explain so Donnie can understand. Also, is some of your anger toward your mother getting directed toward Donnie? If so, you might want to acknowledge that.)

I took a vacation to Texas with a friend to see you. I was hoping to _____ (what did you want to accomplish?) Instead, I ended up feeling hurt and devalued because you had other things to do and didn't seem interested that we were there. Although I hate to admit it, there's part of me that is still angry about that. I realize now that I probably didn't _____ [...check with you about whether you wanted us to come? ...or maybe I should have been more sensitive about _____ (plans you already had?) ... or maybe I should not have assumed _____. Lindsay, try to use the above section to take more responsibility for what happened.] At any rate, it was a very big disappointment to me, and although I've tried to convince myself that it didn't matter and that I didn't need or want a relationship with you anymore, I realize now that that simply isn't true. The fact that I still feel hurt and angry about it helps me realize how important you are to me.

I know there are also hard feelings about Dad's appointing me trustee to the estate. Donnie, this was Dad's decision. It was not my fault nor was I the cause of his decision. I did not say anything to you because I wanted to preserve what little relationship we had as a family. I don't know all that happened with you and Dad's property, nor do I need to know. I know Dad was upset with you, but that is between you and Dad. It does not involve me. The neighbors said you took some of Dad's things. Donnie, if you did things that were less than honorable, then that is on you. My hope is that whatever happened, we will both be able to let those things go and start fresh because we are all that is left of our family.

Sometimes, I can't quite understand what happened in our family. I realize that in many ways, we don't really even know one another. As children, I was too jealous of the attention you got to see who you really were. Now with these many years that have separated us, I've missed knowing you and your family as adults. I hope we can move forward from here. I wish you peace and offer my love. Lindsay

I had no further contact with Lindsay, so I'm not sure how this story ends, but I know that the second letter has a greater probability of producing her desired effect than the first because false forgiveness seldom yields authentic results. I also think that Lindsay would benefit from writing a letter to her mother and then doing some inner work to develop a nurturing "internal mother." It's also quite possible that Lindsay never mailed the second letter if she wasn't yet ready to be more vulnerable with her brother and also herself; only she would know.

Appendix K

Integrative Letters

This appendix provides examples of letters that people have written so they could abide and reckon with difficult issues, such as: death of a loved one, childhood abuse, broken relationships, divorce, and adoption. Each letter is a glimpse into the world of its writer, a story unto itself. The purpose of each letter is to integrate the aspect of self dealing with difficulties rather than trying to banish or hide these aspects from themselves or others. This approach requires the person to exert honesty, courage, and humility so they can access the energy of their larger selves. They can then be restored to wholeness by integrating the part of self that has been left broken, neglected, or unheard.

When I counsel people, I usually don't jump to letter-writing immediately. I take at least one session to assess the issue and to determine if the person is ready, willing, and able to reckon with it. Then, I often give people this appendix to read, or specific letters that relate to similar issues they are facing. Reading other peoples' letters gives them ideas for approaches to their own dilemma. It also instills them with courage. I tell people that when they write the letter they should consider the seven tasks of living and dying healed: forgive me, I forgive you, I love you, thank you, good-bye, let go, open up.[1] If they have completed their Life Story, then I ask them to review it to see if there are people or events that they could write letters to so that their relationship with the person or thing could be changed. If they have banished wounded parts of their own selves, I ask them to write letters back and forth between the wounded self and the conscious self. I usually start by having the conscious self ask questions to the wounded self, such as, "What do you need in order to heal, feel nurtured, and cared for?"

Letters to Heal Neglect and Foster Self-discovery

Abiding and reckoning with feelings of insecurity can be important in healing issues that affect identity, such as adoption, neglect, or abuse. Letter-writing helps develop perspective so forsaken aspects of self can be integrated home. The first letter demonstrates that it's never too late to grow the inward parent we need. We can grow an inward mother to nurture the unmothered child living within. Rather than writing a letter to retrieve her childhood, however, this woman chose to draw a picture of herself as a neglected little girl. She developed an accompanying story:

> "Far out in a silent, marshy, misty bog sits a small simple boat. It has no motor, and it's just floating in one spot as if anchored. It's dark there 24 hours/day, and there is no land in sight. In the boat, sits a young girl about five years old, her melancholy face expressionless. She is alone, looking into the darkness trying to see something although she doesn't know what she's seeking. I can only see her upper body. Her legs and feet are hidden by the boat. She makes somber, detached eye contact with me. She's afraid to speak. If she did, who would listen? She has been there for so long, unnoticed and unloved. She doesn't grow any bigger as the years go by. She just waits and waits.
>
> I have an overwhelming desire to reach her, to remove her from the boat. But how do I do it? Then, I hear how others have coaxed their abandoned child home, and I decide to reach her via a long, narrow, wobbly bridge which floats on the water. She won't come out of the boat. Next I try a sleek motorboat, but this makes too much noise, and it's too fast. She's too frightened to come out. Now, I step into a small, shallow rowboat and row, ever so slowly. The water remains calm. As I extend my hand to her, she reaches out, and I gently help her into my boat."
> (C. Steiner)

Later this woman told me she was reading a storybook to her boys: "I noticed my little girl looking longingly from me in that small abandoned boat. In my mind, I once again stepped ever so carefully into that quiet rowboat and silently made my way over to her. As I reached my hand out to her, she hesitated, but then slid her hand into mine as I assisted her back into my boat. Funny how I could keep on reading to my children while I did this simultaneously."

The next letter was written by Suzanne, a woman who discovered she was adopted. Her letter to her birth mother reflects her journey:

Dear Sara,

I can't imagine how hard it was for you to give me up, give me away as I thought of it as a child. You were a scared, confused young woman of 17. It must have been very hard, as I've since learned from your sisters, Joyce and Barbara.

As an egocentric child, I never thought of how hard it was for you. I just thought of how hard it was for me. I was told in hushed secrecy that I was adopted; the feeling and the implication I received was that there was something wrong with me, that I was somehow defective, unloved, and unwanted by my own mother!! I was even told I was born with two strikes against me.

Adoption was a subject kept secret in that era, and my adoptive mother, Lillie, would get very upset if I even mentioned it, let alone asked about you. She didn't even tell my younger sister, who was her biological child, until she was 16. Needless to say, my sister had figured it out by then. I didn't look like anybody else in the family. Also, Lillie became very upset when I wanted to tell my fiancée. My fiancée!!

Nobody told me that you married my father, but you fought a lot and so you divorced shortly after you gave birth to me. You weren't living with him, and I'm not sure he even knows about me. Aunt Joyce said that when you got back to Jacksonville from Tampa, where you went to have me, that you told him there was no baby.

Nobody told me that you and my grandmother took me from Lillie for a little while. Nobody told me how afraid you were of your father, and how tortured you were by your decision to not keep me. Nobody told me that you always wondered about me and had tried to find me. Nobody told me that even though you bore three sons, your life was so unhappy that you took your own life.

I only found these things out years later when I was almost fifty. I had gotten serious about finding you; it was a long and complicated search. I learned a lot about adoption and adoptees at a time when it was one of society's shameful subjects. When I found your name on the property tax rolls, I was ecstatic. How crushed I was when I found out you were long dead. I felt as if you had died right then because for me, you had. I try not to be jealous of my friends who still have their parents.

Now that I know how much you suffered, how can I blame you? I can't. I won't. But I am so, so sorry I never got to know you. I look for clues from my relatives and have a surge of pleasure when they tell me, "You look so much like Sara." I look for clues, but don't find many from your three sons, my half-brothers. But your Steve has a lot in common with my Tommy.

I miss you, Sara, as I have missed you my entire life. Lillie's long gone now, and I miss her too. Once, in the throes of a fever, I had a dream or a hallucination, I'm not sure which. You, Lillie, and my grandmothers surrounded me in a circle, holding hands. You were all loving me, helping me fight the fever, and I could see the circles of women around you, going back generations. I felt connected to all humanity. It was a wonderful dream, and I cherish the memory.

So what can I say to you, dear Sara? The simple things, really. The heart of it all:

I miss you.

I love you.

I forgive you.

Please forgive me.

Goodbye.

Love, Your daughter Suzanne

Suzanne said that this letter helped her let go of her feelings of inadequacy that she had harbored since childhood. As a result, she was able to open up to her feelings of self-worth.

The next letter is a good example of a young woman who felt guilty for not standing up for herself or speaking her needs to her perfectionist father. Although Rachel and her father now got along, Rachel continued to harbor feelings from a past incident that subtly sabotaged their relationship. The letter also reveals how perfectionist people project their own needs onto others; they try to control external factors to avoid discomfort rather than making the inward journey to reckon with personal imperfections.

Dear Dad:

Thank you for loving and caring for me. Thank you for only

wanting the best for me. You never want me to make a mistake, but I learn from mistakes. Some of them will be painful, but I will grow and become stronger because of them.

You may still believe that quitting ice skating was a mistake, but I know it was one of the best decisions I ever made. Did I love ice skating? Yes. Do I sometimes miss ice skating? Yes. But skating became something that hurt me. I dedicated my life to skating and I didn't receive the rewards. Instead I received injuries, fear, disappointments, and failures. Of course, I had victories, joy, and courage, but those were few and far between.

I'll never forget the championships in Canada when I performed so poorly. Afterward, you didn't greet me at the edge of the rink like usual. You stayed in your seat and made me come to you. You were ready to leave before awards were presented because I wouldn't be on the podium. Well, what I needed was a hug from you and for you to tell me you were proud of me anyway. I went back and watched the tape, and it really wasn't that bad. I remembered it being bad because of your reaction.

I love you Dad. I have forgiven you for your behavior during the final year of skating and my retirement. I know the loss of my skating career was a loss for you as well. Ice skating became a family venture and a family loss. I have forgiven you for not talking to me for a month after I quit. When you did talk to me, you usually said things that made me cry. When you said you were disappointed with me, what you should have said is that you would miss ice skating and the competition.

I want you to know I didn't make a mistake in quitting skating. I also didn't make a mistake skating for 13 years. I quit when it was time. I know you only want the best for me. I know you love me. I know you want to protect me. Because I know you, I forgive you for disappointing me, for not protecting me when I needed protection and support. I needed your encouragement to get rid of ice skating. It was my life, but it was draining the life out of me. I love you.

Rachel chose not to send the letter to her father. "I don't need to give it to him because the anger is gone now. I have forgiven him, and now I can speak my needs – not only to him, but to others as well."

Josh had suffered an experience that still haunted him years after it had originally occurred. In order to abide and reckon with the secret guilt he held, Josh wrote a letter to a woman whose name he didn't even know. Here is the letter:

Dear ???:

We would not know each other if we met today, but I have thought of you often during the past 23 years. I wonder if you are married, on welfare, happy, an alcoholic, or even if you are alive. On what was to become one of the worst nights of your life, we met. I was one of the police officers assigned to tell you that your husband had been killed during a robbery. My partner and I were chosen to notify you because we were mature, had common sense, and were professional. We were supposed to take you to the hospital to identify the body. When you answered the door with a toddler and pregnant, I was no longer the perfect cop who could handle anything. I held back tears as I lied to you. I said your husband had an accident. I wanted to cry and hold you, but a tough cop can't do that in front of his partner. We placed you in the back seat of our cruiser where we didn't have to look in your eyes, and of course I didn't sit with you. We took you to the station like a criminal, dumping the job of telling you on the commander.

I look back on those days and remember how I loved my work and fellow officers. I was young, proud of my profession, and good at it. I made plenty of arrests; I rarely lost a case in court. I was confident I could handle any situation. I loved the excitement, the danger, the chases, the gunplay, the parties. I was as happy at work as I was at home. Perhaps I loved my job more than my wife and two kids because I no longer have them. I also no longer have my best friend, my partner who was with me that night we knocked at your door. He was later shot to death with his own gun.

I was unable to tell my first wife about you nor was I able to tell my present wife. It starts by being able to tell myself, which I'm now ready to do. I've been crying the whole time I've been writing you, and if I met you now, I would also cry. Just be very sure you know I'm very sorry for what I did not do and say in your time of need. I did not know then what I know now. I ask your forgiveness. I hope and pray you are now happy and at peace.

One of the things I learned about myself that night was that I really do care about people and want to help others. For me, the only way I could do this was by leaving the police force. After that night with you, it no longer felt the same. I no longer felt so cocky and sure. I no longer got pleasure out of chases and arrests. Winning a court case didn't seem to matter so much. I'm a nurse now. If you saw me working, you might not recognize me because you'd see me holding and comforting people. And oh yes, you'd see me crying. I'm not afraid to do that anymore. I'm learning that I have feelings — the man, the veteran, the ex-policeman can cry, care about, and comfort others.

Because of you, many have been spared my macho, cavalier attitude. Because of you, I have brought comfort and compassion to others. I thank you for that. I know it was a high price for you to pay. My guilt has been a high price for me to pay too. Maybe I've held onto it long enough. Maybe, it's time for me to realize that out of your tragedy came a blessing for which I can be grateful. I now have a new life with a wife and two children I love, patients I enjoy caring for, and the fulfillment of being a source of comfort for others.

If I could find you, I would want to tell you this story in hopes that the knowledge of your impact on my life would be a source of comfort to you.

Even though he was unable to express his regrets to the woman he had let down, Josh stated that he experienced significant healing from writing the above letter. "The world opened up in a new and different way," he told me.

This letter addresses unfinished business from a divorce. Although it is written to her ex-husband, Vicki had no need to send it to him because the intent of the letter was really to clarify things within herself.

Dear Mark:
I feel pent-up resentment and bitterness as I start this letter. I'm angry at you for leaving me and our children. You've missed so much. You've left me alone. You've abandoned those you love,

and we struggle not to feel responsible for your choices. I rationalize away the guilt.

Jamie asks me, "Why wasn't I good enough for him to stay?" Being an alcoholic is not the end of the world, but not being willing to change was the end of the world for her and for us. You were unable to cope with the pain that alcohol buried. You weren't brave enough to be honest with the past, a past that you weren't responsible for. You were so afraid to face a past that you had already survived.

I now question Love. I question God. I feel betrayed by Love. When I married you, it never occurred to me that our marriage would not last. Only now am I finally letting myself feel the outrage and shock of saying, "Yes, I'm divorced." I didn't see another way of living without getting a divorce. We had known each other since we were 17. We were married for 20 years, had four beautiful daughters, and the only road I could see was to go on without you. It's hard for me to imagine the you I loved: healthy, eyes bright blue, crooked nose, nice smile. The last time I saw you was at mediation. You were straggly looking, a broken blood vessel in your eye. I remember the last phone call. Your voice was nasty and angry. How does someone with so much promise, potential, love, and support throw it all away for nothing? All the chances you had, and still you did not change. You never went into recovery. I've even felt guilty for that.

The first time I remember allowing myself to feel your loss was the day our first grandchild was born. I was in the delivery room and YOU WEREN'T. You MISSED IT! When I was going home, it hit me like a ton of bricks. I almost yelled, "Where are you?" A moment when all I should feel is joy was also filled with sadness and loss. I felt so alone because you weren't with me. I didn't plan on being a grandparent alone. How beautiful our daughter has done for herself. I'm so proud of her. How beautiful is our first perfect granddaughter.

I feel the loss of dreams, a future where I would grow old with my partner. I feel bereft because the comfortable relationship that I thought would be here is gone. I found myself looking around for you at Jamie and Tiffany's graduation. They deserved to have a father there smiling proudly and being supportive. If you could have seen them, you would have been so proud.

And, oh my God, I'm so proud of Jamie's accomplishment of graduating from boot camp. She looks amazing in her uniform and the way she carries herself. Our little girl is now working at the Pentagon! She came dangerously close to the addiction demon, but she has made good choices and is a beautiful strong woman.

Your alcoholism broke your relationship with Tiffany when she was so young. She didn't feel the sting of pain as strongly as Jamie did because she had already barricaded herself off from you.

Nikki still struggles with the loss and abuse. She's still not out of the woods or on the other side of her journey. Her road is longer and different from the others.

I don't want you back. I can't imagine you back. I feel so bad for you. You're probably in the same condition I see many of my patients. Their bodies are poisoned from alcohol. Their brain is poisoned. They have end-stage liver disease. I do want to know when you die because something inside of me will then know that it's over. I think I could be there. I don't want you to die alone. I just realized that I still feel tied to you.

I'm sorry we couldn't have lives together. I just couldn't stay on the roller coaster of your addiction. I had to make a life for myself, raise the girls, and be strong. I needed to put the children and myself first. The breakup of our marriage disrupted my belief system. Then, I realized that I had never challenged my childhood beliefs. In choosing to divorce, be strong, and move on, I have become a better person. The tragedy of our marriage was necessary. I've used the pain to create change. It has been a healthy change for me, our children, and the people who are close to us. I'm now a far different woman. Though my experience has jaded me, I'm now willing to reestablish a belief in love and the value of having a person close to me.
Vicki

Letters to Heal Broken Relationships

I met with Lee, a patient in the nursing home, who had a strained relationship with his son. Whenever the son visited, the meeting was fraught with tension and left them both feeling dissatisfied. Lee had Parkinson's disease, and it was sometimes difficult for him to talk to his son. I met with both of them, but I had difficulty understanding the dynamics of their relationship. After the son left, I remained with Lee. I explained the benefit of abiding with his feelings so he could authentically reckon with the difficulties in their relationship. Lee said he was willing to have me help him construct a letter to his son:

Dear Son,
I'm writing this letter to tell you some things I find hard to tell you in person. I've wanted to say these things for a long time, but I get tongue-tied when I speak with you. One thing I want to tell you is how proud I am of you. You graduated with top honors. You've become a respected physician. You are disciplined. You're a good husband and father. You have succeeded despite many obstacles. One of the main obstacles you faced was me. I drank too much. I used drugs. You needed a father. Instead, you had me. I only caused you and your mother hardship. I'm so sorry about that. I look back and wish things could have been different. I feel sad that my drinking and drugging hurt you so much, probably in ways that are deeper than you or I even realize. I hurt knowing that I did this to you.

I was thinking about you the other day. Remember how your mother wanted you to go into the Navy? Then, I took you to see the movie *Apocalypse Now* and that ended the Navy prospects. I'm thankful you didn't go into the Navy. I have never gotten over Korea. The war has never been over for me. I never want you, or anyone else I love, to see the things I've seen.

I also want to tell you how much it meant to me when you went to the AA meeting with me. That was probably not easy for you, but it helped me a lot. The Lord has also helped me. I had a revelation in Korea. They thought I was dead, but I saw light. They called it a "near-death experience," and I have never forgotten it. Since then, I've always known the Lord is with me. Even though I struggle with depression and PTSD, the Lord is with me.

Son, I love you. I'm proud of you. I'm sorry I let you down.

You deserved so much better than what I gave you. I pray for you now. I'm so pleased you are successful. I'm just saddened that I haven't been part of your success. Know that I love you.
Dad

After the son received this letter, it was reported to me that the relationship flourished. Probably the essential factor was that the son simply needed an acknowledgement and apology for the ways he had been wronged by his father. Expressing his love and telling his son that he was proud of him were also probably long-awaited messages.

Letters from Dying Parents to their Children

The following letter is from a dying father who was willing to abide and reckon with difficulties with his troubled teenage son. It gave the father a sense of peace to know that he was able to leave some advice with his son. He hoped that one day, his son would be able to benefit from his wisdom:

Dear Alex,
I write this letter to you realizing I'm nearing the end of my life. You are heavy on my heart and mind these days. We've not been especially close. I wish that were not so. If we were closer, you might feel more support and personal warmth from me. That is a regret I have. I feel much love for you, yet I've been inadequate in connecting with you. I know it's hard for you to reveal your true self to others. I get glimpses sometimes. I wish I knew you better and that you felt safer in revealing yourself to me.

I have a deep concern for you. You are young, yet growing up fast. Many of your actions now will have effects for the rest of your life. One of my hopes for you is that you complete your high school education. One of the ways I tried to show my love and support for you was to provide home schooling, which didn't really work out. My concern comes from my desire for your future.

You have had difficulty with the law. I know this complicates your life greatly and will continue to adversely affect you in ways you may not yet understand. I hope you will mature enough soon to resist urges to do things that will only lead to trouble for you. These misdeeds will haunt you for many years if you are unable to apply some self-control.

I know your girlfriend is on your mind. It must be very hard to have her so far away. With her pregnancy, she is probably very needy and puts some pressure on you to fulfill those needs. I hope you two will be able to put your own needs aside and think about your baby. You two are so young, so needy. Life is already very hard for you. I hope you will consider letting the baby have a good home with an adopted family.

I know you may not be coping very well with my dying. It's causing everyone a lot of pain. I know it's hard for most teenagers to show their feelings or accept help. There may be a part of you that just wants to run away and get away from it all. This is understandable. Still, I hope you will stay and be with us during this time. I love you.
Dad.

Later, Alex wrote a note and placed it on the Old Rugged Path hanging in the hallway of our Hospice unit. The note read: "I love you Dad. You're the greatest dad in the world. I will see you on the other side. I won't let you down."

A few years later, Maria, the patient's wife, told me her son was doing well. She thought the influence of this letter was partially responsible. "It really had an effect on him, and I think he started thinking more about the decisions he was making."

Letters from the Bereaved

Letting go of the world with their loved one in it and opening up to a world *without* their loved one is the central feature of grief recovery for the bereaved. Integrative letter writing can help accomplish this.

The next letter allows the writer to abide and reckon with ambivalent feelings of loss. Most relationships bear some ambivalent feelings. This letter addresses the "good" and "not-so-good" aspects of their relationship. Sometimes it's tempting to only reflect on the "good" or to "canonize" someone by death. This letter is more healing because it is complete; it addresses both.

Dear Richard,

I couldn't cry at your funeral. I think it was mostly shock because I did cry later. We both knew you were facing serious problems from your cancer. How sad you had to die when you were barely 65. Then I get angry because I remember the doctor telling you if you smoked another cigarette, you'd die. You walked out in the parking lot and lit up. Three days later, you died. No warning. You just said you felt like passing out and then went down. You tried to tell me something just before you fell, but couldn't say it. Sometimes I fantasize that you were going to say: "I know I'm dying" or "I'm sorry for the pain I caused." Common sense tells me it wasn't being sorry because that part of you had died long before your body died.

The first year after you died, I had some sadness, some crying when something would remind me of you, but mostly I felt angry. You not only took away your own life with your drinking, your secretiveness, your deceitfulness and irresponsibility, but you destroyed our life together. I guess one reason I didn't cry at your funeral was I had already cried as I realized you could not change, and I had already mourned the loss of us many years before. I had emotionally separated from you then and that's why I thought I wouldn't miss you.

The second year, I began to feel less angry and to remember more of the good things. I wished you were here when I saw *Mr. Holland's Opus*. It was so like you years ago when you were a bank president. I'd also find myself telling you something I read or was on TV. I miss you carrying the groceries in or the garbage out, taking care of the car and the cats. You had a good sense of humor. Most people liked you, though they didn't know about your secret life the way the kids and I did.

Anyway, I think it must be a relief for you to be able to not have to struggle with living a life you couldn't manage. In many ways, it's a relief to me too. I'm lonely a lot, but I'm doing so much that keeps me active and busy. I miss a companion and there were many times when you could be a pretty good one.

I don't think I've completely forgiven you, but I have come a long way and I know I will eventually. Anyway, Richard, I miss you. I hope you are at peace."

Guilt sometimes corrodes grief recovery. Letter-writing can bring light to this dark place. These next two letters helped resolve guilt for Victoria who tirelessly took care of her aging mother, yet she felt guilty because there were times when she allowed herself to complain about it.

Dear Mom,

I love you so much. As a child you were my protector, teacher, and mentor. As an adult, we became best friends. We could confide in each other with things we could trust to no one else. We had so much fun! Remember the window shopping, dancing, or just playing cards or games at home late into the night?

You were always so proud of me. You said I was smart because I got a full scholarship to nursing school. You were also proud that I was an Army nurse, teaching others.

It was difficult for me to watch you as disease and debility took that vibrant, independent, strong, and fun-loving woman from me, replacing her with someone who was angry, argumentative, ungrateful, and sometimes outright mean. Through those eight years when you were housebound and later confined to bed, I struggled to hang in there with you. I had promised that you would not die in a hospital. After all that you had given me, I had to keep that promise, and I had to help Dad.

I was so busy taking care of you, raising a teenager, and working that I never really slowed down enough to just be in the moment with you. There was more than one occasion when I left your house railing to God, "Please put her out of MY misery!" Instead of focusing on how your pain and lack of oxygen had taken its toll on you, I focused on my exhaustion. Please forgive me for not appreciating how illness had robbed you and how that made you feel. I know that I missed some valuable opportunities to love and support you, and I'm sorry for that.

Throughout my life, you have taught me so much and you continue to do so, even after death. You see, I take what I've learned from our experience and bring it to work. Now, I'm helping veterans and their families go through the dying process. I encourage them not to miss any opportunity with their loved ones and that no matter what they are feeling – guilt, anger, sorrow, hope – that they know that these are normal feelings and it's

okay. Now, I can hear the pride in your voice as you refer to me as your daughter – the hospice nurse.
Love, Victoria

Despite writing this letter, Victoria's guilt persisted. As I frequently do when this occurs, I had her assume the perspective of her mother. The return letter responds:

Dear Victoria,

You have always been my beautiful girl inside and out. I've always been so proud of you. I taught you always to do your very best at whatever you take on. No one could ever ask more of you than that and to do less would be cheating. Cheating yourself of the opportunity to realize your full potential also cheats the receiver of the fullness of what you have to give. This did not change when I was dying. You must forgive your humanness. Everyone gets tired and frustrated at times. After all, you are not God and you don't have inexhaustible resources. But you didn't really let that stop you – you always came back again and again. This allowed me to die the way I wanted to – at home surrounded by my family and things familiar and important to me.

I wasn't always easy to be around, but that didn't stop you either: having dinner with me so Dad could have a break, cleaning my house, managing my doctor visits and medications, just playing a game of cards with me. You were always there, and I knew I could count on you to help me and to help Dad. I knew that you didn't want my suffering to continue, but I needed reassurance that you would continue to love and support Dad since I would no longer be the mother/protector I had always been.

Remember the week before my death? I got up in the middle of the night and managed to get onto my scooter and out the front door. When I fell off the porch, you didn't scold me. Instead, you promised that you'd always be there for Dad. That's when I knew that my prayers were being answered and my pain would end soon with my death. That night you gave me the last thing I needed to be able to go. That gift allowed me to finish with this life. I was able to connect with everyone who was important to me and say goodbye, and within one week I was able to die with peace and dignity. Thank you for that.

Thank you and I love you. You'll always feel me near. When you need me most, know that I am still with you. Just be calm and quiet and you'll hear me. Mom

The letter from her Mom reached the aspect of Victoria that had exiled itself in guilt, restoring that part of Victoria into wholeness.

Appendix L

Letter from David to Gail

This appendix provides the reader with the actual letter that David sent Gail. It is comprised from the stories I gathered as we talked about their relationship.

Dear Gail,

You are often on my mind. And I have to admit, you are heavy on my heart. At this time in my life, I think a lot. I think about my life and my family. I think about you. I think about the suffering in the world. The man in the bed next to mine died yesterday. I was upset. I don't understand why people have to suffer. I had hoped I would die the way my father died – suddenly. The hardest thing about all of this is the lingering. I'm just glad I still have my mind. I'm not so good from the chest down, but from the chest up, I still work fine.

I have several regrets in my life. Some of them relate to you. It must have been hard to be a twin. You always had to share, do things together, compete for time and attention without a chance to shine on your own or be an individual with your own identity. I now understand how I made this even harder for you by favoring Fran. It seemed you had your mother and I had Fran. It seemed fair enough at the time. Now, I know it wasn't. Then, I didn't realize how much that hurt you. Now, I understand and I am sorry. I know it must have caused you a lot of grief to know you were not preferred. It added to the difficulties you sustained as a twin. I ask your forgiveness for this. I know I can't force the issue of forgiveness. But I hope one day you'll be able to forgive me and let go of the hurt I have caused you.

I have other regrets that affected you and everyone in our family. I worked too hard. Those 14-hour days kept me away from you all and made me tired and grumpy. I didn't like to listen to anyone (except myself) either. I was more interested in talking. These days, I'm doing a lot more listening and I'm realizing what I must have missed while I was so busy making money and talking. I know you must have suffered from these actions of mine.

I also have fond memories of us together. Remember the vacations at the beach bungalows in Maine? Or, the winters in West Palm? I also remember trying to win you over with some pennies. I would give you a dollar allowance each week. I thought you'd be happier with pennies because you'd think it was a lot of money. I kept exchanging nickels and dimes for pennies each time I needed change. It was my way of letting you know I loved you. But, even with your pennies, I told you to "share them with Fran." You must have gotten pretty tired and angry hearing that phrase all the time. It seems unfortunate that some things I have learned too late.

It may surprise you to know I'm praying now. I join in the prayers, songs, and Bible readings with the staff here. I remember how faithful my mother was. I didn't carry her faithfulness on, but I'm thankful I can draw on it now. Faith seems more important to me now. In fact, my perspective on many things has changed in these last few weeks.

I worry about you and your multiple sclerosis. Two years ago I looked it up so I could understand it better. I do not like to think of you suffering. I want you to be happy. You are my child, and I want you to know I love you.
Dad

Appendix M

Facilitating a Healing Community

This appendix augments Chapter Eight. It provides a suggested format for facilitating a Healing Community based on this book.

I encourage groups to establish an agreed-upon time limit for starting and ending the group; respect that constraint unless renegotiated by the group. Establish confidentiality ground rules: what is said in the group, stays in the group. Explain that violations of this rule will cause expulsion from the group because creating a trustworthy environment is essential. After a few weeks, I encourage people to share phone numbers so that private support can be shared. I would not recommend adding new group members after the second week; new members can threaten the safety of the group. Later, I encourage groups to repeat *The Hero Within* Healing Community. Invite new members to join at that time.

I also encourage the Native American "talking stick" format. (See Chapter Eight.) I've used this format for 20 years in multiple settings with multi-focused groups. For a group based on this book, I'd suggest opening the group by passing a talking stick or some other symbol that the participants find meaningful, such as a stone. The opening pass of the talking symbol should be simple and fairly brief with each person reflecting in general on concepts from the chapter. After the last person speaks, put the talking symbol aside so further discussion can take place without the constraints of the talking symbol. Discuss concepts in the chapter interactively. Then pass the talking symbol again with each person sharing as much or as little about his or her Life Story self-awareness exercise without interruption. Reemphasize that people can pass the symbol without saying anything. Also remind people that they can share parts of their story, omitting confidential information or details that would reveal personal data about someone else that the other person would not want disclosed. Until trust is clearly established, this should not be a "tell-all" group. Anything confidential can be physically covered up until such a time as the person feels confident about self disclosure. During this time, a person can refer to the issue in generalities rather than specifics: "I have a childhood issue that I'm struggling with. Right now, I'm trying to reckon with it by _____." Later, when there is confidence that all group members are trustworthy, the specifics of the issue can be revealed.

After a person shares his or her Life Story self-awareness exercise, the talking symbol should be put in the center of the circle while participants respond openly with comments, questions, support, and encouragement to the person who shared his or her Life Story. As a person shares his or her Life Story, it will resonate with many of the listeners. During this open portion of the meeting when people are responding to the person's story, participants can add anything that the person's story triggered to their own Life Story scroll.

It is difficult not to talk when someone is speaking with the talking symbol. Others will want to ask questions, make comments, or add their own perspective. When the group is first forming, it is helpful to designate someone to remind people not to speak. This is very important; otherwise, respect for listening is not achieved and the gift of hearing the story for both the teller and receiver is missed. After a few weeks, not interjecting will become ingrained within the group, and a designee to control interruptions will no longer be necessary. At the same time, it is also important to have times where people can interact freely and spontaneously, which is why interactive discussion is also built into the format.

If a few people consume too much time, that's okay. Simply stop as the ending draws near and hold the remaining Life Stories until the following meeting. For example, don't try to do one chapter per meeting. Instead, move on to the next chapter after everyone who wants to share his or her Life Story has done so even if it takes two or ten meetings to accomplish. So if a Life Story is long and complicated and its owner talks in detail about its contents, it's conceivable that only one Life Story gets shared at that meeting. However, should one person consistently consume too much of the group's time each week, someone needs to talk to the person to establish better boundaries. The person might benefit from a referral for some one-on-one counseling.

Save enough time to conclude the group with a final passing of the talking symbol. This closing passage should allow each participant to comment on what they experienced during the session. If one person requires excessive support or is in need of one-on-one counseling, contact a professional service. There are many counselors, churches, hospices, 12-step recovery programs, and community organizations that can provide help.

When your group completes the book, decide what you want to do with the scrolls. Some people want to keep them, even post them. It's like their coat of arms or their badge of courage that reflects what they have been through. On the other hand, you might consider burning the scrolls. It is the internal lessons that are kept; the triumphs and hardships were simply the vehicle to achieve the honesty, courage, and humility to live your story. Burning signifies the transitory data of our lives and the internalization of the lessons learned. (Remember: The healer in the Crescent Moon Bear burned the hair!) I would also suggest utilizing a labyrinth. A search on the internet will probably reveal one closeby. Walking a labyrinth with your fellow pilgrims while playing meaningful music can be very integrative.

After the book is completed, I'd suggest starting over and repeating the process. The depth of healing is often much greater the second time. You can think of different ways to depict your story, such as taking an event or time period in your life and creating a symbolic story. (See example in Appendix K, page 240.) You can also invite a few new members. The "seasoned" members' stories will act as guides to give new members *en-courage-ment* for healing. You might then want to branch out to facilitate other new groups, acting as catalysts for precipitating healing in your community or family. Themed groups can also be done. For example, women in a three-generational family who had all been molested by men in their family, came together to share their Life Stories. Imagine the healing that took place in that family!

In summary, the general format for a two-hour meeting includes:

- Facilitator makes a general pass using the talking symbol with each person briefly stating how he or she did with the concepts from the assigned chapter. (10 minutes)
- Facilitator places the talking symbol in the center of the group so people can interactively discuss the content of the chapter. (20 minutes)
- An individual accepts the talking symbol, sharing more personally about his or her experience with the Self-Awareness Exercise. (15-60 minutes)
- The individual places the talking symbol in the center of the group, signifying he or she has completed his or her story. Participants respond with questions, comments, and support to the individual. Participants should not launch into their own personal stories at this juncture unless it is short and offered as direct support to the individual. If the individual's story triggered something for participants

that they want to add to their own Life Story, it can be done at this time. (10 minutes)

- The above two steps are repeated with other individuals for as many times as time allows.
- A general pass of the talking symbol should close the meeting with each participant making a brief comment about how he or she has grown from the experience. (10 minutes)

Endnotes

Prologue

[1]This patient's real name is Marvin Roesler. It is used with the permission of his daughter, Diane Johnstone.

[2]Grassman, Deborah. *Peace at Last: Stories of Hope and Healing for Veterans and Their Families.* St. Petersburg, FL: Vandamere Press, 2009.

[3]This man's real name is Buzz H. and is used with his permission.

[4]Anxious energy usually rises. Think about what happens when you get excited. Your voice usually gets higher; energy gets flighty. You might place your hand on your chest or near your throat, unconsciously anchoring yourself. A calm, centered person's energy usually resides lower and deeper. If a calm person places their hand on an unsettled person's sternum, it can often help him/her feel secure, more stable, and less anxious.

Chapter 1

[1]Remen, Rachel Naomi. *Kitchen Table Wisdom.* NY: Riverhead Books, 1994.

[2]I'm indebted to a colleague of mine, Diane Johnstone, for helping me articulate this concept. After a Dying Healed class that I teach in which we reckon with the distress in our lives, she said, "Why is it that we all run so fast from doing the very things that will free us up?"

[3]This patient's real name is John Bundy and is used with his permission, as well as his wife's, Donna. He knew I was writing this book and asked that I include his story. He was also writing a book, but he died prior to completing it. The title was going to be *Cancer Saved my Life.*

[4]*Webster's New World Dictionary.* NY: Simon & Schuster, 1994.

[5]*Webster's New World Dictionary.* NY: Simon & Schuster, 1994.

[6]*Webster's New World Dictionary.* NY: Simon & Schuster, 1994.

[7]*Webster's New World Dictionary.* NY: Simon & Schuster, 1994.

Chapter 2

[1]Collected Works of CG Jung. Bollingen Ser., No. 20, 2d ed. Princeton NJ: Princeton University Press, 1973, trans RFC Hull, Vol II, Psychology and Religion: West and East, p.75.

[2]Tolle, Eckhart. *The Power of Now: A Guide to Spiritual Enlightenment.* Novato, CA: New World Library, 1999:126-127.

[3]Anxious energy usually rises. Think about what happens when you get excited. Your voice usually gets higher; energy gets flighty. You might place your hand on your chest or near your throat, unconsciously anchoring your-

self. A calm, centered person's energy usually resides lower and deeper. If a calm person places their hand on an unsettled person's sternum, it can often help him/her feel secure, more stable, and less anxious.

[4] *Holy Bible* (New King James Version). Nashville: Thomas Nelson, 1982: Job: 2:11-13.

Chapter 3

[1] The first three lines of this prayer are used by Alcoholics Anonymous. It is part of a much longer prayer that is attributed to various sources, most commonly Reinhold Niebuhr. I have included the line about hardship because I believe that it is the underlying foundation for the truly wise.

[2] Morton, Nelle. *The Journey Is Home*. Boston: Beacon Press, 1985:153.

[3] Frankl, Viktor. *Man's Search for Meaning*. NY: Washington Square Press, 1984: 98.

[4] Frankl, Viktor. *Man's Search for Meaning*. NY: Washington Square Press, 1984: 100.

[5] Frankl, Viktor. *Man's Search for Meaning*. NY: Washington Square Press, 1984: 54.

[6] Frankl, Viktor. *Man's Search for Meaning*. NY: Washington Square Press, 1984: 97.

[7] Frankl, Viktor. *Man's Search for Meaning*. NY: Washington Square Press, 1984: 99.

[8] Remen, Naomi. *Kitchen Table Wisdom*. NY: Berkeley Publishing, 1994: 161.

Chapter 4

[1] Campbell, Joseph. *The Power of Myth*. NY: Broadway, 1988: 123.

[2] Grassman, Deborah. *Peace at Last: Stories of Hope and Healing for Veterans and Their Families*. St. Petersburg, FL: Vandamere Press, 2009. Chapter One reveals more about this aspect of my journey.

[3] Real names used with Ferol Martin's permission.

[4] Online: www.Thinkexist.com.

[5] Tolstoy, Leo. *The Death of Ivan Ilyich*. NY: Bantam Books, 1981:133.

[6] Estes, CP. *Women who Run with the Wolves*. NY: Random House, 1992: 347-350.

Chapter 5

[1] Frankl, Viktor. *Man's Search for Meaning*. NY: Washington Square Press, 1984: 93.

[2] Frankl, Viktor. *Man's Search for Meaning*. NY: Washington Square Press,

1984: 135.

[3]Frankl, Viktor. *The Will to Meaning.* NY: Penguin Books, 1988: 79.

[4]*Holy Bible* (New King James Version). Nashville: Thomas Nelson, 1982: Mathew 5:44.

[5]*National Consensus Project Guidelines* and *National Quality Preferred Practices for Spiritual Domain.* 2004.

[6]On-line: www.Thinkexist.com.

[7]See author's book, *Peace at Last: Stories of Hope and Healing for Veterans and Their Families,* for more information about the effects of war on the soul.

[8]My boss's name was Joy Easterly, and she was a tremendous support for developing the work that I do.

[9]This patient's name was Percy Hipsley. He wanted his name identified, saying he hoped his perspective would enhance understanding of the meetings: "I've been impatient to die for three weeks now, not understanding why I had to keep waiting. Maybe it was for this. Maybe what I say about the importance of these meetings will help someone else. If so, the waiting has been worth it."

[10]Remen, Rachel Naomi. *Kitchen Table Wisdom.* NY: Riverhead Books, 1994: 79-80.

[11]Remen, Rachel Naomi. *Kitchen Table Wisdom.* NY: Riverhead Books, 1994: 300- 301.

Chapter 6

[1]www.brainyquote.com/quotes/authors/m/mother_teresa.html

[2]*Webster's New World Dictionary.* NY: Simon & Schuster, 1994.

[3]*New American Bible.* NY: Catholic Book Publishing, 1970: Matthew 5:44.

[4]For further reading on the process of forgiveness and tools to accomplish it, see *Forgiving the Unforgivable* by Beverly Flanigan (1992). NY: Macmillan.

[5]The presentation was entitled: "Sacred Conversations: The Role of Forgiveness in End-of-Life Care" by Nicholas Gross, social worker, at the 2004 Florida State Hospice Conference for Volunteers.

[6]Peck, MS. *The Road Less Traveled.* NY: Simon & Schuster, 1978.

[7]This quote is from Roy Johnson, a motivational speaker presenting at the 2011 Arkansas State Hospice conference.

[8]Peck, MS. *The Road Less Traveled.* NY: Simon & Schuster, 1978.

[9]Dr. McChesney died unexpectedly three months later. I was thankful this scene occurred prior to her death.

Chapter 7

[1]Houwen, Henri. *The Lonely Search for God.* (Audiotapes) Chicago: The

Thomas More Association, 1974.

[2] *New American Bible.* NY: Catholic Book Publishing, 1970: Luke 15:11-32.

[3] The first five elements are noted in Ira Byock's book, *Dying Well* (1997. NY: Riverhead). I have added the last two elements because I believe the only reason you do the first five steps is so you can achieve the last two: let go of same and open up to new and different, i.e., shift the relationship you have with a problem, situation, or relationship.

[4] Amy McDonald is the Hospice and Palliative Care physician at the Buffalo VA in New York.

Chapter 8

[1] www.quotationspage.com/quotes/Margaret_Mead.

[2] Nouwen, Henri. *The Inner Voice – A Journey Through Anguish to Freedom.* New York: Image, 1998.

[3] For more information about the therapeutic value of talking sticks, go to www.acaciart.com/stories/archive. Also see Appendix I on rituals.

[4] Wylde, Isabella. (1994) An interview with author and analyst Clarissa Pinkola Estés. *Radiance.* Winter Issue.

[5] Hayford, Jack. *How to Live through a Bad Day.* Thomas Nelson Inc: Nashville, 2001: 21-22.

[6] The Zimbabwe art exhibit is located in the tunnel connecting the T-gates to the Atlanta airport. The sculptures can also be viewed on-line at www.atlanta-airport.com. Click on the following: "passenger information," "art program," "permanent exhibits."

Appendix E

[1] George Wallace was the governor of Alabama who resisted the civil rights movement; he was an outspoken racist in the 1960s who opposed Martin Luther King, Jr.

[2] King, ML. Sr. *Daddy King: An Autobiography.* NY: Morrow, 1980.

Appendix F

[1] Byock, Ira. *Dying Well: Peace and Possibilities at the End of Life.* NY: Riverhead, 1997.

Appendix I

[1] Campbell, Joseph. *The Power of Myth.* NY: Broadway Books, 1988.

[2] Campbell, Joseph. *The Hero with a Thousand Faces.* Princeton NJ: 1973.

[3] Williamson, Marianne. *Illuminata.* NY: Random House, 1994.

[4] For more information about the therapeutic value of talking sticks, go to www.acaciart.com/stories/archive.

Appendix K
[1]The first five elements are noted in Ira Byock's book, *Dying Well.* I have added the last two elements because I believe the only reason you do the first five steps is so that you can achieve the last two: let go of same and open up to new and different, i.e. shift the relationship you have with a problem, situation, relationship, or aspect of self.

Index